XML

for
eServer i5 and iSeries

XML

for eServer i5 and iSeries

Steve Bos and David Morris

First Edition

First Printing—May 2004
Second Printing–April 2005

Special Note from authors: Throughout the text we have used the term iSeries to refer to both the IBM eServer i5 and iSeries.

ISBN: 1-58347-050-6

Corporate Offices
125 N. Woodland Trail
Lewisville, TX 75077 USA

Sales and Customer Service
P.O. Box 4300
Big Sandy, TX 75755-4300 USA

www.mcpressonline.com

Contents

Foreword

Leveraging the iSeries with XML

In a relatively short time, XML has earned its place in business and Web applications by providing a common format that allows disparate computer systems to exchange information. Within two years of XML's inception, information technology vendors including Microsoft, IBM, and Netscape have incorporated XML support into their browsers and applications. Even on the IBM iSeries platform, which tends to wait for new technologies to mature before embracing them, XML is beginning to make headway, particularly in the area of Electronic Data Interchange (EDI).

In the past, a lot of information stored on computers became obsolete because the applications used to store and process that information were using proprietary formats understood only by those applications. Those of us who have been using the iSeries and its predecessors, the AS/400 and System/38, understand the value in being able to migrate information to new hardware and applications without conversion. This capability is not common on other platforms; for example, it would be very difficult and costly to extract the information contained in a spreadsheet created just 15 years ago using version 1 of Lotus 1-2-3. XML uses a simple nonproprietary format that transcends these limitations, allowing data to live beyond the applications used to create the files in which it is stored.

XML is proving to be a versatile language, capable of describing and delivering rich, structured data from any source. With the advancement of XML standards and technologies, the benefits of using XML are obvious. The iSeries is the perfect companion for XML; capable of using every technology. Together, they will leverage the platform to new heights.

This book is geared toward those who are new to XML and familiar with the iSeries. It explains the basic concepts of XML and continues to dive into more advanced topics, including XML Schemas, namespaces, security, and Web services. It also takes a look at the available technologies for the iSeries and how they work together in using XML.

By the time you finish this book, you will not only know the basics of XML; you will also be able to validate data and structures, secure XML data, and program for XML documents. All of this will help position you to take advantage of XML technology on the iSeries.

—Steve Bos

1

XML: Where Did It Come From? Where Is It Going?

In this chapter you will learn:

- ✓ What XML is
- ✓ Why XML was created
- ✓ The history of XML
- ✓ How XML is used on the iSeries (formerly AS/400) platform
- ✓ Where XML is going in the future

This chapter provides an introduction to XML, explaining why XML is important, its history, and uses for it. I will also introduce you to some ways in which you can use XML on your iSeries platform to exchange information and create Web applications. Finally, in this chapter, I will give you some insight into where XML is going.

Defining XML

Extensible Markup Language (XML) is a dialect of Standardized Generalized Markup Language (SGML). The World Wide Web Consortium created this new dialect of SGML to provide a simple and easy-to-use alternative to SGML for describing data exchanged between software applications. Although XML is a simplified version of SGML, it is powerful enough to describe almost any data in a format understood by the majority of computers in use today.

In a relatively short time, XML earned its place in business and Web applications by providing a common format that allows disparate computer systems to exchange information. Within two years of XML's inception, computer vendors such as Microsoft, IBM, and Netscape have incorporated XML support into their browsers and applications. Even on the iSeries platform, which tends to wait for new technologies to mature before embracing them, XML is beginning to make headway, particularly in the area of Electronic Data Interchange (EDI).

A lot of information stored on computers in the past has become obsolete because applications used proprietary formats understood only by similar applications. Those of us that have been using the iSeries and its predecessors, the AS/400 and System 38, understand the value in being able to migrate information to new hardware and applications without conversion. This capability is not common on other platforms. For example, it would be very difficult and costly to extract the information contained in a spreadsheet created just 15 years ago using version 1 of Lotus 1-2-3. XML uses a simple, nonproprietary format that transcends these limitations, allowing data to live beyond the applications used to create it.

The main difference between XML and other markup languages is that XML is a *meta*-markup language. In other words, it describes information about the markup, but it does not describe the domain-specific implementation. This characteristic allows XML to be adapted to fit many more needs than other markup languages such as HTML. The ability to adapt to new uses makes XML much more powerful than HTML.

With XML, you define document elements and attributes, which are then used to mark up your information. An element can represent some piece of information such as an address, a telephone number, or a person's name. Attributes are associated with an element and identify information that is typically not printed or displayed. For example, a payment type might be stored as an attribute for a payment element.

Figure 1.1 shows how a payment is defined using XML:

```
<payment type="ET">
   <amount>500.00</amount>
   <unit>USD</unit>
</payment>
```

Figure 1.1: XML defined payment.

In this example there are three elements: payment, amount, and unit. The payment element contains the amount and unit elements and has a type attribute. This example also shows how XML elements are nested. Unlike HTML tags, XML tags must be opened and closed in order. The unit closing tag in this example, which is nested in the payment tag, has to be closed before the payment tag is closed. Another difference between HTML and XML is that XML is case sensitive. A <Unit> tag is not the same as a <unit> tag.

The X in XML

The X in XML stands for the *x* in *extensible*. For this reason "Extensible Markup Language" is frequently written as "eXtensible Markup Language" and helps justify the XML acronym; apparently, e is out and X, as in X-treme, is in. This new technology with the hip acronym is supported by all of the major software vendors and describes data in a widely recognized, platform-independent manner. Although this book focuses on using XML on the iSeries platform, the platform-independent nature of XML is one of its chief strengths.

When comparing XML to Hypertext Markup Language (HTML), you find many similarities. Both are used in Web-based applications, and both use a similar syntax to describe the content of documents. Unlike most other markup languages including HTML, which restrict you to a fixed set of tags, XML allows you to create new tags. Like HTML, XML tags describe the elements within a document, but XML is a meta-markup language, which allows you to use XML to describe your own *domain-specific* elements. Domain-specific elements are elements that are useful in describing content related to a specific area. For example, there is a domain-specific Chemical Markup Language (CML) that allows chemists to describe data in a way that facilitates the exchange of chemical information.

You can create new elements that meet your needs and use them internally, or you can work within your industry to create a universally recognized markup. There are several organizations helping industry develop and publish new markups. The two largest of these are *XML.ORG*, sponsored by the non-profit Organization for the Advancement of Structured Information Standards (OASIS), and *BizTalk*, which is a Microsoft subsidiary. The URLs for these two organizations are *www.xml.org* and *www.bizztalk.org*. The goal of XML.ORG and BizTalk is to accelerate the adoption of XML as the standard way of exchanging data electronically.

As you have seen, XML allows you to create your own markup tags. If you go to the XML.Org or BizTalk Web sites, you will find complete, industry-specific markups. You can use and even extend these markups with your own elements. To prevent the possibility of name collisions, XML uses a concept called a *namespace*. An XML namespace associates elements and attributes with Universal Resource Identifiers (URI). A URI looks a lot like a Universal Resource Locator (URL) and like a URL, a URI describes a universally unique domain.

Describing Document Content

The syntax provided by XML allows you to describe the content of a document. This capability allows you to describe the content of any document and, just as important, to separate the content of a document from the document's presentation. Style is another term for the presentation format.

It is time for you to see a document that has been marked up using XML. The following example compares a recipe encoded with HTML (Figure 1.2) to the same recipe encoded with XML. I could have created my own markup for the XML version of the recipe; instead, I used Recipe Markup Language (recipeML), which is a full-blown XML markup developed to facilitate describing and exchanging recipes. The recipeML Web site is *www.formatdata.com/recipeml/*.

```
<h1>Smores</h1>
<ul>
   <li>2 Graham crackers
   <li>2 Marshmallows
   <li>2 Chocolate squares
</ul>
<p>Place two marshmallows on a graham cracker.<br>
   Place chocolate square on each marshmallow.<br>
   Cover with graham cracker.<br>
   Bake in 300 degree oven for 5 minutes.</p>
```

Figure 1.2: HTML recipe for smores.

If you are familiar with HTML, the example shown in Figure 1.2 should be easy to follow. If you are not, the following description should help. In this document, the <h1> tag describes a top-level heading, the <ul> tag describes an unordered list, <li> tags are list items, the <p> tag begins a paragraph, and <br> is a line

```
<recipe>
   <head>
      <title>Smores</title>
   </head>
   <ingredients>
      <ing>
         <amt><qty>2</qty></amt>
         <item>Graham crackers</item>
      </ing>
      <ing>
         <amt><qty>2</qty></amt>
         <item>Marshmallows</item>
      </ing>
      <ing>
         <amt><qty>2</qty></amt>
         <item>Chocolate squares</item>
      </ing>
   </ingredients>
   <directions>
      <step>Place two marshmallows on a graham cracker.</step>
      <step>Place chocolate square on each marshmallow.</step>
      <step>Cover with graham cracker.</step>
      <step>Bake in 300 degree oven for 5 minutes.</step>
   </directions>
</recipe>
```

Figure 1.3: The same recipe as in Figure 1.2, but marked up using XML.

break. I did not have to include the final </p> tag, because HTML does not require you to close a paragraph; the browser can insert the paragraph close, which can lead to problems and inconsistent results among different browsers.

The XML representation of the smores recipe shown in Figure 1.3 is quite a bit longer than the HTML representation shown in Figure 1.2. The extra information helps describe the data in a more meaningful way.

These two examples show how XML focuses on describing content rather than presentation. The recipeML example has a distinct structure and uses the descriptive <ing> tag to identify an ingredient. The HTML example uses generic tags, such as <li> to describe list items without regard to whether they are ingredients or some other element, and has no discernable structure. Also, XML follows a stricter set of rules. All tags in XML must be properly nested and have tags, whereas HTML tags can appear in any order, and in some cases closing tags are optional.

The XML example does not contain the heading and style tags that help a browser determine how to display this recipe. I will be covering these items in detail (and provide examples) when we get to syntax in Chapter 2 and style in Chapter 8.

Ensuring Documents' Integrity

One important feature of XML is that it provides built-in assurances that the form and content of information is correct and reliable. There are several ways that XML provides this assurance:

- Documents must be well-formed, adhering to XML's syntax.
- Documents can conform to a Document Type Definition (DTD) or a Schema.
- XML is prohibited from attempting to fix or understand malformed documents.

Although XML gives you the flexibility to create new tags and content as necessary, all XML documents, as well as your extensions must conform to XML's rules. There are two sets of rules; the first set ensures that the basic syntax and structure of a document are correct, the second set of rules is provided by a DTD or an XML Schema and applies domain-specific validation.

When a document follows certain XML rules, the document is considered to be well-formed. Programs that process XML documents check for conformance to these basic rules and are allowed to identify errors, but the XML specification specifically prohibits the correction of errors or interpretation of any document that is not well-formed. In addition, programs that process XML documents cannot ignore errors.

A well-formed document begins with an XML declaration and contains elements that are properly nested. The document must also have one and only one root element. In addition, attribute values must be surrounded by double quotes ("), and the characters < and & may be used only at the beginning of tags and entity references.

DTDs provide another type of validation. A DTD provides rules ensuring that the actual tags, attributes, entities, and content meet certain criteria. The rules applied by a DTD can enforce the use and order of an XML document's components. For example, the DTD for recipeML specifies that a recipe must have ingredients but nutritional information is optional. Furthermore, the recipeML DTD specifies that ingredients must appear before directions and nutritional information. Chapter 3 describes DTDs in detail.

A Schema is similar to a DTD in the validations it can perform, but it goes a step further in supporting type checking. Unlike a DTD, which can check the structure and order of tags, a Schema can make sure that the data contained within an element conforms to certain rule. For example, with a Schema you can validate a date element to be a valid date in a pre-defined format. One drawback to using a Schema over a DTD is that it takes a lot more typing to build a Schema.

Comparing XML and HTML

Many of the same people contributed to the development of both XML and HTML. The languages are also both subsets of Standardized Generalized

Markup Language (SGML). Because of this, their syntax and structure are similar; where they differ is in purpose. HTML's primary purpose was the exchange of information over the Web. XML is designed for the exchange of information by any means.

Because both HTML and XML use similar syntax and structure to mark up documents, anyone familiar with HTML has a head start in understanding XML. HTML and XML also use the same Universal Character Set (UCS) specified by the Unicode Consortium. The use of this character set makes it easier to translate documents between languages. Finally, both HTML and XML can use Cascading Style Sheets (CSS) to apply a consistent look and feel, or style, to documents. Cascading Style Sheets are a simple mechanism that associates display formatting (such as fonts, colors, and spacing) with document tags.

Now let's look at some of the differences. First and foremost is *purpose.* HTML was designed to "mark up" information displayed using a Web browser. XML is designed to structure information and does not care how the information is used. HTML directly supported formatting using tags like <font>, <emphasis>, and <bold>, whereas XML does not. With XML, you must use CSS to format a document for display using a browser.

Browsers have ignored many HTML errors (for example, missing end tags). When these errors are encountered, the browser would do its best to display what it could. A parser interpreting an XML document, on the other hand, can report errors but is prohibited from processing any document with errors.

You may have notice that I refer to HTML in the past tense. The reason is that XML is replacing HTML. A new hybrid version of HTML that is part HTML and part XML began replacing HTML back in 1999. This reformulated version of HTML known as XHTML retains HTML's functionality while conforming to XML's rigid syntax. Documents marked up using XHTML are validated using one of three DTDs. These DTDs define the HTML-like elements of an XHTML document and ensure compliance.

Why XML was Created

Documents marked up with XML have many benefits over documents that are stored as plain text or are marked up using a less capable markup like HTML. The following list describes some of those benefits:

- Data marked up with XML is self-describing.
- Organizations can exchange data in a common predefined format.
- Search engines can search documents intelligently.
- XML can be extended to new domains.
- Document presentation is independent of a document's data.
- Most browsers in use today support XML directly.
- Widespread support ensures tools availability.

XML simplifies many Web development tasks that are difficult to do in HTML. One example of this is the ability to search a document intelligently. With XML, you can search for specific content rather than trying to discern meaning from the words contained within an HTML document. For example, you could search a Web catalog site for blue 18-speed mountain bikes priced between $500 and $1,000. There is little danger this search will get a hit for Blue Mountain coffee priced at $18 per pound.

When you need to exchange information over the Internet, XML is often the best answer. With XML, you do not need specialized import and export support to handle the conversion of data from one format to another. It is easy to transform data described using XML from one format to another format. This ability to transform data is one of XML's most important features and helps facilitate the exchange of information between different databases running on more than one platform.

Another benefit of XML is that it is more rigidly structured. Because XML editors check documents to ensure that their structure is valid, browsers do not have to waste time trying to figure out the intention of a document that contains unmatched or invalid tags. The requirement that documents be valid helps ensure that browsers from different vendors display data more consistently.

Building Perspective: The History of XML

Thousands of people have contributed to the development of XML. Many of those people came up with similar ideas at similar times. Because of this, it is impossible to give a single unified history of XML, and it is likely that I have not given credit to some important contributors and their accomplishments. Keep this in mind as you read the following and remember that XML is the result of the dedicated work of many and not one person's brainchild. The following timeline shows the sequence of events leading up to today's XML:

- 1945 Bush describes foundation of hypertext markups
- 1965 Nelson coins term *hypertext*
- 1967 Tunnicliffe evangelizes use of generalized markup
- 1967 Rice develops GenCode
- 1969 IBM researchers led by Goldfarb develop GML
- 1986 SGML recognized as an ANSI standard
- 1987 Apple introduces HyperCard
- 1990 World Wide Web proposed
- 1993 Mosaic browser released
- 1996 XML's initial working draft released by W3C
- 1998 XML 1.0 working draft becomes recommendation
- 1999 XML new working groups formed, namespaces recommended

The concept of markup languages began with Vannevar Bush's July 1945 *Atlantic Monthly* article "As We May Think," which described his vision of a hypertext system he called memex. Later, around 1965, Theodor Holm Nelson coined the terms *hypertext* and *hypermedia*. Later he wrote the book *Computer*

Lib/Dream Machines, published in 1974, which helped influence the development of the World Wide Web.

Several independent groups laid the foundation for XML late in the 1960s, when they began using descriptive markup tags to supplement written information. Before this, specialized codes were used that did not describe the type of data, but rather a specific typeface, font, or style. One person who recognized the value in separating document content from format was William Tunnicliffe, who evangelized this concept in a presentation that he gave to the Canadian Government Printing Office in 1967.

Shortly after Tunnicliffe's speech, a group led by book designer Stanley Rice developed GenCode, which defined a set of generic markup tags. Norman Scharpf recognized the significance of GenCode and created the Gencode Committee to oversee its development. This committee went on to contribute to the development of Standardized General Markup Language (SGML).

At about the same time, another research group at IBM led by Charles Goldfarb, with Edward Mosher and Raymond Lorie developed the Generalized Markup Language (GML). If you are ever going to be tested on this, remember that this acronym also happens to reflect their initials. One significant feature of this new markup is that it introduced the concept of a nested element structure.

Combining the concepts of GenCode and GML, the American National Standards Institute (ANSI) presented a working draft of the first version of Standardized Generalized Markup Language (SGML) in 1980. This final version of SGML became a recognized international standard in 1986 with the publication of ISO 8879.

Following Bush and Nelson's initial activity, hypertext development faded until 1987, when Apple introduced HyperCard. Developers quickly saw that hyperlinked text was a much better way to organize and navigate text stored on computers. Apple and Microsoft incorporated this feature of hypertext links into both the Macintosh and Windows help systems.

In the late 1980s, Tim Berners-Lee, working with Robert Cailliau at the European Particle Physics Laboratory (CERN), began work on a distributed information system. In 1990, they proposed a distributed information system based on hypertext that they called the World Wide Web. They also created the first Web browser and introduced the initial version of Hypertext Markup Language (HTML). In 1993, Marc Andreessen, working for the National Center for Supercomputing Applications at the University of Illinois, released the first easy-to-install and easy-to-use Web browser, Mosaic for X.

David Raggett at Hewlett-Packard Laboratories created HTML+ in 1993 to support forms, tables, and figures. In 1995, the HTML Working Group proposed HTML 2.0, which was the first version of HTML described by a formal specification. Late in 1999, the World Wide Web Consortium (W3C) recommended version 4.01 of HTML. This was the final version of HTML; XHTML, an XML-compliant HTML derivative, is HTML's replacement.

In 1996, the W3C Generic SGML Editorial Review Board, chaired by Jon Bosak of Sun Microsystems, with support from the W3C's Generic SGML Working Group, began the first phase of XML and developed the original XML specifications. Soon after this, two new XML groups were formed: an XML Working Group and an XML Special Interest Group.

The first phase of XML culminated on February 10, 1998, when the W3C issued the XML 1.0 Recommendation. Following this recommendation, the second phase of work began. By late 1998 the W3C had restructured the XML effort and directed it toward a new XML Coordination Group. The actual definition was broken down and handled by five new working groups: the XML Schema, XML Fragment, XML Linking, XML Information Set, and XML Syntax Working Groups. These groups are part of the W3Cs Architecture domain

The second phase of XML resulted in the Namespaces in XML Recommendation, issued in January 1999, and the Style Sheet Linking Recommendation, issued later that year in June. The third phase of development continues the work of the second phase and adds a new working XML Query Working Group.

Setting Standards

Like most Internet technologies, standards define XML. Several groups contribute to the development of Internet standards, including the World Wide Web Consortium (W3C), the Internet Engineering Task Force (IETF), and the Organization for the Advancement of Structured Information Standards (OASIS).

XML's Creator, the W3C

The group credited with creating XML is the W3C. Their mission is to provide an open forum for the discussion and promotion of interoperability standards. In addition to the original XML standard, recommendations submitted by the W3 include Mathematical Markup Language (mathML), XHTML, versions of the Document Object Model (DOM), and XSL Transformations (XSLT).

The W3C strives to achieve the following goals:

- To promote technologies that provide for universal access to the Web
- To develop a software environment conducive to effective Web use
- To guide Web development to ensure that legal, commercial, and social need are met

The membership of the W3C works within a set of guidelines. The membership first approves proposals for new initiatives, known as activity proposals, and assigns the activity to a W3C Working Group. The W3C organizes these activities under four domains: the Architecture Domain, the User Interface Domain, the Technology and Society Domain, and the Web Accessibility Initiative.

The first stage of a new proposal in the W3C is a Working Draft. During the Working Draft stage, changes are expected. Following the Working Draft, a proposal evolves to become a Candidate Recommendation, then a Proposed Recommendation, and finally a Recommendation.

Guiding Internet Development at the IETF

The IETF is a loosely self-organized group that helps guide the development of the Internet and its technologies. This group is the principal source of new Internet standards and specifications. The mission statement of this group includes the following items:

- To identify and propose solutions and protocols that address Internet problems
- To make standards recommendations
- To facilitate technology transfer from researchers to the Internet community
- To provide a forum for the exchange of Internet information

The IETF is open to anyone, and its participation has grown considerably from twenty-one back in 1986 to thousands in more recent years. Each year they hold three conferences to discuss and propose Internet standards, as well as working group meetings and online discussion. Most standards start out as Internet Drafts that, after discussion and approval, are published as Requests for Comment (RFCs) and are refined until their recommendations are completed. The processes for proposing and accepting these standards are very structured; this structure reduces obstacles that might sidetrack and delay standards adoption.

OASIS: Promoting Interoperable Standards

Another group that has contributed to the development of XML and its related standards is OASIS. This nonprofit consortium creates interoperable industry specifications based on public standards such as XML, SGML, and HTML. Members of OASIS are companies and individuals with a personal stake in furthering the use of interoperability standards.

OASIS does not create and recommend new standards as the W3C and IETF do. Instead, OASIS focuses on furthering the adoptions of standards. One function of OASIS is the recommendation of specific application strategies that meet certain interoperability goals. The XML Cover Pages sponsored by OASIS provides a comprehensive online reference for XML, SGML, and their related technologies. The XML Cover Pages Web site is located at *xml.coverpages.org*. Another resource sponsored by OASIS is XML.ORG, which provides an independent resource for the use of XML in industrial and commercial settings. The XML.ORG Web site is located at *www.xml.org*.

Corporate and individual membership in OASIS is not cheap. Individual membership starts at $250 USD per year, and a corporate membership starts at $2,500 USD for companies with fewer than ten employees.

Each of the standards groups mentioned here maintains a Web site. Their Web sites are located at *www.w3.org*, *www.ietf.org*, and *www.oasis-open.org*. Each of these Web sites provides a wealth of information related to XML and the Internet. Visit these Web sites to read the original standards specifications or to follow the development of Internet standards.

Transform and Style with XSL

Almost every computer program takes some sort of input and converts it to another form of output. Sometimes the support for formatting the output is embedded in the language, as in the venerable RPG cycle; added to the language, like Java servlets; or defined by an open standard, such as the Common Gateway Interface (CGI). Extensible Style Language (XSL) gives XML the ability to add style to documents or transform information from one format to another.

Two specifications describe XSL. The first specification, which was the first released and is the most widely adopted, is XSL Transformation (XSLT) language. The second specification describes an XML vocabulary for specifying formatting semantics, known as XSL Formatting Language. It is somewhat confusing, but both XSL and the XSL Formatting Language share the same abbreviation (XSL). Chapter 8 describes XSLT and XSL Formatting Language in more detail.

The initial 1.0 version of XSLT became a W3C Recommendation in November of 1999. Before becoming a Recommendation, XSLT was stable, so the preliminary support that vendors provided for XSLT closely matched the Recommendation.

Because of this, early adopters of XSL have used the transformation language. The most common use of the transformation language is to take an XML document and transform it to HTML for display on the Web.

Transforming XML to HTML is a workaround for the limited support of XML in browser clients. Performing the transformation on a server and sending out the result to a client gives consistent results and is a bridge between the new XML technology and the majority of Web users, who do not run the latest browser. I suspect that this may become a long-term strategy, especially for open Internet applications, because it helps transcend the subtle differences among various vendors' browsers.

XSLT does not restrict you to converting XML to HTML. I have seen this technology used in very creative ways. For example, I have seen XSLT used to convert database files described by XML to Structured Query Language (SQL) statements, which actually created the tables, indexes, and views that the XML data described. You can also use XSLT to transform data to different Electronic Data Interchange (EDI) formats from a common XML format.

The second XSL specification, XSL Formatting Language, has not enjoyed the same stability that XSLT has had. However, after several false starts, XSL Formatting Language is finally on track to widespread adoption. The formatting language describes how to present a document, and is much more capable than a style sheet.The XSL Formatting Language uses formatting objects to take elements described in an abstract tree-like representation of a document and renders those elements in the document's actual presentation. The formatting language and formatting objects are extremely powerful, supporting features such as sorting, expressions, and complex document elements. With this power comes complexity. XML is supposed to be a simple alternative to SGML; you may want to put off adopting XSL Formatting Language until XML and CSS no longer meet your needs.

Tools of the Trade

For many people, a new project, whether Java, XML, or home improvement, is an excuse to acquire and use new tools. I am one of these people; in my case a home improvement project usually involves a couple of hours, some supplies, and a new tool—a tape measure, handsaw, or if I am really lucky, a power tool.

XML is a tool lover's dream. There are hundreds of cool new products to add to your toolbox, which support every aspect of XML. I don't understand why, but the majority of these new tools are also free. The Internet is the best place to find these XML tools and resources. Here are some sites with useful tools to get you started:

www.alphaworks.ibm.com: This Web site provides access to IBM's emerging alpha-code technologies. At this site you will find dozens of XML tools, including XML Interface for RPG, XML Lightweight Extractor, XML Parser for Java (XMLJ), XML and Web Services Development Environment, Xeena, and the XSL by Demo WebSphere Studio plug-in.

msdn.microsoft.com/xml/: Microsoft's XML site contains XML fixes, updates, and product previews for Internet Explorer (look for the Xmlinst.exe Replace Mode Tool). On the downloads page you will find tools such as Internet Explorer Tools for Validating XML and Viewing XSLT as well as XML Notepad.

xml.apache.org: This Web site, which is related to the well-known Apache Web server, contains quite a few open-source tools, including Xerces, Xalan, Crimson, and Xang. Although the names are odd, these tools are some of the best available; visit the Web site to find out whether Xerces is a markup language for Greek mythology, or an XML parser written in Java.

java.sun.com/xml/: You will find several Java-related XML tools at Sun's XML site, including Java API for XML Processing (JAXP) and Java API for XML Messaging (JAXM).

www.w3.org/People/Raggett/tidy/: XML Tidy is a handy freeware utility by Dave Raggett that converts HTML to XHTML. Be sure to read the Getting Started guide. If you prefer a Windows interface, download the TidyGUI version, which is also on this page.

You can use any text editor, such as Code/400 or Notepad, to edit your XML documents, but eventually you will want to get an editor that helps you with the job. Quite a few are available; some are even free or have free trials. IBM's Alphaworks Web site has several editors, including Xeena. You can go to Microsoft's Web site and download XML Notepad; the direct URL is *msdn.microsoft.com/xml/notepad/intro.asp*. If you want an open-source editor, Conglomerate provides support for both Windows and Linux; their Web site is *www.conglomerate.org*.

iSeries XML Solutions

The final section of this book describes two complete iSeries (formerly AS/400) solutions. These solutions show how to use XML on the iSeries platform and may give you some ideas on how XML can help you in your environment. In addition to XML, these solutions use RPG IV, Java, servlets, and the Apache Web server running on the iSeries. I include enough information to set up and get started with these solutions. Where appropriate, I have listed resources describing where you can get more details.

Building an XML File Viewer

The first solution describes an XML file viewer that uses XML to describe database files in a manner similar to Data Description Specifications (DDS). This solution allows you to create database files from this definition. After creating a file, you can add some data to the file and then view the formatted data with a Web browser. To view the data, a Java application builds an XML data stream from the data and then displays the results in a browser.

This solution contains two parts. The first part shows how to describe database files using XML. The first step creates an XML document that describes a database file. A DTD ensures that the XML document is valid and conforms to several rules. Next, a process converts the XML description to a DB2 database file residing on your iSeries system. The actual conversion uses XSL Transformations (XSLT) to convert the XML definition to the SQL statements used to create the table.

The second part is a file viewer that uses an XML database definition to display database file information in a browser. First, information contained in a database file is converted to an XML document using IBM's XML Lightweight Extractor (XLE). A Cascading Style Sheet helps to format the resulting XML document for display using a JavaServer Page (JSP) in a browser.

The browser-based file viewer uses a simple Java servlet that runs on your iSeries server. In order to focus on the XML parts of the application and not be sidetracked by WebSphere's complexities, I used the very capable and easy-to-configure Jakarta servlet engine. The Jakarta servlet engine is an open-source project supported by the Apache organization. There is nothing in the example that is specific to Jakarta, so it will run just fine if you already have WebSphere running and want to use WebSphere.

Building an XML Data Interchange

One application that many iSeries shops run is Electronic Data Interchange (EDI). This solution describes how to create an industry-specific markup language and DTD. This new markup language is used to exchange information in a common format. The Timber Exchange (TIMEX) markup language is specific to the timber and logging industry, but the concepts are valid for any industry-specific solution.

I begin this example by describing the elements of the TIMEX markup language. Following that, I show you how to create the TIMEX DTD, which ensures TIMEX documents adhere to some rules. Trading partners use the TIMEX DTD to ensure validity of information before sending the information.

On the receiving end, I show you how to use the XML Interface for RPG, which is a free tool that validates and parses XML documents. After determining that the information is correct, I show you how to interpret and write the XML-formatted data to a DB2 database file.

This example walks you through the steps necessary to create a new markup that supports the timber and logging industry, but these techniques apply to all industry-specific markups. If someone has already defined a widely accepted markup in your industry, use it; if none is available, now is your chance to become an industry leader and define your own markup.

Chapter Highlights

In this chapter, you learned about the problems that XML solves as well as some XML history and background.

- XML is extensible because it is a meta-markup language.
- With XML, content is separated from style.
- Well-formed documents comply with XML's syntax and structure.
- An XML document can use a DTD or Schema for additional validation.
- Search engines search XML documents more effectively.
- XHTML is now replacing HTML.
- XML uses CSS, XSL, and XSLT to provide style.

In the next chapter, I will start to describe the parts and structure of an XML document as well as basic XML syntax.

2

XML Basics

In this chapter you will learn:

- ✓ The parts of an XML document
- ✓ XML's basic syntax
- ✓ How to read and write XML documents
- ✓ How to apply basic style to XML documents
- ✓ How to check XML documents to see whether they are well-formed and valid

In the last chapter, I introduced you to XML and gave some reasons why XML is such an important technology. If you have done much work with HTML, this section will seem familiar, because HTML and XML are very similar markup languages. The introduction is brief; after all, you are probably eager to begin building your own XML solutions.

Building your own XML applications is not that hard once you understand a few of XML's rules. This chapter introduces you to those rules and shows you how to create a simple XML document. You will also learn how to use a style sheet to format this XML document for viewing in a Web browser.

As you begin feeding XML documents to your Web browser, your results may be different from the examples shown, because different Web browsers support XML differently. Remember also that XML applications cannot process XML documents that contain errors. You may also experience some of the incompatibilities between some Web browsers and XML. Because of these difficulties I have included some instructions that will help you in case your browser is not up to XML's expectations. Older versions do not support XML at all; in general, you will need version 5+ of the major Web browsers.

Creating XML Documents

An XML document is textual in nature and uses standard ASCII characters. To create an XML document, you combine character data and markup tags. You can use one of the editors described in Chapter 1, or simply start your favorite text editor; Notepad will work fine for most simple XML documents. The following XML example is simple but represents a complete XML document. Variations of this example appear throughout this book.

```
<?xml version="1.0"?>

<!-- Sample log delivery XML document -->
<deliveries>
   <load scale-type="DTL">
      <scale-ticket>12345</scale-ticket>
      <weight>42168</weight>
      <weight-uom>LBS</weight-uom>
      <scale-uom>US</scale-uom>
      <delivered-date>
         <month>10</month>
         <day>29</day>
         <year>2001</year>
      </delivered-date>
      <log>
         <species>WESTERN LARCH</species>
         <grade>PEELER</grade>
```

Figure 2.1: A simple XML document describing log deliveries (part 1 of 2).

```
            <large-end-diameter>15</large-end-diameter>
            <small-end-diameter>12</small-end-diameter>
            <length>32</length>
        </log>
        <log>
            <species>WESTERN LARCH</species>
            <grade>PEELER</grade>
            <large-end-diameter>13</large-end-diameter>
            <small-end-diameter>9</small-end-diameter>
            <length>32</length>
        </log>
    </load>
</deliveries>
```

Figure 2.1: A simple XML document describing log deliveries (part 2 of 2).

The first line of the log delivery document shown in Figure 2.1 describes the type of content. It is unlikely that XML will see a new version anytime soon, so you will see this line a lot. Following that line is a blank line. XML ignores this line just as it ignores all forms of white space, including spaces, tabs, carriage returns, and line feeds. A comment, enclosed by <!-- and -->, follows. The next line in the delivery document starts the root element <deliveries>, which is closed by the </deliveries> tag. An XML document can only have one root element, so you cannot have another element that follows the </deliveries> closing tag.

The entries contained within the document root describe a typical load (to keep this example short, I removed all but two logs) of logs delivered to a lumber mill. This load of logs has a scale-type attribute. These attributes are associated with a load and therefore enclosed in the <load> tag.

The Building Blocks of XML

If you are familiar with HTML, you will find the basic building blocks of XML are familiar. All XML documents consist of XML text, which in turn consists of character data and markup. Markup is everything but your content and includes start tags, end tags, comments, and entity references. Delimiters surround markup. The most commonly used are tag delimiters, which are the less-than (<) and greater than (>) signs, and entity delimiters, which are the ampersand

(&) and semicolon (;). The main components you will use when creating an XML document are

- Elements enclosed in tags, such as <recipe> . . . </recipe>
- Attributes, which add further information to tags, such as menuitem="Y"
- Entity placeholders for text or binary files, such as &REPLACEMENT
- Processing instructions to embed non-XML information
- Comments that describe an XML document
- Text supplies the most common form of XML content

All XML documents use some combination of these components. XML supplies strict rules that describe how and where these components may be used.

The Element

The most basic part of an XML document is an element. Elements describe the logical structure of an XML document. Each element represents a logical component of an XML document. Matching tags enclose elements that support either content or structure. Elements that support content contain text or binary information and are the reason that an XML document exists. Elements that support structure make it easier to understand a document by providing a way of grouping other elements.

An element nested in another element is a subelement. Every XML documents has one high-level element known as the root element. The elements beneath the root element are subelements of the root. If a subelement contains other subelements, it is a branch. If it does not contain a subelement, it is a leaf.

The hierarchy just described sounds a lot like a tree. The term *tree structure* is often used when referring to an XML document.

Using Attributes

Attributes are associated with an element and add further information. Going back to the example in Figure 2.1, the <load> element has a scale-type attribute that is set to DTL. In many cases, you have to decide between creating a new element and adding an attribute to an existing element. In most cases an answer of yes to any of the following three questions indicates that you should use an element rather than an attribute.

1. Is it common to include this item in output?
2. Does this item contain structure; in other words, can it be broken down into subcomponents, such as a month, day, and year for a date?
3. Can an element contain more than one of these items?

If you are not certain of the answer to one of these questions, it is usually better to go with an element because elements offer more flexibility.

Entity References

An entity is a way to refer to some part of an XML document. That part can be some text, a snippet of XML, or an entire file. You can include an entity in a document using an entity reference. An entity reference to some text defined and used in the same document is an internal general entity. An internal general entity is a good way to ensure that frequently used text is consistent throughout a document. An abbreviated example in which an internal general entity is used to replaces the reference &WL with the text WESTERN LARCH is shown in Figure 2.2:

```
<!ENTITY WL “WESTERN LARCH”>
. . .
<log>
   <species>&WL;</species>
```

Figure 2.2: Internal general entity and reference to it.

Processing Instructions

With HTML it is common to see proprietary extensions supported via comments embedded in an HTML document. This practice is dangerous, because it is very easy to lose a comment or cause some unintended action with a documentation comment. XML avoids this danger by explicitly supporting processing instructions. A processing instruction is a string of text between <? and ?>.

Using Comments

Comments in an XML document are surrounded by the <!-- and -->. The purpose of a comment is to add descriptive information to the XML document. Comments should not be used be used to add proprietary extensions. You can use comments to prevent XML markup from being recognized, as follows:
<!-- This embedded log tag is not processed <log> -->

Content

The most important part of an XML document is its content. That is the reason that the document exists. Content is interspersed throughout an XML document and can be part of an element, attribute, or entity. Text is the most common form of content, but XML also supports binary content such as an image file, voice clip, or spreadsheet.

Avoid Terse XML Documents

Even someone with no knowledge about the timber industry can derive some meaning from the log delivery summary shown in Figure 2.1. You may not know that Western Larch is a type of tree or that CUBIC is a way of measuring trees, but you should be able to see that something was delivered on October 29, 2001, that weighed 42,168 pounds. This ability to derive meaning comes from the use of descriptive tags. If the Deliveries, Load, and DeliveredDate tags had terse names like Dlvs, Ld, and DlvDt, it would be much more difficult to derive any meaning from this document.

You should avoid being terse when you create your own tag names. This is one of XML's design goals. One reason you might use short names is to cut down on the amount of typing that you have to do. Most XML editors make it unnecessary to key a tag more than once in an XML document. Another reason you might use short names is to reduce the overall size of your XML documents. Compression tools do a great job at compressing XML documents because repeated information takes up very little space.

Basic Syntax and Structure

All XML documents have to conform to some basic rules. An XML document that conforms to the rules is known as a *well-formed document.* Documents that do not follow the rules cannot even be processed and are not considered XML documents.

The following list sets forth some of XML's rules:

- If included, an XML document declaration starts on line one.
- Every XML document must have one root element.
- All elements must have matching begin and end tags.
- Elements must be properly nested.
- XML is case sensitive.
- White space outside of elements is ignored.
- Attribute values must be enclosed in single (') or double (") quotes.
- Use & for ampersand (&) and < for less than (<) inside markup.

XML Names

You can use any name for the elements (tags) of an XML document, as long as the name follows a few simple rules. First, names must start with a letter or an underscore (_) character. The rest of the name is any combination of letters, digits, underscores, periods (.), hyphens (-), or colons (:). Names cannot have embedded spaces or start with any form of XML; therefore, names like

<xmlmyname>, <XML-myname>, or <XmlMyname> are invalid. The colon character is used to separate names from namespaces, so it is best to avoid using a colon in an XML name.

Names are case sensitive, so <myname> is not equivalent to <Myname>. When assigning names, it is best to be consistent. The most common convention is to use lowercase letters with words separated by hyphens, for example <date>, <my-name>, or <street-address>.

Eventually, you will experience a name collision where your naming conflicts with someone else's and the meaning you apply to the name is different. XML provides for resolving these conflicts by using *namespaces*. A namespace allows you to associate a name with a domain-specific namespace. For more information on XML namespaces and to see how XML resolves name collisions, see Chapter 6.

Rules for Elements

Every element must have a start tag and an end tag. This means that for every beginning tag like <log>, there must be a corresponding ending tag of </log>. This is different from HTML, where the browser will insert the closing tag if you leave it out. This is particularly common with paragraph <P> and list item <LI> tags.

Elements with no content are *empty tags*. You can close an empty tag using the special notation />, like: <date-type format="*ISO" />. Be sure to include the blank space before the closing />.

Every document must have one element that contains all others. This top-level element is the *root* element, also known as the *document element*. The root element in Figure 2.1 is the deliveries element. The entire XML document is enclosed between the starting <deliveries> tag and the closing </deliveries> tag.

All elements within a document nest within one another. In other words, an element embedded in another element must open and close within the enclosing element. For example, the following sequence is valid: <log><species> . . .

</species></log>, whereas this sequence is invalid: <log><species> . . . </log></species>. The second sequence is invalid because the log element does not completely enclose the species element.

Place attributes associated with an element in the element's starting tag. The value follows the element name and is enclosed in quotes (') or double quotes ("). Although single quotes are valid, it is good practice to enclose double quotes for attribute values. The following example shows a scale-type attribute for a load element: <load scale-type="DTL">

Document Declaration

An XML document can include an optional XML declaration that specifies the version of XML used as well as some other attributes. If a document includes an XML declaration, it must be the first thing found in the document, starting in the first position of the first line. It is good practice to include an XML declaration. One exception to this is XML documents that are combinations of more than one XML document. Chapter 3 goes into more detail about combining documents using entities. The following is a simple XML declaration: <?xml version="1.0" ?>

As I mentioned, an XML declaration may also describe some other attributes. One of these is the *encoding declaration*. The encoding declaration is optional and describes the character set used in the document. All XML parsers must accept Unicode and the International Organization for Standardization (ISO/IEC) 10646 character sets. Chapter 3 also describes the use of various character sets in detail. The following XML declaration shows the encoding declaration for Western European Latin, referred to either as ISO-8859-1 or sometimes by the nonstandard name Latin-1: <?xml version="1.0" encoding="ISO-8859-1" ?>

The default encoding is UTF-8, which is a superset of ASCII. This means that UTF-8 is fine for XML documents that use the ASCII character set. The Unicode character set is assumed if you leave out the encoding declaration. Because any XML document that uses anything other than Unicode must have a document declaration that starts in position one, it is possible for the parser to use this fact to determine the encoding.

Another attribute supported in a document declaration is the *standalone document declaration*. Specifying standalone="yes" indicates that there are no external markup declarations that affect the information passed from the XML processor to the application. Specifying standalone="no" indicates that there may or may not be any external markup declarations. A standalone document declaration is not commonly used.

Processing Instructions

The document declaration in the preceding section is a processing instruction. A processing instruction begins with <? and closes with ?>. Processing instructions send instructions to an XML processor or application. In HTML it is common to see proprietary extensions supported through the use of comments. For example, IBM's WebSphere Studio product uses HTML comments to associate JavaScript with the prompt screen that Studio originally used to create the Java script.

One of the most common uses for processing instructions is to associate a style sheet with an XML document. The following example shows a typical processing instruction that associates a Cascading Style Sheet (CSS) with an XML document: <?xml-stylesheet href="dessert1.css" type="text/css"?>

Using Special Characters

In some cases you will need to refer to special characters within the content of an XML document. XML requires that some special characters may appear in their literal form only in the context of markup and not within character data content. You are most likely to encounter this limitation with the less-than sign (<) and ampersand (&), which can appear in their literal form only as markup delimiters. To prevent the interpretation of a special character, you must *escape* the character by referring to the character indirectly using an entity or a numeric character reference. If you have more than one character that you want to escape, you may want to use a character data (CDATA) section.

The simplest way to refer to a special character is to use a predefined entity reference. An entity reference starts with an ampersand (&) and ends with a semicolon (;). XML has built-in support for the following entities:

- & for the ampersand (&)
- < for the less-than sign (<)
- > for the greater-than sign (>)
- ' for the apostrophe (‘)
- " for the double quote (“)

Figure 2.3 shows a snippet of a recipe marked up using the recipeML discussed in Chapter 1. It shows how to place an ampersand in a recipe ingredient.

```
<ingredients>
   <ing>
      <item>salt &amp; pepper to taste</item>
   </ing>
</ingredients>
```

Figure 2.3: Marked up recipe from chapter 1.

In this context, using the ampersand symbol directly would make the document invalid. For more information on embedding special characters, see Chapter 3, which describes how to create entities that refer to other special characters such as the copyright symbol.

An alternative to using an entity reference is a numeric character reference. This type of reference allows you to use a special notation to identify any character that is part of the ISO/IEC 10646 character set (which covers most languages). This notation starts with an ampersand and pound sign (&#) followed by the decimal number for the character, and ends with a semicolon (;). The numeric character reference for an ampersand is &. The hex equivalent can also be used by specifying an x after the &# like ©, which represents a copyright (©) symbol.

Character Data Sections

In an XML document, anything contained between a less-than sign (<) and a greater-than sign (>) is markup. Anything else in an XML document is character data that represents content. In some cases, you may want to embed XML markup or plain text that contains special characters in the content of an XML document. The best way to do this is to use a character data (CDATA) section.

To start a CDATA section you use the notation <![CDATA[and to end the section, you use]]>. You can embed any combination of tags, special characters, and text inside a CDATA section, and an XML processor will treat it as text.

```
<codesample>
<![CDATA[
   import java.io.*;
   import java.util.*;
   import java.util.zip.*;
   class listzip{
      public static void main(String args[]) {
         try {
            File f = new File(args[0]);
            if(!f.exists()){
               f = new File(args[0]+".zip");
            };
            if(f.exists()) {
               try{
                  ZipFile zf = new ZipFile(f);
                  System.out.println("Contents of " + args[0] + ":");
                  Enumeration ze = zf.entries();
                  for (;ze.hasMoreElements();) {
                       ZipEntry zpe = (ZipEntry)ze.nextElement();
                       System.out.println("" + zpe.getName() +
                         "\t" + zpe.getSize() +
                         "\t" + zpe.getCompressedSize());
                  };
               } catch(ZipException ex) {
                  System.out.println(args[0] + ": " + ex.toString());
               };
            } else {
               System.out.println(f.getAbsoluteFile() + " doesn't exist.");
            };
         } catch(ArrayIndexOutOfBoundsException ex) {
            System.out.println("Usage:\tjzip <zipfile>");
         } catch(Exception ex) {
            ex.printStackTrace();
         };
      }
   }
]]>
</codesample>
```

Figure 2.4: Java code embedded in XML by means of CDATA.

One rare exception is when you want to embed a CDATA close (]]>) within a CDATA section; in that case, use]]>. Figure 2.4 shows an example in which a Java source code sample is embedded in an XML document.

White Space and Comments

Within an XML document white space, which consists of any combination of spaces, tabs, carriage returns, and line feeds, helps to improve the readability of a document. In most cases, an XML processor ignores white space that is not part of a document's content. However, an XML processor must return white space that is part of a document's content to an application when an XML document is processed.

To tell an application that white space in content is significant and should be preserved, use the special attribute xml:space. This attribute signals how an application should process this white space and is included in a Document Type Definition (DTD).

Comments are surrounded by the <!-- and --> notations. There are a few rules associated with comments. The first is that you embed comments in an XML document anywhere outside of markup, that is, anywhere that is not inside a beginning (<) or ending (>) of a markup instruction or tag. In addition, a comment cannot start an XML document with a document declaration, because if a document declaration is used, it must be first. Finally, a comment cannot have an embedded double hyphen (--).

Viewing XML Documents

After working so hard to create your XML documents, you are probably anxious to see what they look like in a Web browser. If you are using an older browser (say, something released in the last century), you should go to your browser vendor's Web site and get the latest version. Remember that the W3C recommended XML in 1998, so most browsers did not support large parts of the specification until after the year 2000.

To view an XML document in a Web browser, you can open it from a browser using the **File → Open** dialog. Alternatively, you can publish your XML document to a Web server. In most cases, it does not matter which technique you use. Figure 2.5 shows how the log delivery document looks in a Web browser. In this case, I used the Apache Web server running on my iSeries system.

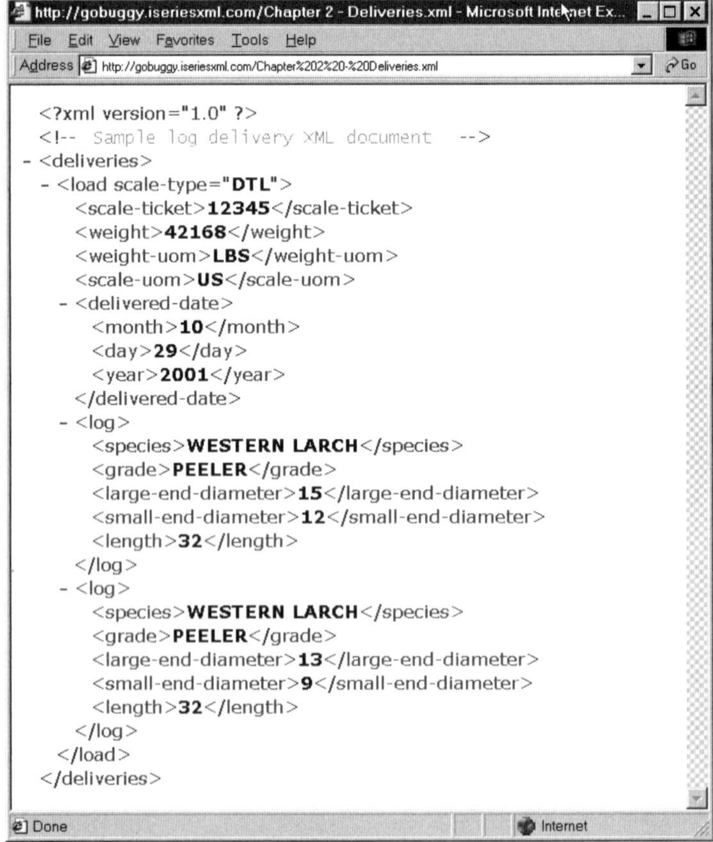

Figure 2.5: How Internet Explorer 5.5 renders the log delivery XML document shown in Figure 2.1.

When you look at Figure 2.5, you may feel cheated. Internet Explorer did little more than render the log delivery document in an outline format. It is great that you can click on the "-"s and "+"s to collapse or expand a level of the document, but this is not something you want to display when the shipping clerk looks at the day's deliveries. With other browsers, you may not even get the outline feature; all you get is the raw XML document.

The reason the document shown in Figure 2.5 displays the way it has is that it has no style. Chapter 8 covers how to apply style to your XML document in detail, but realizing that a document without style is boring, I will take this opportunity to go over some style basics.

The simplest and most widely supported style mechanism is Cascading Style Sheets (CSS). Other ways to apply style to a document include using Extensible Stylesheet Language (XSL) or converting the XML document to HTML. One way to convert an XML document to HTML is to use an XSL Transformation (XSLT). All of these methods of applying style are covered in depth in Chapter 8.

You can use a CSS with either HTML or XML. The W3C has released several versions of CSS starting with CSS1, which became a recommendation in December of 1996. The W3C recommended CSS2 in May of 1998. The development of CSS came out of early arguments relating to formatting and HTML. Because of this, CSS targets HTML, and, although it works for styling XML documents, it is not capable of formatting XML documents that are radically different from HTML. With that warning in mind, Figure 2.6 shows a simple CSS.

```
deliveries {
   margin: 0.5in;
   border: solid;
   display: block;
}
log {
   text-align: left;
   display: block;
}
species {
   font-weight: bold;
}
```

Figure 2.6: A simple Cascading Style Sheet (CSS).

I entered the CSS shown in Figure 2.5 using the Windows Notepad. The main limitations in this example are that there are no headings and that the column data is not in a tabular format. If the deliveries document had been an HTML document, it would have included headings and a table that defined the columnar data. Figure 2.7 shows how Internet Explorer renders the delivery XML document with the CSS from Figure 2.6.

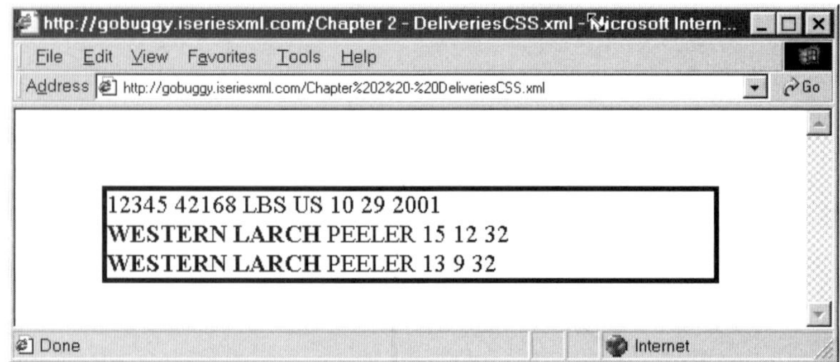

Figure 2.7: The delivery document from Figure 2.5 with the CSS from Figure 2.6.

To create the example shown in Figure 2.7, I copied the Deliveries.xml document shown in Figure 2.1 to a new XML document named DeliveriesCSS.xml. Next, I inserted the following after the document declaration, which associates the CSS with the new XML document:

```
<?xml-stylesheet href="deliveries.css" type="text/css"?>
```

As you can see, CSS has some limitations. In particular, it is very difficult to add presentation structure such as columns and headings to an XML document using CSS. For this reason, it is best to use CSS with HTML or the XML-compliant version of HTML, XHTML.

One method of adding presentation structure to an XML document such as the delivery document is to convert the document to an HTML or XHTML document using an Extensible Stylesheet Language Transformation (XSLT). The resulting document can, and probably should, use a CSS.

Earlier I mentioned that XML ignores white space; this is not entirely true. A tag that occupies a new line causes a space to be inserted with Internet Explorer 5.5.

Checking Your XML Document

As you start using XML, you are likely to create documents containing errors. An XML document with errors is useless, so you need to check your documents before delivering them to your users. Quite a few tools will check your XML documents. The easiest way to check an XML document is to run the document through a parser.

There are two types of checks performed on an XML document. The first type of check ensures that a document is *well-formed*. A well-formed document complies with XML's basic syntax and rules. The other type of check uses a Document Type Definition (DTD), which describes what tags and attributes are valid and in what context the tags and attributes are valid. A document that conforms to the rules of a DTD is *valid*. Chapter 3 describe how to build and use a DTD.

Validating XML Documents with a Web Browser

One feature found in more recently released browsers is a built-in XML parser. This means that you can use the browser to check your XML document for errors (remember that documents with errors are not processed, but the parser can report errors). When Internet Explorer encounters an error, you get a display similar to the one shown in Figure 2.8.

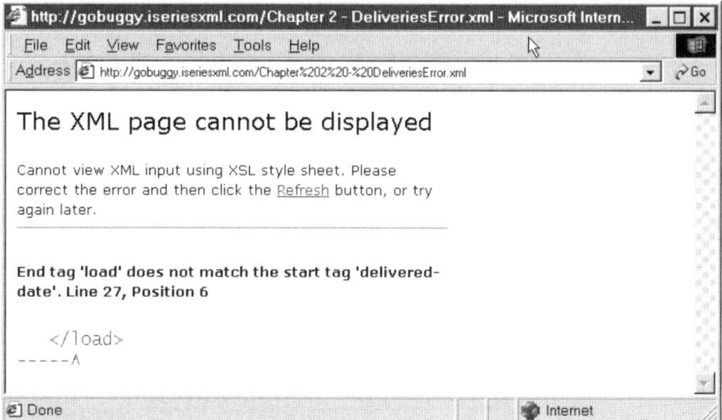

Figure 2.8: Internet Explorer reporting a validation error.

In this case, the closing </delivered-date> tag is missing. Mistakes like this are easy to make, especially when you are using a text editor that does not automatically close tags and perform syntax checking as you go.

Web Sites That Validate XML Documents

Several Web sites will check an XML document. Most of these sites allow you to specify a URL or cut and paste XML text into a test window.

> *www.networking.ibm.com/xml/XmlValidatorForm.html:* This page uses a servlet to check an XML document. Although the documentation states that this page checks an XML document to see whether it is valid, documents that are well-formed work fine. This page uses a servlet to build a Document Object Model (DOM) tree view of your XML document. You must type the XML document in directly or use cut and paste.
>
> *www.xml.com/pub/a/tools/ruwf/check.html:* This page checks an XML document to see whether it is well-formed. You can enter a URL or type the XML document in directly.
>
> *www.stg.brown.edu/service/xmlvalid/:* This page checks an XML document to see whether it is well-formed and valid. To be valid, your document must refer to a DTD. You can enter a local file or a URL or type the XML document in directly.
>
> *www.cogsci.ed.ac.uk/~richard/xml-check.html:* This page checks an XML document to see whether it is well-formed and, optionally, whether it is valid. You must enter the URL for your XML document.

These Web sites provide a way to see quickly how various parsers will check an XML document to see whether it is well-formed and valid. If you find yourself constantly referring to one of these pages, it may be time to build your own XML validation tool using a parser.

Preventing Errors with an XML Editor

Another way to catch errors is to edit your XML documents with a specialized XML editor. These specialized editors check the syntax of an XML document as you make changes. Some XML editors ensure only that a document is well-formed; others allow you to specify a DTD and perform a check for validity. There are quite a few editors to choose from, and many of them are even free.

One free and easy-to-use XML editor is Microsoft's XML Notepad. This editor only checks documents to see whether they are well-formed. The direct URL for XML Notepad is *msdn.microsoft.com/xml/notepad/intro.asp.*

Chapter Highlights

In this chapter you learned a lot about XML's syntax.

- Embed the ampersand (&) and less-than sign (<) in markup using the & and < escape sequences.
- Avoid creating terse documents.
- A well-formed XML document is syntactically correct.
- A valid XML document conforms to the rules of a DTD.
- Use CDATA to embed text containing special characters in XML documents.
- XML parsers ignore white space that is outside of markup.

In the next chapter I will take you through some of the more advanced parts of XML and introduce you to some XML applications.

3

The Basics of DTDs

In this chapter you will learn:

- ✓ What DTDs are used for
- ✓ How to create a DTD
- ✓ The syntax of a DTD
- ✓ How define elements and attributes
- ✓ More about general and parameter entities
- ✓ When to use a DTD and when not to

By now you have an idea of just how flexible XML is. In some cases this flexibility presents a problem. Sometimes you may need to restrict an XML document to something that a particular application understands. Such restrictions are often necessary when you have an application that relies on an XML document for input. Most applications work with a certain set of input. One way to restrict the options available in an XML document is to use a Document Type Definition (DTD). A DTD allows you to specify which elements and attributes may appear, when they may appear, and in what order.

All XML documents must be well formed. When a document complies with the rules of a DTD, it is also valid. Often these two terms are used together, so when you read that a document is well formed and valid, you know that it complies with the rules of a DTD.

A DTD uses a formal syntax that is somewhat different from XML's syntax. This syntax borrows from regular expressions and supports capabilities such as pattern matching and sequencing notation. UNIX programmers are familiar with regular expressions because they are an integral part of the UNIX operating system and utilities like *grep*. You even see some of this notation used in DOS, SQL, and Java Script, so even if you are unfamiliar with UNIX, it is likely that you have had some exposure to regular expressions.

You may already be using DTDs without knowing it; they have been around for over 30 years. DTDs are part of the Standard Generalized Markup Language (SGML), the parent of XML and HTML. Unlike SGML, where all documents have to use a DTD, XML imposes enough rules that a DTD is not required. One type of XML document that uses a DTD is XHTML. The DTDs for XHTML are available at *www.w3c.org*, and an XHTML document type declaration often specifies the files using their W3C URL.

Validating XML Documents

When an XML document is to be validated, it includes a document type declaration that identifies a DTD that the document satisfies. The DTD lists the elements, attributes, and entities that the XML document uses and the permissible relationships between them. The DTD may describe items that the XML document does not include. To be valid, the document must use only those items described by the DTD. If it uses elements not described or puts elements in a relationship that is not described, it is invalid.

Even when an XML document is valid, there is still a lot of flexibility allowed. For example, a DTD does not specify the values or type of data that an element contains. You can't tell a DTD to allow numeric values, the length of a value, or other such rules. A DTD also does not tell you what the root element is or how many instances of an element may appear. A DTD is just your first line of defense; further editing must be done using an application or a schema definition.

When to Use a DTD

You know at this point that a DTD is not required for XML documents. One of the first questions you have to answer is whether you even need a DTD. In many cases, a DTD is a requirement imposed upon your XML document. For example, XHTML needs to specify one of several DTDs. Even if a DTD is not imposed on you, there are several reasons you might want to use a DTD, such as the following:

- A DTD provides a clear definition of what your applications expect in XML documents.
- For complex documents, DTDs help XML authors determine relationships between markup and other rules such as sequence.

In most cases, if you are working with more than a few documents that share a common structure, you should create a DTD. In some cases you have to use a DTD to support certain features, such as the inclusion of non-XML content in an XML document.

As you have seen, a DTD is not required, and in some cases the value of a DTD does not outweigh the cost of creating a DTD. This is true when you have very large XML documents or will never run them through a validating parser. Another case where you might not use a DTD is in a program-generated XML document.

Using a DTD

A parser uses a DTD to test the validity of an XML document. Not all parsers support the use of a DTD. Those parsers that do support a DTD are known as validating parsers. Most validating parsers allow you to turn off DTD validation. In most cases, a DTD is stored in a document file that is separate from the XML documents that reference it. This allows you to use one DTD to validate many

XML documents. An XML document may also reference more than one DTD or may combine internal DTD definitions with external definitions.

Interpreting a Simple DTD

Even if you do not plan to use DTDs, it is useful to understand how a DTD works. Often, looking at the DTD for an XML document will help you understand more about the applications that process the XML document. For example, knowing that the DTD for PCML (see Chapter 11) allows you to define data within a *struct*, and that you cannot use *struct* within data, implies that a structure groups data.

The DTD in Figure 3.1 is about as simple as they come, but it goes a long way toward describing the allowed content of an XML document. This DTD describes the elements in a recipe XML document. This is a very simple example; in actual use, a recipe DTD would most likely be more complex and support additional elements.

```
<!ELEMENT recipe (name, ingredient+, instruction+)>
<!ELEMENT name (#PCDATA)>
<!ELEMENT ingredient (quantity?, description)>
<!ELEMENT quantity (#PCDATA)>
<!ELEMENT description (#PCDATA)>
<!ELEMENT instruction (#PCDATA)>
```

Figure 3.1: A simple recipe DTD used to validate recipe markup.

First, this DTD would probably be stored as a separate document referred to by an XML recipe document. However, it is also possible to define a DTD like this within the XML document that it describes within the document type definition. The extension for a DTD is usually .dtd, although it is not a requirement.

Each line of this DTD is an element declaration. All XML documents have at least one element, and elements are the main component of an XML document. An element declaration defines which elements you can use, the children of those elements, the types of data those elements contain, and the allowed attributes.

Because a DTD defines the hierarchy of this XML document, the topmost element declaration is the root element, although this is not a requirement. The recipe DTD starts with the root element declaration, which is recipe. From the recipe element declaration, you can see that a recipe is composed of a name element, ingredient elements, and instruction elements. This tells you that these three elements are all that are valid within a recipe element.

Looking more closely at the recipe element definition, you will notice that the name, ingredient, and instruction elements are separated by commas and that the ingredient and instruction elements are followed by a plus (+) sign. The commas and plus sign tell you more about the relationship between these elements and the recipe element. The comma ensures that the elements appear in the order specified, so you must include the name before ingredient elements and ingredient elements before instruction elements. The plus sign indicates that the recipe must have one or more ingredient and instruction elements. The name element, which has no special symbol, must appear once and only once.

Within the ingredient element definition, you see that it lists a quantity element and a description element. The quantity is followed by a question mark, which indicates that it may or may not occur.

The name, quantity, description, and instructions elements do not specify other elements; they specify that they contain #PCDATA, which stands for parsed character data. Parsed character data is raw text that may contain entity references (such as *&* or *'*) but does not contain other markup. In this case, the name, quantity, description, and instruction elements contain only text and may not contain other elements.

You can see that even a short DTD is useful when you are trying to make sure that an application is capable of processing a particular XML document. An application that uses XML documents based on the recipe DTD needs to understand six elements. Knowing the hierarchical relationship of those elements reduces the number of possibilities that the application needs to handle.

The recipe DTD is also useful to the author of recipe XML documents. Not only can the author read the DTD and understand what is expected, but some XML editors allow you to specify a DTD. Those editors can help the author by showing what elements are valid and help prevent the author from making mistakes.

The Document Type Declaration

An XML document starts with a prolog, which may contain an XML declaration, document type declarations, processing instructions, comments, and white space. If you are going to use a DTD to validate your document, the *document type declaration* is the part of this prolog where you specify the DTD. Be careful not to confuse the document type *declaration*, which is a line in the XML document that specifies a DTD, with the Document Type *Definition,* which is the DTD itself.

The document type declaration may include the DTD itself or refer to an external DTD. The document type declaration also identifies the root element of the XML document. A typical prolog containing a document type declaration looks like this:

```
<?XML version="1.0" standalone"no"?>
<!DOCTYPE recipe SYSTEM "simplerecipe.dtd">
```

The document type declaration is shown on the second line, following the XML declaration. The *<!DOCTYPE* tag starts the document type declaration, after which the root element, *recipe* in this case, is identified. The next part of the document type declaration, *SYSTEM "simplerecipe.dtd"*, instructs the processor to obtain the DTD from the external document simplerecipe.dtd.

Frequently, a document type declaration uses a Uniform Resource Identifier (URI) to refer to a DTD. With a URI this same reference might look like:

```
<!DOCTYPE recipe SYSTEM "http://www.iseriesxml.com/xml/dtd/
  simplerecipe.dtd">
```

Internal DTDs

The DTD does not have to be external. Instead of referring to a DTD in an external file, the document type declaration may contain the DTD itself.

Figure 3.2 shows how the simple recipe DTD from Figure 3.1 would look as such an *internal* DTD.

```
<?XML version="1.0"?>
<!DOCTYPE recipe [
   <!ELEMENT recipe (name, ingredient+, instruction+)>
   <!ELEMENT name (#PCDATA)>
   <!ELEMENT ingredient (quantity?, description)>
   <!ELEMENT quantity (#PCDATA)>
   <!ELEMENT description (#PCDATA)>
   <!ELEMENT instruction (#PCDATA)>
]>
```

Figure 3.2: An internal DTD included directly in an XML document.

Using an internal DTD allows an XML document to be self-contained, but it prevents you from reusing the DTD. There is a time when an internal DTD is useful: when you need to *extend* an external DTD to support a particular document. An XML document can have internal declarations and also reference a SYSTEM or PUBLIC URI. When you mix internal and external DTDs, the part that is contained within the XML document is the *internal DTD subset*, and the part brought in from an external document is the *external DTD subset.*

When you use an external DTD subset, you should specify *standalone="no"* in the XML declaration. There are rare cases when you do not have to do this, but since *standalone="no"* is always permitted, the simplicity of this rule outweighs the work involved in determining whether you can get away without setting *standalone="no"*.

Public vs. System IDs

The *SYSTEM* keyword indicates that an entity is stored at a location identified by a URI. Another way that you can reference an entity is by a *public* ID. You use the *PUBLIC* keyword in place of the *SYSTEM* keyword when you want a document validated using a DTD that is so well known and stable that the validating parser may be able to *recognize* it and validate the document on the basis of its own information without actually retrieving the DTD from its network location. In most cases, the URI is also included in case the validator does not recognize the public reference. Here is a typical public reference to the XHTML DTD:

```
<!DOCTYPE html PUBLIC "-//W3C//DTD XHTML 1.0 Strict//EN"
  "http://www.w3.org/TR/xhtml1/DTD/xhtml1/DTD/xhtml1-strict.dtd">
```

With this document type declaration, the XML parser may recognize the public name or go to the URI. In reality, most of the time public IDs are not recognized and the DTD is retrieved using the URI.

DTD Syntax

Much of the syntax for DTDs is the same as for XML documents. They use much of the same notation and share the same rules for comments and white space. The main difference is in their use. A DTD describes to a parser the rules of an XML document, whereas an XML document contains content.

Element Declarations in Detail

When you use a DTD to validate an XML document, you have to identify which elements may be used. That is the purpose of an element declaration. The simple recipe example shown in Figures 3.1 and 3.2 contains some examples of element declarations. The syntax of an element declaration looks like this:

```
<!ELEMENT name (content)>
```

An element declaration starts off with the *<!ELEMENT* tag. This tag contains the name of the element and then its *content model*. The name of the element can be any valid XML name. The content model describes what the element contains. There are five types of content shown in Table 3.1. The names of the elements defined in Table 3.1 are all creatively named *name*.

Table 3.1: Types of Content in DVD Elements

Content Type	Usage	Type of content allowed
Text	<!ELEMENT *name* (#PCDATA)>	Parsed character data
Element content	<!ELEMENT *name* *(child | child2)*>	Contains only an element of type *child* or *child2*
ANY	<!ELEMENT *name* ANY>	No restriction on the type of content
EMPTY	<!ELEMENT *name* EMPTY>	Cannot contain any content
Mixed content	<!ELEMENT *name* (#PCDATA I *child*)*>	Contains a mixture of parsed character data and elements of type *child*

Restricting Element Content to Text

One of the simplest forms of element declaration is that for elements that contain parsed character data. Parsed character data is simply text that does not contain markup. You can embed entity references such as *&*, but you cannot have embedded elements. The declaration for an element that contains parsed character data looks like this:

```
<!ELEMENT precipitation (#PCDATA)>
```

This element declaration allows the *precipitation* element to contain text and nothing but text.

Elements Containing Elements

One of the most common element notations indicates that an element contains other elements. This sort of element declaration builds a hierarchical picture of the relationship between elements. For example, you may want to define a catalog that contains sections and products. Products have a description and price. The element declarations for *catalog*, *section*, and *product* might look like this:

```
<!ELEMENT catalog (section+)>
<!ELEMENT section (product+)>
<!ELEMENT product (description, price)>
```

These element declarations allow an XML document to have one *catalog* root element containing one or more *section* child elements. Although you cannot specify that an element is a root element, the hierarchy defined here infers that *catalog* is the root. Each section contains one or more *product* child elements. Each product contains a *description* child element and a *price* child element, in that order.

As you can see, it is possible to pack a lot of meaning into a few statements. A lot of this is possible because of the available choice notation, such as the plus (+) signs and commas in the preceding example, which provides an important part of an element declaration. The next section describes this notation in detail.

Choice Notation

The notation used in an element declaration is very important. Depending on the symbols used, you can force child elements to appear in a certain order, or force the use of zero, one, or more child elements. You can combine these symbols to impose many types of restrictions using parentheses.

A comma separating child elements denotes a sequence. Child elements separated by commas must appear in the order in which they are listed in the element declaration. In the following example, the *weather* element must contain both *precipitation* and *sunshine* child elements in that order. The parser will flag an error if you specify sunshine before precipitation.

```
<!ELEMENT weather (precipitation, sunshine)>
```

A pipe (|) character separating child elements denotes a choice. If you want to have one of several possible child elements, separate the child elements with the pipe character. In this example, there may be either a precipitation or a sunshine element:

```
<!ELEMENT weather (precipitation | sunshine)>
```

Another type of notation that you can use tells the parser how many of a child element or group of child elements may appear. You can place symbols after a child element or parenthesized group of child elements to specify that zero or one, one or more, or any number of that element or group must appear as content. The absence of any symbol following a child element or group indicates that one and only one of that element or group must appear. The symbols used to indicate the number of elements are the question mark (?), the plus sign (+), and the asterisk (*). A question (?) mark indicates that zero or one child elements are required. The plus (+) sign indicates that at least one child element must be included. Finally, an asterisk (*) indicates that any number, including zero, of a child element must appear. Here are some examples:

```
<!ELEMENT product (price, suggestedprice?, discount*, supplier+)>
```

The preceding example indicates that a product must have one, and only one retail price; zero or one suggested prices; any number of discount codes; and one or more suppliers. Because commas separate the child elements, they must also appear in the order listed.

One of the most powerful notations is parentheses. Parentheses allow you to group child elements to form even more descriptive content models. You can separate child elements within parentheses using a comma or pipe character to indicate a sequence or choice. You can also suffix the parentheses with a ?, *, or +, to indicate a quantity other than one. In addition, parentheses may contain nested parentheses.

The following example shows how to combine child elements using parentheses. In this case an order discount may have a discount percentage or a coupon with an amount or percentage, but not both.

```
<!ELEMENT discount (discount | coupon, (amount | percentage))?>
```

Table 3.2 summarizes the symbols used when creating the content model for an element declaration. As you can see, there really aren't that many options, but together they allow you to impose quite a few useful restrictions on elements and their children.

Table 3.2: Summary of Element Declaration Notation

Symbol	Usage	Use
(and)	<!ELEMENT *name* (*child, (child1 | child2)*+)>	Parenthesis group choices
?	<!ELEMENT *name* (*child?*)>	Zero or one *child* elements allowed
*	<!ELEMENT *name* (*child**)>	Any number including zero *child* elements may appear
+	<!ELEMENT *name* (*child+*)>	One or more *child* elements allowed
	<!ELEMENT *name* (*child*)>	When ?, *, or + are not specified, a *child* element must appear once
,	<!ELEMENT *name* (*child, child1, child2*)>	Child elements must appear in the order listed
|	<!ELEMENT *name* (*child | child1 | child2*)>	One of the child elements listed

ANY and *EMPTY*

An element declaration that specifies *ANY* places no restrictions on the type of content. It can be parsed character data, elements, or empty. You still have to declare the subelements contained in an *ANY* element declaration in their own element declarations. Because the purpose of a DTD is to supply some guidelines on structure, *ANY* is seldom used.

Another type of content specification is *EMPTY*. This one is easier; it means that an element may not have content. Remember that you can use shorthand notation such as *<name />* for elements with no content.

Mixed Content

Mixed content is a mixture of parsed character data and elements. An element declaration for mixed content might look like this:

```
<!ELEMENT weather (#PCDATA | precipitation | sunshine)*>
```

The content model starts with with *#PCDATA* and is followed by any number of element names. You must specify *#PCDATA* first in the content model. This specification says that the weather element contains some parsed character data (text) and any number of precipitation and/or sunshine elements. The weather element might look like this:

```
<weather>
    Today's weather forecast calls for low clouds.
    <precipitation>Slight drizle possible</precipitation>
</weather>
```

With mixed content, you have to specify the asterisk (*) following the content model. An asterisk indicates that the number of elements that appear within another element is unrestricted. Using the weather tag as an example, this means that there can be any number of precipitation or sunshine elements.

Attribute List Declarations

A DTD must also declare all of the attributes that elements use. To declare an attribute list, you use the *<!ATTLIST* tag. An attribute list declaration lists all of the attributes that may be used within a given element along with the attributes' types and default values. A typical attribute declaration looks like this:

```
<!ATTLIST precipitation type CDATA #REQUIRED>
```

With this attribute list declaration, the *precipitation* element must contain a *type* attribute. Using *CDATA* indicates that the type attribute contains character data. The final *#REQUIRED* is the default declaration.

Attribute Types

Including *CDATA*, there are ten different attribute types. Table 3.3 shows those types along with a short description of each.

Table 3.3: Allowable Attribute Types

<table>
<tr><th>Type</th><th>Allowable Content</th></tr>
<tr><td>CDATA</td><td>Any character string, use <, >, &, ', or "e; if necessary</td></tr>
<tr><td>NMTOKEN</td><td>Valid XML name with one exception, it may start with any character</td></tr>
<tr><td>NMTOKENS</td><td>Multiple NMTOKENS separated by white space</td></tr>
<tr><td>Enumerations</td><td>Not a keyword, but a list of possible values separated with the pipe (|) character</td></tr>
<tr><td>ENTITY</td><td>The name of an unparsed entity declared in the DTD</td></tr>
<tr><td>ENTITIES</td><td>Multiple entities separated by white space</td></tr>
<tr><td>ID</td><td>A valid and unique XML name used to identify the element</td></tr>
<tr><td>IDREF</td><td>A reference to the ID of another element</td></tr>
<tr><td>IDREFS</td><td>A list of IDREFs separated by white space</td></tr>
<tr><td>NOTATION</td><td>Rarely used, allows the name found in a <!NOTATION declaration</td></tr>
</table>

CDATA

An attribute that specifies *CDATA* allows any text allowed in a well-formed attribute. The only real restriction is that you have to use an entity reference to include certain characters. To include a less-than sign (<), a greater-than sign (>), an ampersand (&), or possibly an apostrophe (') and quote ("), use an equivalent entity reference <, >, &, ', or "e;.

NMTOKEN and NMTOKENS

A *NMTOKEN* is similar to an XML name, except that a *NMTOKEN* is slightly less restrictive. Remember that XML names must start with a letter or an underscore (_) character, and the rest of the name is any combination of letters, digits, underscores, periods (.), hyphens (-), or colons (:). Names cannot have embedded spaces or start with any form of XML. A *NMTOKEN* must follow these rules except that there is no restriction on the starting character, so a name token like *123* or *-nameless* is valid.

NMTOKENS can specify a list of *NMTOKEN* values. You use white space to separate individual tokens when using *NMTOKENS*.

Enumerations

Another way to specify the type of an attribute is to use an enumeration. "Enumeration" is not an XML keyword. With an enumeration, you specify the possible values separated by the pipe (|) character. Here is an example of how you might use an enumeration:

```
<!ATTLIST precipitation type (snow | rain | drizzle | hail | sleet)
#REQUIRED>
```

In this example, the precipitation element must contain a type that has one of the values *snow*, *rain*, *drizzle*, *hail*, or *sleet*, so the following XML is valid:

```
<precipitation type="snow">Heavy snow expected</precipitation>
```

Each of the values in the list of an enumeration must be valid as a *NMTOKEN*. So you cannot specify names that contain special characters such as a forward slash (/) or semicolon (;).

ENTITY and ENTITIES

An *ENTITY* type indicates that the attribute contains the name of an unparsed entity declared elsewhere in the DTD. You use *ENTITIES* when an attribute may contain a list of entities separated by white space.

ID

An *ID* attribute type indicates that the attribute contains an XML name that is unique within the document. This is similar to a primary key for a database file. You use an ID to associate a unique value to an element. Frequently, a program refers to the element's content using this unique ID. Here is an example of a unique ID:

```
<!ATTLIST product product-number ID #REQUIRED>
```

Remember that the ID must follow XML naming conventions, so it cannot start with a number. Using this example, if the product number starts with 0 through 9, it may be necessary to precede the product number with a character. Here is an example of a product element with a *product-number* ID:

```
<product product-number="pn#2pencil">#2 lead pencil</product>
<product product-number="pn8.5x11">White paper</product>
```

Each of these products listed has its own unique *product-number*. The same document could not contain another product with a product-number of *pn#2pencil* or *pn8.5x11*.

IDREF and IDREFS

Use *IDREF* for an attribute that refers to the ID attribute of another element. This is similar to a foreign key in a database file. You use an *IDREF* to establish many-to-many relationships between elements where containment will not work.

One place where you might see an *IDREF* used is with a bill of materials that tracked parts as components and by use. Suppose, for example, that you manufacture pencils that are made up of erasers, cedar tubes, and soft or hard graphite. Figure 3.3 shows how you might represent your products and their component pieces.

```
<product product-number="pn#1pencil">
   <description>#1 lead pencils</description>
   <component part="pn#1graphite">
   <component part="pn#eraser">
   <component part="pn#cedartube">
</product>
<product product-number="pn#2pencil">
   <description>#2 lead pencils</description>
   <component part="pn#2graphite">
   <component part="pn#eraser">
   <component part="pn#cedartube">
```

Figure 3.3: Example of code to represent products and components (part 1 of 2).

```
</product>

<part part-number="pn#1graphite">
   </description>#1 Graphite</description>
   <used-in product="pn#1pencil">
</part>
<part part-number="pn#2graphite">
   </description>#2 Graphite</description>
   <used-in product="pn#2pencil">
</part>
<part part-number="pn#eraser">Eraser</part>
   </description>Eraser</description>
   <used-in product="pn#1pencil">
   <used-in product="pn#2pencil">
</part>
<part part-number="pn#cedartube">
   </description>Cedar Tube</description>
   <used-in product="pn#1pencil">
   <used-in product="pn#2pencil">
</part>
```

Figure 3.3: Example of code to represent products and components (part 2 of 2).

To establish the relationship between these products and component parts, you would use an *IDREF*. In this case, the *IDREF* might look like this:

```
<!ATTLIST product product-number ID #REQUIRED>
<!ATTLIST part part-number ID #REQUIRED>
<!ATTLIST component part IDREF #REQUIRED>
<!ATTLIST used-in product IDREF #REQUIRED>
```

This set of attribute lists joins products to component parts in a many-to-many relationship that an application can navigate and a parser can enforce.

The *IDREFS* attribute type is the same as an *IDREF* except that it allows multiple IDs separated by white space. In the preceding example, the *used-in* and *component* attributes could have specified *IDREFS* and simply listed their related IDs separated by a blank. Specifying *IDREFS*, the *eraser* part might look like this:

```
<part part-number="pn#eraser">Eraser</part>
    </description>Eraser</description>
    <used-in product="pn#1pencil pn#2pencil">
</part>
```

The attribute list declaration for this version might look like this:

```
<!ATTLIST used-in product IDREFS #REQUIRED>
```

Either way, the same thing is accomplished. In this case *used-in* does not specify any other attributes, such as quantity, so it would work just fine. In a real bill of materials you would probably need other attributes to describe the relationships between products and parts, which would require you to have one element for each relationship and not allow you to use *IDREFS*.

NOTATION

A *NOTATION* type attribute contains the name of a notation declared elsewhere in the DTD. Because no widely deployed software supports this method for indicating the element type, notation type attributes are not often used. In theory, the ability to tie an attribute to a notation has more capability than a simple enumeration, because you could theoretically tie information associated with the notation back to the element containing the notation reference. If you do use a notation type attribute, it would look like this:

```
<!NOTATION gif SYSTEM "PNG.exe">
<!ATTLIST image type NOTATION #REQUIRED>
```

Attribute Default Declaration

The last part of an attribute list is the default declaration. There are four possible declarations. The following list describes the four default declarations:

#IMPLIED: Use *#IMPLIED* when an attribute is not required and the attribute does not have a default.

#REQUIRED: Use *#REQUIRED* when an attribute is required. When an attribute is required, there is no default.

#FIXED: When *#FIXED* appears ahead of a literal default value, it means that the default value must be used and cannot be changed. You use *#FIXED* like this:

```
<!ATTLIST part uom CDATA #FIXED "US">
```

In this case, even if a part does not specify a *uom* attribute, a default is supplied. The default has the value of *uom="US"*. Unfortunately, that is also the only value allowed. For this reason, *#FIXED* is rarely used. Chapter 8 describes one case in which *#FIXED* sets the namespace for a particular element.

Literal Value: Use a literal value enclosed in double quotes when you want to supply a default value for an attribute. Specify a literal value like this:

```
<!ATTLIST part uom CDATA "US">
```

In this case, even if a part does not specify a *uom* attribute, a default is supplied. In contrast to the *#FIXED* example, *US* is simply the default and can be overridden.

Entity Declarations

Entities are the building blocks of an XML document. They allow you to break up documents into smaller, more manageable pieces. Recombined, the pieces form new documents that are more flexible and easier to maintain than the monolithic original. For the same reasons, programmers have moved away from huge programs to programs built from components; this is why more programmers are using Integrated Language Environment (ILE) and Java on the iSeries.

There are two basic types of entities: general and parameter. You use general entities within XML document content and parameter entities within a DTD. Both of these are used in similar ways. The biggest difference is that the notation used to refer to a general entity starts with an ampersand (&), whereas a parameter entity reference starts with a percent (%) sign.

Entity Review

In Chapter 2, I introduced you to general entities such as & and <. In this chapter I showed you how to create and refer to internal general entities and unparsed external entities. An internal general entity allows you to reuse some text within your XML document. You use an unparsed external entity to include such things as images and sound in an XML document. What I didn't mention in Chapter 2 and 3 was that those statements were part of an internal DTD. Now that you are building an understanding of DTDs, it is time to look at entities in more detail.

XML provides support for five predefined entities. You use those entities within markup that cannot contain one of these special characters. The predefined entities start with an ampersand (&) and end with a semicolon (;). They are *&* for the ampersand (&), *<* for the less-than sign (<), *>* for the greater-than sign (>), *'* for the apostrophe ('), and *"* for the double quote (").

Internal Entities

You can create your own general entities. A general entity may contain plain text or markup. If you include markup in a general entity, you need to ensure that markup is well formed. For example, you cannot have an entity containing a start tag but no end tag. Figure 3.4 shows how to declare entities in an internal DTD.

```
<?xml version="1.0" encoding="UCS-2"?>
<!-- Internal DTD follows -->
<!DOCTYPE deliveries[
   <!ENTITY wl "WESTERN LARCH">
   <!ENTITY date "
      <delivered-date>
         <month>10</month><day>29</day><year>2001</year>
      </delivered-date>">
]>
<deliverys>
   <load scale-type="DTL">
         <scale-ticket>12345</scale-ticket>
         <weight>42168</weight>
         <weight-uom>LBS</weight-uom>
         <scale-uom>US</scale-uom>
         &date;
         <log>
            <species>&wl;</species>
            <grade>PEELER</grade>
            <large-end-diameter>15&quot;</large-end-diameter>
```

Figure 3.4: XML document containing a DTD with two entity declarations (part 1 of 2).

```
            <small-end-diameter>12&quot;</small-end-diameter>
            <length>32&apos;</length>
        </log>
        <log>
            <species>&wl;</species>
            <grade>PEELER</grade>
            <large-end-diameter>13&quot;</large-end-diameter>
            <small-end-diameter>9&quot;</small-end-diameter>
            <length>32&apos;</length>
        </log>
    </load>
</deliverys>
```

Figure 3.4: XML document containing a DTD with two entity declarations (part 2 of 2).

If you look in the body of the XML document in Figure 3.4, you will see references to the two entities declared in the internal DTD along with references to the predefined entities for double quote (“) and single quote (‘). In this case it was not required to use the *"* and *'* references. This example redefines those tags as attributes:

```
<log large-end-diameter="13&quot;"
       small-end-diameter="9&quot;"
       length="32&apos;">
   <species>&wl;</species>
   <grade>PEELER</grade>
</log>
```

Redefined like this, the *log* tag attributes cannot have embedded quotes, so you are best off using the built-in entity reference *"*. The *'* reference in the *length* tag is not required but is good practice. In fact, the *large-end-diameter* and *small-end-diameter* attributes could have enclosed their values in single quotes (‘) and used double quotes (“) directly, but again, using an entity reference is good practice.

Notations and External Unparsed Entities

As you learned earlier, unparsed entities allow you to embed files that are not XML in an XML document. You include these as unparsed entities, which may be files containing images, word processor documents, spreadsheets, sound, or

PDF files. You normally embed these types of files in an XML document as external unparsed entities.

The entity declaration for an external unparsed entity associates an entity to a notation declaration using the value that follows *NDATA*. In the following example, this associates the gif notation declaration with the logo entity.

```
<!NOTATION gif SYSTEM "PSP.exe">
<!ENTITY logo
  SYSTEM "http://www.iseriesxml.com/logo.gif"
  NDATA gif>
```

The notation declaration specifies the type of data. In this case, the notation uses the external identifier PSP.exe. Another common way of specifying the external identifier is to use the MIME type, which in this case would be image/gif. XML provides no standard or suggestions for the external identifier, leaving the definition and interpretation of this up to the application.

To refer to an unparsed entity in an XML document, you cannot simply use an entity reference. You have to insert an element with an ENTITY type attribute with a value that is the name of the unparsed entity.

```
<!ELEMENT image EMPTY>
<!ATTLIST image source ENTITY #REQUIRED>
```

Finally, to include the logo image in your XML document, you would use an *image* element with a source attribute value of *logo*. In our XML document, this element would look like this:

```
<image source="logo"/>
```

After you place this in your document, it is up to the application processing the document to put the image into the document. The parser identifies the URI and notation, but it is the application's job to do something with this information.

Another alternative to declaring notation is to simply include the URI of the image directly in the image tag. In this case, the image tag would look like this:

```
<image source="http://www.iseriesxml.com/logo.gif"/>
```

This simpler solution bypasses the notation, which has dubious value anyway. However, the XML specification indicates that you should use a notation, because it provides the external identifier. The XML Working Group at the W3C defined external unparsed entities to accommodate legacy SGML documents. With XML you are free to use the file extension to determine the type of processing, given that the external identifier provided by a notation is of little value because the standard does not state what it should be.

External Parsed General Entities

To store snippets of XML documents in reusable external files, you use an external parsed general entity. This technique is more flexible than an internal general entity, because multiple XML documents share the same external files. With a Web server, particularly when using JSP, there are other ways to include content. Using an entity reference has the advantage of working the same everywhere, whether the content is supplied to a browser or to an application run from a command line.

Text used to form an external parsed general entity does not have to be well formed, but all tags must be complete. This means that you do not have to have a single root element, but you cannot have a tag that starts in one external file end in another. In addition, it is not a requirement for a parser to replace an entity reference. The XML specifications allow a nonvalidating parser to ignore the entity reference.

The declaration of an external parsed general entity looks like this:

```
<!ENTITY copyright SYSTEM "http://www.iseriesxml.com/copyright.xml">
```

Instead of a URI reference, you could also just use a file reference. The file reference may be relative or absolute. If you were processing this entity reference in a servlet on the iSeries, you could specify the file relative to the root of the Web server. On the iSeries, an absolute reference will begin with a forward slash, as follows:

```
<!ENTITY copyright SYSTEM "/legal/copyright.xml">
```

You refer to an external parsed general entity in the same way as you would an internal general entity. You simply include the entity name enclosed in an ampersand (&) and semicolon (;), such as *©right;*.

Parameter Entities

Up to now, all of the entities discussed were general entities. Parameter entities are another type of entity that is always parsed and usually external. You use a parameter entity within a DTD. A parameter entity frequently stores snippets of a DTD in order to prevent duplicating those snippets throughout the DTD. Often, those snippets are common attributes shared by several elements or a link to an outside DTD.

The way you reference a parameter entity is similar to the way that you reference a general entity in an XML document. A parameter entity uses a percent sign (%), as in *%ref;* instead of an ampersand (&) as in *&ref;*. A parameter entity reference appears only in a DTD, whereas a general entity is allowed only in a document's content. The parameter entity definition must precede its reference.

To define a parameter entity, you start with the same *<!ENTITY* opening you saw before, but between this opening and the entity name you place a percent sign (%). Here is a typical parameter entity to define an enumeration:

```
<!ENTITY % precipitation-type "snow | rain | drizzle | hail | sleet">
```

Within a DTD you refer to the *precipitation-type* parameter entity like this:

```
<!ATTLIST precipitation type (%precipitation-type;) #REQUIRED>
```

which expands to

```
<!ATTLIST precipitation type (snow | rain | drizzle | hail | sleet)
#REQUIRED>
```

Unless you work for The Weather Channel, this example may not excite you, but there are other ways to use parameter entities. The technique just shown centralizes markup that appears repeatedly in DTDs. Another and more exciting way to use parameter entities is to carve up a DTD into reusable pieces reassembled into problem-specific DTDs.

To carve up a DTD into pieces and reassemble them, you use an external parameter entity. Instead of replacing a parameter entity reference with some replacement text defined in the DTD, you replace the entity with an entire file. In this type of parameter entity, you specify *SYSTEM* or *PUBLIC* followed by a URI. I covered the differences between *SYSTEM* and *PUBLIC* earlier in this chapter in discussing the document type declaration, but in this case you probably want to use *SYSTEM*. Here is an example of an external parameter entity:

```
<!ENTITY % weather SYSTEM "weather.dtd">
```

In this case, a parameter entity reference to *%weather;* brings the file weather.dtd into the DTD, placing the file contents at the point of the reference. To further illustrate the value of this, the following describes an example from the timber industry.

In the timber industry, the technique used to measure a log, known as *scaling,* varies significantly by region. Depending on where you are in the world, logs are sold by weight, cords, cubic volume, an approximation technique called the Scribner scale, and several other methods. Each of these different scaling methods provides a different set of measurements. To accommodate this, a DTD that supports the basic description of a log, such as species, logger, and hauler, is extended by a regional DTD. The regional description ensures that an XML document transmitted from a Montana scaling bureau provides the required Scribner measurements, whereas a log scaled in Washington provides necessary Cunit measurements.

To tie the various DTDs together that supports this type of DTD, you use a master DTD that looks like this:

```
<!-- Scribner log scale -->
<!ENTITY % logscale SYSTEM "logscale.dtd">
<!ENTITY % logscale-scribner SYSTEM "logscale-scribner.dtd">
%logscale;
%logscale-scribner;
```

The second DTD, which has several counterparts, is dependent on the scaling method. Several versions of this DTD including *logscale-cunit* and *logscale-cords*, ensure that the XML document provides the measurements required by each scaling method.

Earlier I mentioned that parameter entities are usually external. One reason for this is that the XML specification for internal parameter entities allows only complete declarations, unlike external parameter entities, which allow you to define partial declarations. This removes the ability to define such things as enumerations.

There are many ways to use parameter entities. For example, if you need to define a DTD supporting HTML elements, you might start by bringing in the XHTML DTD, which is available on the W3C Web site at *www.w3.org*. In fact, the W3C recommendation "Modularization of XHTML" describes this in detail. That recommendation is also available from the W3C Web site.

Ignoring and Including DTD Content

When you need to create a single DTD from several smaller DTDs, *ignore* and *include* directives are useful. You use the *ignore* declaration to comment out parts of a DTD and *include* to force inclusion. When combined, these two directives provide a way to include DTD statements conditionally.

The *ignore* and *include* directives do not have any keywords and look like the following when included in a DTD:

```
<![IGNORE[
  <!ATTLIST length uom ( IN | FT ) #REQUIRED>
]]>
<![INCLUDE[
  <!ATTLIST length uom ( MM | CM | M ) #REQUIRED>
]]>
```

In this example, suppose you have logs scaled via the same scaling method, with some going to Canada and the others destined for the United States. You could include one or the other set of units of measure using *include* and *ignore* directives.

At first, this may not seem much better than simply commenting out the attribute list that you do not need. This technique does have one distinct advantage over using comments when combined with a parameter entity. In this case, instead of the explicit *ignore* and *include*, you would have something like:

```
<![%us-destination;[
  <!ATTLIST length uom ( IN | FT ) #REQUIRED>
]]>
<![%non-us-destination;[
  <!ATTLIST length uom ( MM | CM | M ) #REQUIRED>
]]>
```

Now, you set the parameter for *us-destination* and *non-us-destination* depending on the destination. This allows you to share DTDs more easily and flexibly. In this case, the parameter entity looks like this:

```
<!ENTITY % us-destination "IGNORE">
<!ENTITY % non-us-destination "INCLUDE">
```

That is all you need to swap in and out parts of your DTD. This feature allows you to share DTDs more easily.

Name Collisions and Overriding DTDs

If you build or use many DTDs, it is likely that at some point you will need to understand what happens when different DTDs provide different definitions for the same name. It may seem that such a situation should be avoided at all costs. Once you understand what happens with name conflicts, you may also see opportunities you can work to your advantage.

Earlier in this chapter, I described how parameter entities allow you to break up DTDs into many small, reusable chunks. Sometimes those chunks might end up defining the same markup. You could also have a name collision between an internal DTD and an external DTD. What happens when those names collide?

Name collisions between external DTDs may or may not even work, depending on the parser you are using. Because of this, you need to avoid conflicts between external documents. You may find that the parser you are using does not care, which is fine if you do not care which DTD takes precedence.

When a name collision occurs between an external and an internal DTD, the internal DTD always takes precedence. I mentioned this opportunity earlier. You can use this to your advantage if you want to customize the requirements of a particular DTD. Using the simple recipe DTD shown earlier in this chapter, you might end up with something like this:

```
<!DOCTYPE recipe SYSTEM "simplerecipe.dtd"
  [
    <!ELEMENT recipe (name, ingredient+, instruction+, source?)>
    <!ELEMENT source (#PCDATA)>
  ]>
```

The recipe name, ingredients, and instructions remain as they were defined in the external DTD shown in Figure 3.1, but now, with this new definition for the *recipe* element, a recipe can also specify an optional source, which was not possible with the original DTD.

Specifying a DTD

Just having a DTD doesn't mean you have to check for validity. There is a whole class of XML processors, called *nonvalidating* processors, which, as their name suggest, do not check the document against the contents of the DTD, whether or not it is provided. In particular, such processors are completely free to ignore any parts of the DTD (such as the external subset, but there are others) that are in other entities.

It turns out that *all* processors *have to* read the internal subset and, on top of that, have to use some of the declarations in it. But the existence of the *<!DOCTYPE* declaration is not a signal to validate. The document type declaration must appear before the first *element* in the document.

One of the most significant design improvements in XML is to make it easy to use with modern compiler tools. Part of this improvement involves making it possible to express the syntax of XML in Extended Backus-Naur Form (EBNF). If you've never seen EBNF before, think of it this way:

- EBNF is a set of rules, called productions.
- Every rule describes a specific fragment of syntax.
- A document is valid if it can be reduced to a single, specific rule, with no input left, by repeated application of the rules.

Let's take a simple example that has nothing to do with XML (or the real rules of language):

```
[1] Word       ::= Consonant Vowel+ Consonant
[2] Consonant  ::= [^aeiou]
[3] Vowel      ::= [aeiou]
```

Rule 1 states that a *Word* consists of a *Consonant* followed by one or more *Vowels* followed by another Consonant. Rule 2 states that a Consonant is any letter other than *a*, *e*, *i*, *o*, or *u*. Rule 3 states that a Vowel is any of the letters *a*, *e*, *i*, *o*, and *u*. (The exact syntax of the rules and the meaning of square brackets and other special symbols, is laid out in the XML specification.)

Using the above example, is *red* a Word? Yes.

1. *red* consists of the letter *r* followed by the letter *e* followed by the letter *d*: r e d.
2. *r* is a Consonant by rule 2, so *red* is: Consonant 'e' 'd'
3. *e* is a Vowel by rule 3, so *red* is: Consonant Vowel 'd'.
4. By rule 2 again, *red* is: Consonant Vowel Consonant, which, by rule 1, is a Word.

By the same analysis, *reed*, *road*, and *xeaiioug* are also words, but *rate* is not. There is no way to match Consonant Vowel Consonant Vowel using the EBNF in this example.

XML is defined by an EBNF grammar of about 80 rules. Although the rules are more complex, the same sort of analysis allows an XML parser to determine that *<greeting>Hello World</greeting>* is a syntactically correct XML document, whereas *<greeting]Wrong Bracket!</greeting>* is not.

In very general terms, that's all there is to it. You'll find all the details about EBNF in *Compilers: Principles, Techniques, and Tools* by Aho, Sethi, and Ullman or in any modern compiler textbook.

Although EBNF isn't an efficient way to represent syntax for human consumption, there are programs that can automatically turn EBNF into a parser. This makes it a particularly efficient way to represent the syntax for a language that will be parsed by a computer.

Chapter Highlights

In this chapter, you learned how DTDs are constructed and about the syntax and keywords used when defining a DTD.

- DTDs document the structure of XML documents.
- There are general and parameter entities referred to using *&entity;* or *%entity;* notation.
- There are two types of entity: parsed and unparsed.
- Commas indicate sequence.
- The pipe character (|) indicates a choice between alternatives.
- For quantity use the suffix *?* for zero or one, * for any number, + for one or more, and no suffix for one and only one.
- *Include* and *exclude* provide flexibility when combining DTDs.

In the next chapter I will show you how to interpret and use DTDs that support your applications.

4

XML Schemas

In this chapter you will learn:

- ✓ What is a Schema?
- ✓ Where did Schemas come from?
- ✓ DTD vs. Schema comparison
- ✓ Components of a Schema
- ✓ Data types available for Schemas

Since DTDs were developed, they have been widely used to assist in the creation of XML documents. The rules defined in the DTD provide the framework to generate the XML. With this capability, a DTD can be passed to an external or internal resource, and a developer can start writing a method for generating an XML document using those rules. The XML is delivered to the system for processing. This type of delivery would have been done using HTTP, HTTPS, or even a Web service or MQ Series.

One of the first things that has to be done once the application has accepted the XML document is to validate the data. The application has to read every node and attribute to ensure that the data is of the correct type. Furthermore, if there is any particular data format requirement, such as a government ID number, the application has to validate the data against that specific format. These tasks also require the generation of some sort of mapping facility for the XML document so that the application can access the data.

Now, this procedure sounds acceptable for one or two documents, but it becomes extremely tedious when hundreds of XML documents are being transferred, which is more likely the case for most organizations. The burden becomes even more challenging when the XML document is large or contains hundreds of elements. A great deal of processing overhead becomes necessary to ensure that the data is valid, not to mention the resources required to develop this code. The possibility of error becomes very high when this type of code is written, making for very challenging debugging.

Another issue that may come up in developing the XML document is the need to support namespaces. The current implementation of DTDs does not let us specify any namespaces.

The W3 Consortium identified the need for an XML description language, and in response the XML Schema specification has been developed. The XML Schema specification makes up for many of the limitations of DTDs and provides a richer and more useful means of defining an XML.

What Is a Schema?

Schemas are basically the successor to DTDs. DTDs provided a great deal of functionality in the early stages of the life of XML. However, as XML documents came into wider acceptance, it was obvious that DTDs lacked in many areas. Therefore, the W3 Consortium decided to pursue a new specification that would address many of the limitations of DTDs.

A schema is very similar to a DTD. Both schemas and DTDs define the building blocks for an XML document. They describe what elements and attributes may be included in the document, as well as defining how they are all related. They describe what nodes can be children to other nodes and what nodes can have attributes. They both provide a predictable and consistent input for the applications accepting the XML.

XML schemas have the ability to describe the allowable content. This is something that a DTD cannot accomplish. The XML Schema specification provides the rules for defining what values are allowed for each element and attribute. It also describes the number and sequence of children a parent node may have. These features make the days of writing classes and classes of validation logic a thing of the past.

Schema History

As you know, DTDs were the original validation-mechanism for XML data. DTDs are used to describe the structure of a Standard Generalized Markup Language (SGML) document. Since XML is a subset of SGML, DTDs were the obvious choice for providing the rules that detailed the structure for an XML document.

DTDs have fallen short in many ways, however. One of their major weaknesses is that DTDs are unable to constrain the data inside the XML document. This omission has forced developers to write custom code for each XML document in order to validate the data, from simple data type and range validation to complex multi-node validation. DTDs also lack the ability to support namespaces.

Acceptance of XML has made it very important to have a language that can provide a means of completely describing an XML document. XML Schemas was not the first specification presented; there were others, which were also used as references to develop the Schema specification. Other specifications that were presented included Datatypes for DTDs, XML-Data, Document Definition Markup Language or XSchema (DDML), Schema for Object-oriented XML (SOX), DCD (Document Content Description for XML), and XML-Data-Reduced (XDR). All of these specifications can be found on the W3 Consortium Web site.

As the creators were developing the XML Schema specification, they were trying to address some key issues. They needed to develop something that was self-describing and more detailed than a DTD's description. Clearly, the problem that DTDs cannot control the data that is entered into an XML document needed to be addressed.

Another goal was to have a human-readable description language. To meet this requirement, the XML Schema designers chose the most obvious language: XML itself. This gives developers the ability to use their existing knowledge of the XML language. No new languages are required to learn Schemas—just a new syntax that describes the XML document. In addition, because the Schema is using XML syntax, it does not require a new tool to develop the document. Most IDEs and XML tools support Schemas.

Other issues addressed were performance and interaction with other specifications. Although a specification may provide all of this wonderful functionality, the actual performance must be acceptable. Having a great deal of system resources tied up into XML validation would make the specification difficult to accept in the programming community. Lastly, what good is a specification if it doesn't work with all the other specifications written? Extra attention was put forth to ensure that this specification worked with the other specifications for XML documents.

And the Result...

The result has been two releases of the XML Schema specification: one released in February 1999 and the second released in May 2001. This book will focus on the specification released in May 2001. Both of these specifications contain three parts: the primer, structures, and data types.

Part 0: Primer

Quite simply, the primer is intended to serve as an introduction to the XML Schema specification, as an alternative to bombarding a reader with an intense technical document. The primer can be used as a preface to the complete specification.

The primer contains an easily understood set of instructions of how schemas are created, focusing on the features of the specifications rather than digging into the extremely technical details of Schemas. The primer is very example-based and is very easy to read. It is the ideal starting point for those who wish to get a better understanding of Schemas. When the details and syntax are needed, the other parts should be referenced.

The primer can be found at *www.w3.org/TR/xmlschema-0/.*

Part 1: Structures

Part 1 of the specification details the rules for structuring an XML document. It provides instructions for declaring elements and attributes. Most important, it defines where they can appear inside a document, in what sequences elements may appear, and whether or not the element is optional. This declaration provides the basic framework for a document. Once the elements and attributes have been declared, the allowable content can be defined for each item.

Some kinds of complex data validation that may be necessary for the data of an XML document must be done inside an application. These tasks include multiple elements and attributes as well as complex data ranges that are dependent on values of other elements or attributes. This type of control is beyond the scope of the XML Schemas specification.

The structures part of the XML Schemas specification can be found at *www.w3.org/TR/xmlschema-1/.*

Part 2: Data Types

Part 2 of the specification focuses on describing the allowable content for an XML document. This provides a mechanism to validate the data inside the XML. The data can be validated on the basis of data typing including byte, date, numeric, and string values. These data types are similar to SQL and Java primitive data types. This approach makes importing and exporting to and from databases simpler because the data will remain in a predictable format.

The predictable format greatly decreases the need for type casting needed inside the accepting applications.

Apart from the type of data, other types of validation can be performed for the data. Ranges can be identified for numerical data, and patterns can be identified for strings. Details regarding the specifics will be discussed later in the chapter.

All of this functionality, combined with the structures described in Part 1, can now be combined to create user-defined types that can be declared and reused.

Part 2 can be found at *www.w3.org/TR/xmlschema-2/.*

Schemas vs. DTDs

As mentioned, schemas and DTDs have a great deal in common, particularly when it comes to defining the structure of an XML document. To really see the difference between DTDs and schemas, the best way would be to see XML documents having the same content under each of the validation systems. Figure 4.1 shows a simple customer information XML document. The document element is named *customer*, and it contains four child elements named *id*, *firstname*, *initial*, and *lastname*. Each one of these items is a string value.

```
<?xml version="1.0" ?>
<customer>
   <id>123456</id>
   <firstname>Joe</firstname>
   <initial>E.</initial>
   <lastname>Smith</lastname>
</customer>
```

Figure 4.1: Simple customer XML document.

The DTD shown (with line numbers added) in Figure 4.2 defines the structure of the document shown in Figure 4.1. The element named *customer* contains four child elements, as seen in line 2. Each of the child elements is then defined (all with the type PCDATA). The child elements are defined in lines 3 through 6.

```
<?xml version=“1.0” encoding=“UTF-8”?>
<!ELEMENT customer (id, firstname, initial, lastname)>
<!ELEMENT firstname (#PCDATA)>
<!ELEMENT id (#PCDATA)>
<!ELEMENT initial (#PCDATA)>
<!ELEMENT lastname (#PCDATA)>
```

Figure 4.2: DTD for customer XML document.

To reference the DTD in the XML document, the line of code shown in Figure 4.3 must be added to the XML document below the XML declaration. This indicates that the DTD in the file customer.dtd will be used to validate the docment.

```
<!DOCTYPE customer SYSTEM “customer.dtd”>
```

Figure 4.3: Referencing a DTD inside an XML document.

Figure 4.4 shows the schema for the same XML (with line numbers added). Like the DTD, it describes an element named *customer*, found on line 3. The child elements, described on lines 6 through 9, are declared inside a complex type, which will be described later.

```
1  <?xml version=“1.0” encoding=“UTF-8”?>
2  <xsd:schema xmlns:xsd=“http://www.w3.org/2001/XMLSchema”>
3     <xsd:element name=“customer”>
4        <xsd:complexType content=“elementOnly”>
5           <xsd:sequence>
6              <xsd:element name=“id” type=“xsd:int”/>
7              <xsd:element name=“firstname” type=“xsd:string”/>
8              <xsd:element name=“initial” type=“xsd:string”/>
9              <xsd:element name=“lastname” type=“xsd:string”/>
10          </xsd:sequence>
11       </xsd:complexType>
12    </xsd:element>
13 </xsd:schema>
```

Figure 4.4: XML schema for the customer information.

To reference the schema in the XML, the code shown in Figure 4.5 is added to the document element. It indicates to the parser that the schema contained in the file customer.xsd is to be used to validate the document. It also instructs the parser to use the 2001 version of the specification.

```
<customer xmlns:xsi=http://www.w3.org/2001/XMLSchema-instance
xsi:noNamespaceSchemaLocation="customer.xsd">
```

Figure 4.5: Referencing a schema in an XML document.

Of course, one of the most obvious differences between a schema and a DTD is the size of the files. The DTD is much smaller than the schema, but that is mainly because the schema goes beyond the structure of the XML. As you can see in lines 6 to 9 in Figure 4.4, where the child elements are declared, there is an attribute indicating the type of data. The most obvious is the *id* for the customer, which is declared as an integer. If a string were passed inside the XML document, the DTD would allow it, but the schema would not, and an error would be initiated.

Table 4.1: A Comparison of DTD and XML Schema Technologies

DTD	XML Schema
Defines the structure of an XML document	Defines the structure of an XML document
Uses ELEMENT tag to define XML elements and its children	Uses elements with complex types to define the elements and the structure of the dccument
Non-XML format	XML format
Difficult to read	Human readable
No support for data type validation	Support for data type validation
Can create entities	Can create own types
No support for namespaces	Support for multiple namespaces

Table 4.1: A Comparison of DTD and XML Schema Technologies, *continued.*

DTD	XML Schema
Can validate based only upon instructions inside of the DTD	Mixed content modules can be used
Cannot validate the data inside an XML	Can provide complex rules for many data types

Why Use Schemas?

There are many reasons why schemas should be used. They provide a skeleton for XML documents that may be used in an enterprise. A schema provides a means of understanding an XML document in an easy-to-read format. If the schema is handed to a developer, the developer knows not only what the structure of the XML is to be but also the allowed data for each of the items in the XML.

The Schema's main purpose is to provide a means of validating a document. It makes sure that all of the elements and attributes are present. This is extremely important, because the accepting application expects the data in a specific format. If the structure and data can be ensured prior to delivery, it helps eliminate steps in the processing.

As in application development, every XML author has their own naming convention for the elements and attributes. This makes it very difficult, without a schema, to determine what data in what format should be used for the values. The Schema may not always help with the naming conventions, but it will help with the data types.

As mentioned earlier, schemas are in XML format. What does this mean? It means that, like any other XML document, a schema can be manipulated using a parser, so the values inside a Schema could be altered simply using a DOM parser. This allows values to be changed dynamically. XML can also be transformed by simply applying an XSL stylesheet, producing another format. This provides the ability to make an XML document, including a schema, into an HTML or another XML document.

Another feature of schemas that has not been mentioned yet is the ability to support additional elements and attributes. The case will arise where a current schema does not have a field that may be required. The new node can be simply added without causing any problems. It cannot be added just anywhere, however; it cannot make the current data invalid.

Finally, XML documents can reference more than one schema. This allows multiple schemas to be used to validate a document. As an example, one schema could be used to validate a customer's information, whereas another could be used to validate the order the customer has made. This type of approach allows for reuse of code and eliminates the need to define the same information more than once.

When to Use a Schema

One of the reasons the Schema specification is used is to ensure that the document has the proper structure and all required data. Additionally, by using a schema, you can ensure that the document contains only valid data. So why not use it all the time? If you use Schemas everywhere, you will incur a certain degree of performance overhead; however, the benefits may be worth it.

Another approach to using XML validation is to reference the validation documents only during the development stage. This approach was used a great deal when DTDs were widely used, mainly because DTDs could only ensure that the document had a proper structure and because using DTDs everywhere led to some performance issues. The other aspect to this approach was that in production the application accepting the XML document had to validate all the data, requiring a great deal of human resources to write this validation code. This is not the best use of your resources, especially when there are a great number of XMLs to write.

As described earlier, schemas can be passed to a developer, internal or external, and the developer will know how to write the XML. The entire structure is identified, along with any attributes an element may have. The data type and any string patterns are easily identified. The schema can be referenced inside the XML document so that developers can validate their documents.

Components of a Schema

Let's start with some simple schema basics. Since the schema is an XML document, it must be well formed. There can be no incomplete elements, or the schema will be invalid. Each attribute also must have the proper opening and closing quotes. The tags are case sensitive, so they must match exactly. Schema documents have the extension *.xsd*. Each element name inside the document has a prefix consisting of *xsd* and a colon. The document element has an attribute indicating the namespace for the document; for example:

```
<xsd:schema xmlns:xsd="http://www.w3.org/2001/XMLSchema">
```

Element Declarations

An element declaration links a name to a type. The name given to the element is a unique name and cannot be duplicated within the current schema. The type describes the type of data that will be included in the element, which may be simple or complex types. Each of these types will be described in detail later in this chapter.

For example, a simple element that describes a customer's first name would contain just the name and type attributes. The name would indicate that the element is named *firstname*, and the type would indicate that the type of data inside the element would be a *string*. The element declaration would look like Figure 4.6:

```
<xsd:element name="firstname" type="xsd:string"/>
```

Figure: 4.6: A simple element declaration.

Element Occurrences

A simple element declaration such as that in Figure 4.6 requires the element to appear once and only once in its context. So declaring the first and last name for a customer requires the XML to contain one and only one first name and one and only one last name for the customer. This requirement works well for this type of information and for unique identifiers. However, it does not work with an order containing one or more line items or for a customer's middle initials, which may or may not be given.

To provide a solution for these two scenarios, the Schema specification allows two *occurrence* constraints to be specified as attributes on the element declaration: one for the minimum number and the other for the maximum number of times the element may occur in its context in the XML. These two attributes provide the ability to specify whether or not an element is required as well how many times it may occur.

The element declaration in Figure 4.7 describes an order item. Each order item must occur a minimum of once, but there is no upper limit to the number of occurrences.

```
<xsd:element name="orderItems" type="xsd:string" minOccurs="1"
 maxOccurs="unbounded" />
```

Figure 4.7: Occurrences example.

The occurrence constraints also provide the ability to make an element optional by simply setting the minimum occurrences (minOccurs) to 0 and the maximum (maxOccurs) to 1. Figure 4.8 shows an example of how this is done.

```
<xsd:element name="initial" type="xsd:string" minOccurs="0"
 maxOccurs="1" />
```

Figure 4.8: Making an element optional.

The minOccurs and maxOccurs attributes can apply to any element. There are no restrictions on the type of element they can be applied to. A summary of how they are used is given in Table 4.2.

Default Values

Back in the days of DTDs, default values were not straightforward. In order for the XML to be valid, a blank element had to be declared. Once the application accepted the XML, it would perform all necessary validation of the data. If the element were left blank, a default value would be set for the variable in the code.

Table 4.2: Examples of minOccurs and maxOccurs

Description	minOccurs Value	maxOccurs Value
Only one element	1	1
Optional, zero or one	0	1
Zero to unlimited	0	*unbounded*
One or unlimited	1	*unbounded*
5 to 100 elements	5	100

Before Schemas, providing default value functionality required pragmatic workarounds. Schemas allow for default values, providing a great deal of advantage. If an element is left blank or not included in the XML document, the parser treats the element as if it had the default value. This feature of the Schemas specification removes the default value code from the application and allows the value to be updated. Because a schema is an XML document, an application could open it up and change the default values.

Default values can be applied only to string elements. They cannot be applied to attributes or to any other data types.

In the example in Figure 4.9, the sendEmail element is a flag indicating whether to send an email to a customer. The element is a string type, so it can have a default value, which for this field is "yes". The default value will be substituted if the element is empty (either *<sendEmail></sendEmail>* or *<sendEmail />*): or if the element is not specified in the XML document.

```
<xsd:element name="sendEmail" type="xsd:string" default="yes"/>
```

Figure 4.9: Default value for the sendEmail element.

Fixed Values

As an alternative to the default value, the *fixed* attribute to the element declaration can be used. It allows a single value to be used for a schema element. The value for the element cannot be anything other than the value declared in the *fixed* attribute in the schema. If any value other than that value is given in an XML document, the document is invalid.

The example in Figure 4.10 populates the sendEmail element with the value "yes". There is no other value that can be used for this element.

```
<xsd:element name="sendEmail" type="xsd:string" fixed="yes"/>
```

Figure 4.10: Fixed value for the sendEmail element.

All of the following are valid examples of the element in XML:

- <sendEmail>yes</sendEmail>
- <sendEmail></sendEmail>
- <sendEmail />

The following examples, however, would all be invalid:

- <sendEmail>no</sendEmail>
- <sendEmail>false</sendEmail>
- <sendEmail>
- <emailAddress>user@domain.com</emailAddress>
- </sendEmail>

The fixed and default attributes cannot be used together. These attributes are incompatible.

Global vs. Local Elements

There are two kinds of elements that can be declared: global and local elements. Global elements are children of the root *schema* element. Once a global element has been declared, it can be referenced inside other (local) complex types using the *ref* attribute. The global element can be referenced many times by other complex types. Global elements should be used when there is a good chance they are going to be reused.

Local elements are typically nested deeper into the schema structure. Local elements may or may not reference other (global) elements. Local elements are used when it makes sense to create a type that will not be used again.

Let's take the schema shown in Figure 4.11 as an example. Inside it are two global elements, named *name* and *homeaddress*. The name element consists of three additional elements that outline the name of the person. The homeaddress element contains five elements, which describe the address for the person. As well, there are two local elements named *customer* and *employee*. The customer and the employee elements are both local because they both have *ref* attributes

```
<?xml version="1.0" encoding="UTF-8"?>
<xsd:schema xmlns:xsd="http://www.w3.org/2001/XMLSchema">
  <xsd:element name="customer" type="customerType" />
  <xsd:element name="employee" type="employeeType" />
    <xsd:complexType name="nameType">
      <xsd:sequence>
        <xsd:element name="firstname" type="xs:string"/>
        <xsd:element name="initial" type="xs:string"/>
        <xsd:element name="lastname" type="xs:string"/>
      </xsd:sequence>
    </xsd:complexType>
    <xsd:complexType name="addressType">
      <xsd:sequence>
        <xsd:element name="address" type="xs:string"/>
        <xsd:element name="city" type="xs:string"/>
        <xsd:element name="state" type="xs:string"/>
        <xsd:element name="zipcode" type="xs:string"/>
        <xsd:element name="country" type="xs:string"/>
      </xsd:sequence>
    </xsd:complexType>
    <xsd:complexType name="customerType">
      <xsd:sequence>
        <xsd:element name="customername" type="nameType"/>
        <xsd:element name="homeaddress" type="addressType"/>
      </xsd:sequence>
```

Figure 4.11: Complex customer and employee schema (part 1 of 2).

```
        </xsd:complexType>
           <xsd:complexType name="employeeType">
        <xsd:sequence>
        <xsd:element name="employeename" type="nameType"/>
        <xsd:element name="homeaddress" type="addressType"/>
        </xsd:sequence>
     </xsd:complexType>
</xsd:schema>
```

Figure 4.11: Complex customer and employee schema (part 2 of 2).

for the name and address elements.

This schema can be used to produce different kinds of XML documents. This is because there are two different local elements. The customer or the

```
<?xml version="1.0" encoding="UTF-8"?>
<customer xmlns:xsi="http://www.w3.org/2001/XMLSchema-instance"
xsi:noNamespaceSchemaLocation="complexcustomer.xsd">
   <customername>
      <firstname>Joe</firstname>
      <initial>E</initial>
      <lastname>Smith</lastname>
   </customername>
   <homeaddress>
      <address>123 street</address>
      <city>New York</city>
      <state>NY</state>
      <zipcode>12345</zipcode>
      <country>USA</country>
   </homeaddress>
</customer>
```

Figure 4.12: Example of a complex customer.

employee schema can be used to generate an XML. Figures 4.12 and 4.13 are examples of both.

```
<?xml version="1.0" encoding="UTF-8"?>
<employee xmlns:xsi="http://www.w3.org/2001/XMLSchema-instance"
xsi:noNamespaceSchemaLocation="complexcustomer.xsd">
   <employeename>
      <firstname>Billy</firstname>
      <initial>E</initial>
      <lastname>Roberts</lastname>
   </employeename>
   <homeaddress>
      <address>123 street</address>
      <city>Boston</city>
      <state>MA</state>
      <zipcode>34567</zipcode>
      <country>USA</country>
   </homeaddress>
</employee>
```

Figure 4.13: Example of a complex employee.

Attribute Declarations

Attributes are declared very similarly to elements. An attribute declaration consists of a name and the type of data that the attribute will hold. The name is a unique reference to the attribute and cannot be duplicated anywhere else in the schema.

The major difference between elements and attributes is that you cannot describe any child information for the attribute. Because attributes are pieces of data that are within the element tag, they cannot hold any child information. Attributes can use only simple types for the data they can contain. Complex types typically have many child elements, while a simple type only has one value. The order in which attributes are added cannot be controlled.

Figure 4.14 shows an example of a schema with an attribute. In this example, we define customer information with an ID attribute. The ID attribute contains integer data.

```
<?xml version="1.0" encoding="UTF-8"?>
<xsd:schema xmlns:xsd="http://www.w3.org/2001/XMLSchema">
<xsd:element name="customer">
   <xsd:complexType content="elementOnly">
      <xsd:sequence>
         <xsd:element name="firstname" type="xsd:string"/>
         <xsd:element name="initial" type="xsd:string"/>
         <xsd:element name="lastname" type="xsd:string"/>
      </xsd:sequence>
      <xsd:attribute name="id" type="xsd:int" />
   </xsd:complexType>
</xsd:element>
</xsd:schema>
```

Figure 4.14: Customer schema with an attribute.

The XML in Figure 4.15 shows an example:

```
<?xml version="1.0" encoding="UTF-8"?>
<customer xmlns:xsi="http://www.w3.org/2001/XMLSchema-instance"
  xsi:noNamespaceSchemaLocation="customerwithattribute.xsd" id="1">
   <firstname>Joe</firstname>
   <initial>P</initial>
   <lastname>Smith</lastname>
</customer>
```

Figure 4.15: Example of a customer XML with an attribute.

Optional and Required Declarations

When you declare an attribute, the attribute is not required. This rule is different from the rule for elements, which *are* required unless they are declared to be optional by setting *minOccurs="0"*. To make an attribute required, the *use* attribute is placed in the attribute declaration.

To make an attribute (for example, the *id* attribute of the customer) required, the *use* attribute is added to the attribute declaration with a value of *required*, as in

```
<xsd:attribute name="id" type="xsd:int" use="required" />.
```

Although an attribute is not required, the attribute may still be declared as optional. The following is the syntax for an optional attribute:

```
<xsd:attribute name="id" type="xsd:int" use="optional" />.
```

Global vs. Local Declarations

Global and local attributes act very similarly to global and local elements. A global attribute may be reused throughout the schema and is a child of the *schema* root element.

Local attributes are typically nested deeper into the schema structure. Local attributes may or may not reference other (global) attributes. They are used when it makes sense to create a type that will not be used again.

Data Types

The Schema specification allows for the writers of a schema to use three different types of data to be used as the contents for an element. The three types are simple types, complex types, and the built-in schema specifications.

Simple Types Built into Schemas

One of the powerful features of XML Schemas is the ability to validate the values passed inside an element. This was a weakness of DTDs, because they allowed any type of data to be passed. Built into the Schema specification is the ability to support a wide variety of types. They are very similar to the types of data used in Java and SQL. They range from string to numeric to date and time data types. These types can then be used to create user-defined types, which will be described later in this section. These simple, built-in types are listed in Table 4.3.

To describe text, such as a customer's first name, the type that would be used is *xsd:string*., as in *<xsd:element name="firstname" type="xsd:string" />*. In the string data type, anything can be passed into it.

On the other hand, if there is a need to have a numeric field such as a customer number, the *xsd:integer* type would be used. It would ensure that the value inside the element would be an integer:

```
<xsd:element name="id" type="xsd:int"/>.
```

Table 4.3: Examples of the Built In Types

Type	Example
String	This is a string
normalizedString	This is a string
Token	This is a string
Byte	–1, 126
unsignedByte	0, 126
base64Binary	GpM7
HexBinary	FFF0
Integer	–123456, 1, 0, 123456
positiveInteger	1, 123456
negativeInteger	–1, –123456
nonNegativeInteger	0, 123456
nonPositiveInteger	–1, –123456
unsignedInt	0, 123456
Long	–123456, 0, 123456
unsignedLong	0, 123456
Short	–1, 12345
unsignedShort	0, 12345

Table 4.3: Examples of the Built In Types, *continued.*

Type	Example
decimal	1.234, 123.567, 0
float	–1, 123, 123.45E-2
double	–1, 123, 123.45E-2
boolean	true, false
time	15:32:12.123
datetime	2003-01-01 15:32:12.123
duration	P\p{Nd}{4}Y\p{Nd}{2}M
date	2003-01-01
gMonth	01
gYear	2003
gYearMonth	2003-01
gDay	01
gMonthDay	01-01
Name (XML 1.0 Name type)	phoneNumber
Qname (XML Namespace)	foo:phoneNumber
NCName (XML Namespace)	phoneNumber
anyURI	http://www.ibm.com
language	en-US
ID (XML 1.0 ID attribute)	No example
IDREF (XML 1.0 IDREF attribute)	No example
IDREFS (XML 1.0 IDREFS attribute)	No example
ENTITY (XML 1.0ENTITY attribute)	No example

Table 4.3: Examples of the Built In Types, *continued.*

Type	Example
ENTITIES (XML 1.0 ENTITY attribute)	No example
NOTATION (XML 1.0 NOTATION attribute)	No example
NMTOKEN (XML 1.0 NMTOKEN attribute)	US
NMTOKENS (XNK 1.0 NMTOKENS attribute)	Canada, US, UK

Simple User-Defined Types

User-defined types can be derived from existing simple types by imposing other constraints in addition to type on the data. The restriction element is used to identify these additional constraints on the data, also known as "facets." These types are called *simple types,* and their declarations are enclosed in an *xsd:simpleType* element.

Enumeration lists can be used to provide a list of acceptable values for an element. The only legal values for these elements are the values that have been declared in the enumeration list. Figure 4.16 shows an example of an enumeration list in which there are three countries available: the United States, Canada, and the United Kingdom.

```
<xsd:simpleType name="country">
   <xsd:restriction base="xsd:string">
      <xsd:enumeration value="USA"/>
      <xsd:enumeration value="CAN"/>
      <xsd:enumeration value="UK"/>
   </xsd:restriction>
</xsd:simpleType>
```

Figure 4.16: Enumeration list simple type.

Minimum and maximum values can be placed on numeric values to ensure that the values fall within an acceptable range. This is done with the *minInclusive,* and *maxInclusive,* elements. As the *minOccurs* and *maxOccurs* attributes do for the number of occurrences of an element, these attributes provide the range in which a value can fall. There are also *minExclusive,* and *maxExclusive* attributes.

Figure 4.17 shows an example of a data range for an order value. The value uses the integer data type and must fall between 1 and 999. This type of restriction ensures that the number is greater than zero and less than 1,000.

```
<xsd:simpleType name=“orderValue”>
   <xsd:restriction base=“xsd:integer”>
      <xsd:minInclusive value=“1”/>
      <xsd:maxInclusive value=“999”/>
   </xsd:restriction>
</xsd:simpleType>
```

Figure 4.17: Simple type for integers within a given range.

To ensure that the values for strings are acceptable, there are a few methods to restrict the values. One is based on string patterns (regular expressions). This method looks at the contents of the string and ensures that it can be matched to the regular expression pattern in the schema.

Figure 4.18 shows an example of how a North American phone number would be declared. The phone number pattern is described inside the *xsd:pattern* element. In the *value* attribute, the pattern for the string is found. In this example the first character is a parenthesis. The next five characters, *\d{3}*, indicate that the next characters must be exactly three digits (*\d*), which make up the area code for the phone number. The next two characters are a closing parenthesis

```
<xsd:simpleType name=“naPhoneNumber”>
   <xsd:restriction base=“xsd:string”>
      <xsd:pattern value=“(\d{3}) \d{3}-\d{4}”/>
   </xsd:restriction>
</xsd:simpleType>
```

Figure 4.18: Simple type with pattern restriction for North American phone numbers.

and a space. Next there must be three digits (the exchange). A hyphen and then the final four digits of the phone number follow.

The patterns are not limited to numeric data. Any character data may also be restricted using this approach. The *pattern* element is used with some slightly different values.

For example, suppose the following are the requirements for a component number:

- The first character is either a B or a C.
- The next three characters must be numeric.
- The last three characters must be within the range A through G.

Such a component number would be described with the syntax shown in Figure 4.19.

```
<xsd:simpleType name="componentNumber">
   <xsd:restriction base="xsd:string">
      <xsd:pattern value="B?C\d{3}[A-G]{3}"/>
   </xsd:restriction>
</xsd:simpleType>
```

Figure 4.19: Simple type with pattern restriction for a component number containing alphabetic and numeric portions.

Another restriction that can be placed on string values is the length of the string. Similarly to other range restrictions, minimum and maximum values are specified to ensure that the data falls within the acceptable range. For string data, the *minLength* and *maxLength* elements are used.

Figure 4.20 shows how the minimum and maximum lengths can control the length of the string. The product number requires a minimum length of 10 and cannot be longer than 20 characters.

```
<xsd:simpleType name="productNumber">
   <xsd:restriction base="xsd:string">
      <xsd:minLength value="10" />
      <xsd:maxLength value="20" />
   </xsd:restriction>
</xsd:simpleType>
```

Figure 4.20: Length restrictions on a string type.

Lists

As an alternative to having multiple elements to contain an array of items, a list element can be used to define a group of items. The list is essentially a white space-separated string.

A list of countries, each of which is on the enumeration list from Figure 4.16, would be defined as shown in Figure 4.21.

```
<xsd:simpleType name="countryList">
   <xsd:list itemType="country"/>
</xsd:simpleType>
```

Figure 4.21: List of enumerated countries.

The element that would contain the values would look like the following: *<country>CAN USA</country>*.

Obviously, if one of the values were not in the country enumeration list, it would be invalid. Note that the list does not need to use another simple type; the item type can be any of the data types provided in the specification. The list can be an array of integers or strings; it really depends on the purpose of the element.

Unions

With the union element, two types can be combined to create a single, multi-purpose element. This allows values constrained in two different types to be combined to validate a single type. In Figure 4.22, we have a shipping date-type element that will contain the value from one of two simple types: One of the sim ple types is a date, and the other is an enumeration list containing alternate values.

```
<xsd:element name="shippingDate" type="xsd:date" />
<xsd:simpleType base="shippingAlternates">
   <xsd:restriction base="xsd:string">
      <xsd:enumeration value="TBD" />
      <xsd:enumeration value="NA" />
   </xsd:restriction>
</xsd:simpleType>

<xsd:element name="shippingDateType">
    <xsd:union memberTypes="shippingDate shippingAlternates"/>
</xsd:element>
```

Figure 4.22: Union data type.

The element can contain one of the following elements:

- <shippingDateType>2003-01-01</shippingDateType>
- <shippingDateType>TBD</shippingDateType>
- <shippingDateType>NA</shippingDateType>

Complex Types

A complex type has a defined structure containing attributes, child elements, or both. Whenever an element is to contain a child or an attribute, it must be defined in a complex type. Complex types replace the nested element declarations from DTDs.

The complex type shown in Figure 4.23 describes a set of customer information. In this element declaration, the customer element will contain a *firstname*, an *initial*, and a *lastname*. It will also contain an ID attribute.

An example of a valid XML using this schema is shown in Figure 4.24.

```
<xsd:element name="customer" type="customerType" />
<xsd:complexType name="customerType" content="elementOnly">
   <xsd:sequence>
      <xsd:element name="firstname" type="xsd:string" />
      <xsd:element name="initial" type="xsd:string"/>
      <xsd:element name="lastname" type="xsd:string"/>
   </xsd:sequence>
   <xsd:attribute name="id" type="xsd:int"/>
</xsd:complexType>
```

Figure 4.23: Complex data type.

```
<?xml version="1.0" encoding="UTF-8"?>
<customer xmlns:xsi="http://www.w3.org/2001/XMLSchema-instance"
  xsi:noNamespaceSchemaLocation="customerwithattribute.xsd" id="12">
   <firstname>Joe</firstname>
   <initial>P</initial>
   <lastname>Smith</lastname>
</customer>
```

Figure 4.24: XML document using the complex date type shown in Figure 4.23.

User-defined types may also be used in place of the base simple types provided by the specification. This allows personal names to be used in both customer and employee elements.

Annotations

Three elements provide the ability to add annotations to an XML schema. These annotations are added for the benefit of both human readers of the schemas and other applications. The three elements are *documentation*, *appInfo*, and *annotation*. The *annotation* element is always the parent for either the *documentation* or *appInfo* element.

The *documentation* element is for human readers. This type of information could be comments or copyright information. It is recommended that the *xml:lang* attribute be used with this element. This attribute provides the language in which the comments are written. This also allows multiple comments to be placed inside the annotation element. The *appInfo* element is used to provide information for other applications, tools, and stylesheets.

Best Practices

There is a lot to absorb in the Schemas specification. With all of this functionality, it can be very easy to get carried away and structure anything and everything. However, doing so can detract greatly from the flexibility of the specification, and the Schemas become increasingly difficult to use. So, when developing a schema, use the KISS rule: Keep it simple, stupid. Having simpler schemas will provide greater flexibility.

Another good idea is to use simple types to constrain complex data. This is a great way to ensure your SKU numbers are in a valid format and to ensure that phone numbers are valid. However, one can get carried away with this practice as well.

Wrap-up

There are a many similarities between the Schemas and DTD specifications. However, where DTDs left off is where Schemas have taken over. Schemas provide the same constraints to the structure as DTDs. They provide a means of defining the structure of an XML document by way of a readable XML syntax.

But Schemas do not stop there. They also provide a means to describe the data inside each of element by way of built-in data types and user defined simple and complex types.

References
www.w3.org/XML/Schema

5

Programming with XML

What you will learn:

- ✓ The types of parsers that are available
- ✓ How to use the various parsers
- ✓ Available XML tools for the iSeries

Now that the structure of XML documents is understood, documents that contain iSeries information can be created. But how do the XML documents get populated with the data from iSeries resources?

There are a great many tools that can be used to generate XML data automatically. In many cases they provide a solution that would fit most of the technical requirements. However, what if the tool does not provide enough functionality? When the features of the tools are not adequate, you are left with developing your own solution.

There are many tools and components that can assist in the development of XML-aware applications. They can read and generate XML documents that interact with the iSeries. Some of the available tools are the following:

- XML parsers: DOM and SAX
- DB2 XML Extender
- XForms

With these tools, XML-aware applications can be created using various programming languages on the iSeries. including Java, RPG, COBOL, and ILE C. They can use both the Simple API for XML (SAX) and Document Object Model (DOM) parsers. Other tools such as the DB2 XML Extender can be used to extend the capabilities of the DB2 database and provide interfaces that utilize XML as the import format.

Parsers

One of the most essential components of XML technology is the XML parser. An XML parser is a software processor that understands the structure of an XML document. With the understanding comes the ability to manipulate and validate the data.

Parsers are used by a wide variety of XML technologies to access the data inside an XML document. Parsers are used "under the hood" by many XML technologies that read and write XML documents. Also, they provide the only way for a developer to retrieve information from an XML document. When requested, the parser will return information from the XML document.

A parser can also validate data inside an XML document. An XML document may have a reference to either a DTD or an XML schema. Both of these control the structure and type of data found inside an XML document, as described in Chapters 3 and 4. When opening an XML document, the parser will ensure that the data inside conforms to the rules established in the DTD or schema. If the data does not meet the requirements, the document is considered invalid, and the parser will not allow processing to continue.

Types of Parsers

There are two basic parser types available: the DOM and SAX parsers. Each provides its own unique view of the document and various methods for accessing data.

The key to understanding the specification rather than the specific implementation is that the specification outlines all of the functionality required for the parser. Each implementation of the specification will have the same functionality but with its own naming conventions. So, if the specification is understood, it is just a matter of knowing how to use the various implementations of the parser.

DOM

A Document Object Model (DOM) parser allows applications to access and update the data and structure of an XML document dynamically. The DOM parser presents the XML as a hierarchy of nodes. Each node may contain other nodes as well as attributes.

The DOM specification details the objects and interfaces that must be used when implementing this parser. IBM, Inso EPS, SoftQuad, Arbortext, Software AG, and JavaSoft submitted the DOM specification to the W3 Consortium. The specification is currently in Level 3 Core Version 1.0, which was last updated in November 2003. Microsoft and Apache, to name a few, have developed implementations of the DOM specification. Level 3 Core Version 1.0 will be used for this book.

All that is required to use the DOM parser is an implementation. As just mentioned, implementations are available for COM developers and for Java development.

DOM Interfaces

The DOM specification outlines the objects that must be implemented. Each type of object has its interface, as described in the following paragraphs.

Document Interface

The most important object is the document object. It is the document element, or the root element of the XML document. There can only be one document for an

XML file, because it cannot have any parent nodes. The document interface acts as a factory for creating elements, text, comments, and other XML objects. Once these objects have been created by the document, they will be associated with the document that created them.

Table 5.1 lists the attributes required in the implementation of the document interface. Table 5.2 lists the methods that must be implemented for the document interface.

Table 5.1: Attributes of the DOM Document Interface

Attribute Name	Description
doctype	The doctype returns the Document Type Declaration for the document. If the value has not been set, doctype returns a null. This attribute uses the DocumentType node. This is a read-only attribute.
documentElement	This attribute provides an easy way to access the document element of the document. It returns an element interface and is a read-only attribute.
documentURI	The documentURI returns the location of the document. This is a read-only attribute.
inputEncoding	inputEncoding specifies the encoding type of the document. It will return a null if the type is unknown. This is a read-only attribute.
strictErrorChecking	When this attribute is set to true, strict error checking will occur on the document. When set to false, it does not report every error encountered during execution.
xmlEncoding	This read-only attribute specifies the encoding used for the XML document. A null value will be returned when there is no encoding type specified.
xmlStandalone	This attribute indicates whether or not the XML is a stand-alone document.
xmlVersion	xmlVersion returns the version number specified in the XML declaration element. This is a read-only attribute that will return null if there is no value specified.

Table 5.2: Methods of the DOM Document Interface

Method Name	Description
adoptNode	This is a new method that was introduced in Level 3 DOM. It allows an element from another document to be added to the current document. This will move the entire subtree into the destination document.
createAttribute createAttributeNS	This method will create an attribute interface. The name of the attribute will be passed when executing this method. To add the attribute to an element, the setAttributeNode must be executed. The createAttributeNS creates an attribute using a namespace URI.
create CDATASection	This creates a CDATA section inside the XML document.
createComment	The createComment method creates a comment inside the XML document.
createElement createElementNS createTextNode createDocument- Fragment	These methods each create a unique type element interface. The name of the element is passed in the method and if the element is to be part of a namespace, the namespace URI is also passed. The new element will be added to the destination element by using the appendChild method.
getElementById getElementsByTag- Name getElementsByTag- NameNS	These methods will search the document for the element based upon the criteria entered. The getElementById method will only return a single element, but the others will return a group of elements inside a NodeList interface. If there are no elements found with the ID search, a null value will be returned. If there are no elements found in the other searches, a node list with zero nodes will be returned.
importNote	This method will import a node from another document without changing any values.
normalize- Document	This new function to Level 3 essentially acts as if it has saved and reloaded the document.
renameNode	This is a new function to the Level 3 Core. The renameNode method renames a node to a new name.

Node Interface

The node interface is used as a base interface for many other interfaces in the DOM. Inside an XML document, any individual node can be referenced using the node interface.

Table 5.3 contains a list of the key methods for the node interface type. Table 5.4 lists the available attributes for the node interface.

Table 5.3: Methods for the DOM Node Interface

Method Name	Description
appendChild insertBefore	These methods add the node to the list of children. The insertBefore method uses a reference node as the node that the new node will precede.
cloneNode	The cloneNode method makes a copy of the node structure. When used on a node, it does not carry any of the data or the parent information. When used with an attribute, it does copy the data and child nodes. By default, when elements are cloned, the data is copied but not any child nodes. To copy the child nodes, a deep clone must be used. Cloning an Entity Reference interface makes a copy of the entire subtree regardless of whether a deep clone is performed.
compareDocument Position	Compares the position of the current node to the position of the node passed in. The return is a short value indicating the relative position.
getUserData	Retrieves the object associated with the key. In the event that an object, such as a node or attribute, has been associated with the current node using the setUserData, that object will be retrieved.
hasAttributes	Returns a true or false value indicating whether the node has any attributes.
hasChildNodes	This attribute returns a true or false value indicating whether the node has any child nodes.
isDefault Namespace	The isDefaultNamespace checks to see whether the specified namespace is the default namespace for the document.
isEqualNode	This method tests two nodes and determines whether they are equal. To be equal, the nodes must be the same type, have the same name, local name, namespace, prefix, node value, attributes, and child nodes.

Table 5.3: Methods for the DOM Node Interface, *continued*

Method Name	Description
isSameNode	The isSameNode method checks to see whether the current node is the same as the node passed. It is conceivable that the same node may have been returned in two different queries. This method will check whether the node is the same.
isSupported	This method tests to see whether this node supports the submitted feature.
lookupNamespace-URI	This method returns the namespace URI based upon the given prefix.
lookupPrefix	This method returns the given prefix for the current node.
normalize	This new function to Level 3 essentially acts as if it has saved and reloaded the node.
removeChild	This method removes the node from the subtree.
replaceChild	This method replaces a node with a new node.
setUserData	This method associates an object with the key for the current node. The object can be retrieved later by calling the getUserData method on the same node.

Table 5.4: Attributes for the DOM Node Interface

Attribute Name	Description
attributes	This attribute returns the attributes specified for the node. If there are no attributes, the return value is a null.
childNodes	The childNodes attribute returns a collection of the children to the current node.
firstChild lastChild nextSibling previousSibling	Each of these attributes returns a child node. A null value will be returned if the requested node does not exist.
namespaceURI	This read-only attribute returns the namespace for the current node.
nodeName	This attribute returns the name of the node.

Table 5.4: Attributes for the DOM Node Interface, *continued*

Attribute Name	Description
nodeType	This attribute returns the type of node.
nodeValue	This attribute returns the value of the node.
ownerDocument	This attribute returns the owner document interface.
parentNode	This attribute returns the parent node.
prefix	This attribute returns the namespace prefix.
textContent	This attribute returns the text content for the current node. Depending upon the node type, it will return different parts of the node.

There are a few types of nodes, each of which implements the node interface. One thing to note is that each implementation does not necessarily take on all of the methods and attributes of the node interface.

Attribute Interface

The attribute interface, known as the *Attr* interface, is an interface representation of an attribute of a node. To retrieve the value of the attribute, the nodeValue attribute can be used. In the example in Figure 5.1, you will see that ID is an attribute of the customer node.

```
<customer ID="123456">
. . .
</customer>
```

Figure 5.1: Attribute.

This implementation does not take on all of the available methods and attributes of the node interface. Attributes do not contain any child nodes and so cannot make use of any such methods and attributes. In the same way, parent and sibling attributes return null values.

The attribute *specified* indicates whether the attribute was explicitly entered into the XML document. This deals with values that have been provided by an XML schema. In the event that there was no value entered for the attribute and there was a default value in the XML schema, the *specified* attribute will be set to *false*.

CDATASection Interface

The CDATASection is the interface that contains a section of text inside an XML document. It allows for almost any sequence of data inside the interface.

```
<script>
<![CDATA[
function add(a,b) {
  return a + b
}
]]>
</script>
```

Figure 5.2: Example of a CDATA section.

In Figure 5.2, the data is surrounded inside the CDATA tags with the closing tag being the]]> sequence. This allows for data that may normally been escaped to be passed into the XML document without fear of losing functionality.

Comment Interface

This interface places comments inside the XML document. This will properly escape the values inside a node, as shown in Figure 5.3.

```
<parentNode>
<!-- This is a comment node inside of the parent node -->
</parentNode>
```

Figure 5.3: Example of an XML comment interface.

Document Fragment Interface

The Document Fragment Interface is very similar to the document interface. It contains the ability to create node interfaces and create a subtree. The biggest difference, however, lies in the fact that the interface is a scaled-down or "lightweight" version of the document interface. This allows for a subtree to be generated using the document fragment and then inserted into the document interface. This type of functionality is possible with the document interface; however, it may be difficult depending upon the application implementation.

Document Type Interface

The document type interface allows for the editing of the entities inside a DTD. When requested, the interface will return a list of all the entities inside the DTD and provide the means of updating the values.

Element Interface

The element interface represents an element that can be found inside an XML or HTML document. The element interface is very similar to the node interface; however, the element interface has more attribute-related methods and attributes.

Table 5.5 lists the methods implemented inside the element interface. The attributes listed in Table 5.6 have been implemented in the element interface.

Table 5.5: Methods of the DOM Element Interface

Method Name	Description
getAttribute getAttributeNS getAttributeNode getAttributeNodeNS	These methods return the attribute value based upon a name. The method returns the attribute value based upon the name and namespace. The getAttributeNode and getAttributeNodeNS methods return an attribute node based upon the name and, if applicable, the namespace.
getElements-ByTagName getElements-ByTagNameNS	These methods will return a listing of nodes based upon the name and namespace provided.

Table 5.5: Methods of the DOM Element Interface, *continued*

Method Name	Description
hasAttribute hasAttributeNS	The hasAttribute and hasAttributeNS will determine whether an attribute exists in the element based upon the name and namespace.
removeAttribute removeAttributeNS	These methods will remove an attribute based upon the name and the namespace. If the attribute contains a default value from either the DTD or the schema, then a new attribute will appear.
removeAttribute-Node	This method removes an attribute based upon the attribute interface entered. Similarly to the removeAttribute and removeAttributeNS methods, a new attribute will appear if there is a default value specified.
setAttribute setAttributeNS setAttributeNode setAttributeNode-NS	These methods will set the value of an attribute. The name, the value, and, if necessary, the namespace will be used to set the value. If the attribute does not already exist, then the method will create the attribute. The setAttributeNode and setAttributeNodeNS methods add a new attribute based upon an object rather than values.
setIdAttribute setIdAttributeNS setIdAttributeNode setIdAttributeNode-NS	These methods set the ID for the attribute based upon the name and the namespace provided. The setIdAttributeNode and setIdAttributeNodeNS will set the ID of the attribute based upon the node submitted rather than the values.

Table 5.6: Attributes of the DOM Element Interface

Attribute Name	Description
schemaTypeInfo	This attribute returns the type information associated with this element from the schema.
tagName	This attribute returns the name of the element. This attribute acts a little differently from the nodeName attribute inherited by the node interface. When used on an XML document, it will return the name of the element with the case preserved. When used with an HTML document, the name of the tag is returned with the name in uppercase regardless of the case inside the HTML.

Entity Interface

An entity interface represents an entity found inside a DTD. This implementation allows for the editing of the values for the entity. The nodeName attribute returns the name of the entity.

The entity interface has a few additional attributes worth noting, listed in Table 5.7.

Table 5.7: Attributes of the DOM Entity Interface Other Than nodeName

Attribute Name	Description
inputEncoding	This attribute returns the encoding used for the entity.
notationName	This attribute returns the name of the notation for unparsed entities. When the entity has been parsed, it returns a null value.
publicId	The publicId attribute returns the public identifier for the entity. If there is no identifier, a null will be returned.
systemId	This attribute returns the system identifier for the entity. If there is no identifier, a null will be returned.
xmlEncoding	This attribute returns the XML encoding for the specified entity.
xmlVersion	This attribute returns the XML version for the entity.

Entity Reference Interface

This interface allows for the creation and manipulation of entity references. An entity reference allows for value substitution during parsing. This functionality is very common in HTML development. For example, if a blank character is needed to ensure spacing but not permit a line break, a * * is entered into the HTML code. The * * must be transformed into the hex value for a non-breaking blank character.

```
<!ENTITY entityName "Entity Value">
```

Figure 5.4: Entity reference format.

Figure 5.4 provides the structure of an entity reference node. An entity reference contains only two components: the name and the value of the entity. The DOM implementation provides a means of creating these nodes, which are not a normal, well-formed XML node.

```
<!ENTITY nbsp " " -->
```

Figure 5.5: Example of an entity reference for a blank character.

```
<customerName>Joe Smith</customerName>
```

Figure 5.6: Using an entity reference inside an XML document.

Figures 5.5 and 5.6 show how an entity reference would be declared and how it would be used. Figure 5.5 declares a simple entity with the name of *nbsp* and a value of * *. In Figure 5.6, the entity reference is used in the customerName node. The name is preceded by an & character and followed by a semicolon.

Notation Interface

The notation interface defines a notation reference for use inside a DTD. A notation element is used to identify a program to process a type based upon the data format or identify the type of data format. The notation node is read-only in the DOM 3 implementation and contains no child nodes.

Processing Instruction Interface

The processing instruction interface contains a processing instruction that is used to hold process-specific information. This interface provides the ability to link a Cascading Style Sheet (CSS) or even an Extensible Stylesheet Language (XSL) stylesheet to the XML document. During parsing, the XSL can be retrieved and then applied to the XML document.

The interface provides a mechanism to identify the document and the type of document that will be associated with the XML. The implementation also gives a means of attaching additional information regarding the specific processing instruction.

Text Interface

The text interface represents any text contained inside an element or attribute interface. This interface is used to manipulate the text that is placed inside an element or attribute. The text interface provides access to the text contained in the current element as well as all children.

Table 5.8 lists additional methods for the text interface. The text interface has the additional attributes listed in Table 5.9.

Table 5.8: Methods for the DOM Text Interface

Method Name	Description
replaceWholeText	This method replaces the text in the current node and all values from the adjacent elements.
splitText	This method splits the text into two parts based upon the incoming index. The first part will be the text up to the index value, and the other part will be the remaining text.

Table 5.9: Attributes of the DOM Text Interface

Attribute Name	Description
isElementContent-Whitespace	This attribute returns true if the text inside the element contains any whitespace.
wholeText	The wholeText attribute returns all of the text from all of the adjacent elements.

Using the DOM Parser

To use the DOM parser requires the following simple steps:

1. Create the Document Builder, which is created by the Document Builder Factory.

2. Load the XML file into a document by using the *parse* method from the Document Builder.

3. Perform the necessary actions (for example, read or update values).

4. Save the document if necessary.

To show how all these steps come together, we will use the XML document shown in Figure 5.7. This XML document contains some simple customer data.

```
<?xml version="1.0" ?>
<customer id="12345">
   <firstname>Joe</firstname>
   <initial>E.</initial>
   <lastname>Smith</lastname>
   <addresses>
      <address type="home">
         <street>123 Avenue</street>
         <city>New York City</city>
         <state>New York</state>
         <zipcode>12345</zipcode>
      </address>
      <address type="mailing">
         <street>123 Street</street>
         <city>Atlanta</city>
         <state>Georgia</state>
         <zipcode>23456</zipcode>
      </address>
   </addresses>
</customer>
```

Figure 5.7: Customer information in an XML document.

The Java code shown (with added line numbers) in Figure 5.8 parses the document and sends the information to the system output stream. This Java example uses the Apache implementation of the DOM known as Xerces version 2.6.0. For more information about the Apache implementation, visit *xml.apache.org/*.

```
public class domRead {
   public static void main(String args[]) throws Exception
   {
      DocumentBuilder db =
        DocumentBuilderFactory.newInstance().newDocumentBuilder();
      Document xml = db.parse(new InputSource(new FileReader(new
        File("customerinformation.xml"))));
      Element documentRoot = xml.getDocumentElement();
      displayElementDetails(documentRoot);
      NodeList firstNameList =
        documentRoot.getElementsByTagName("firstname");
      if (firstNameList.getLength() > 0)
      {
         Element firstName = (Element) firstNameList.item(0);
         displayElementDetails(firstName);
      }
      NodeList addressList =
        documentRoot.getElementsByTagName("address");
      for (int i = 0; i < addressList.getLength(); i++)
      {
         Element addressElement = (Element) addressList.item(i);
         displayElementDetails(addressElement);
         for(int x = 0; x <
           addressElement.getChildNodes().getLength(); x++)
         {
            if (addressElement.getChildNodes().item(x).getNodeType()
              == Node.ELEMENT_NODE)
            {
               Element childNode = (Element)
                 addressElement.getChildNodes().item(x);
               System.out.print(childNode.getParentNode().getNodeName()
                 + " - ");
               System.out.print(childNode.getNodeName() + " - ");
               if (childNode.hasChildNodes() &&
                     childNode.getFirstChild().getNodeType() ==
                       Node.TEXT_NODE) {
                     Text textNode = (Text) childNode.getFirstChild();
                     System.out.println(textNode.getNodeValue());
               }
            }
         }
      }
   }
   private static void displayElementDetails(Element inElement)
      throws Exception
   {
```

Figure 5.8: The Java code to parse the customer information XML (part 1 of 2).

```
37        if (inElement.getParentNode() != null)
38        System.out.print(inElement.getParentNode().getNodeName()
            + " - ");
39        System.out.println(inElement.getNodeName());
40        for(int i = 0; i <
            inElement.getAttributes().getLength(); i++)
41        {
42           Attr attribute = (Attr)
               inElement.getAttributes().item(i);
43           System.out.print(attribute.getName() + " - ");
44           System.out.println(attribute.getValue());
45        }
46    }
47 }
```

Figure 5.8: The Java code to parse the customer information XML (part 2 of 2).

As just described, the first step to using the DOM is to create the Document Builder using the Document Builder Factory. This is done on line 04. The next step is to use the Document Builder to ready the XML document. On line 05, the Document Builder opens the customerinformation.xml (Figure 5.7) into the Document object.

The next thing that is done, on line 06, is to retrieve the document element from the document using the getDocumentElement method. Using the displayElementDetails method, the information about the element is displayed. In this method, the node name (line 39), the parent node name (line 37 and 38), and the entire attribute information (lines 40 to 45) are displayed.

On line 08 the first name element is retrieved using the getElementsByTagName method. The result is a node list class containing all of the nodes found with the name *firstname*. To ensure that there were results returned from the query, the value returned from the getLength method on the node list is checked (line 09) to see whether it is greater than 0.

One of the next actions is to display all of the addresses contained in the XML. Line 14 queries the document element and retrieves all of the address nodes. The results of the query would be the two address nodes. On lines 15 through 33, the information about the addresses is shown. On line 21, the child node is checked to ensure that it is an element. If the address element contained an attribute, the attribute would also be returned as a child. Also on line 26, before the value of the address child element is displayed, the element is checked to see whether it contains any child nodes and whether it is a text node. This test is important because the text value of the element is contained in a child node with a type of text node.

In Figure 5.7 there are two address nodes located inside the *addresses* element. If there were additional address elements located in the document, not necessarily in the addresses element, they would also be returned in the query. To refine the search, the getElementsByTagName could be executed against the addresses element rather than the document element.

```
#document - customer
id - 12345
customer - firstname
addresses - address
type - home
address - street - 123 Avenue
address - city - New York City
address - state - New York
address - zipcode - 12345
addresses - address
type - mailing
address - street - 123 Street
address - city - Atlanta
address - state - Georgia
address - zipcode - 23456
```

Figure 5.9: Output of the execution.

The result of running the domRead application on this XML file is shown in Figure 5.9.

Writing to an XML Using DOM

Writing to an XML document using the DOM parser is very similar to reading from the document. The document still needs to be opened, and the elements will be queried. The difference comes when accessing the values of the elements and attributes.

The first step to writing an XML is to create an element. To create an element, the createElement method is executed on the Document object. The Java code shown in Figure 5.10 creates a birth date element and then add it to the document element. Note that the new element does not need to be added to the document element. It can be added to any other element inside the XML document.

```
Element birthDateElement = xml.createElement("birthdate");
documentRoot.appendChild(birthDateElement);
```

Figure 5.10: Creating an element and adding it to a document.

The second step is to add a value to the element. Simply creating a text class and then appending it to the element can accomplish this task. This can be seen in the code example in Figure 5.11.

```
Element birthDateElement = xml.createElement("birthdate");
Text birthDateText = xml.createTextNode("12/15/1968");
birthDateElement.appendChild(birthDateText);
documentRoot.appendChild(birthDateElement);
```

Figure 5.11: Adding a value to an element.

Existing text can be changed in one of two ways: The old text node can be replaced, or it can be edited. To replace the text node of an existing last name element from Figure 5.7, the code in Figure 5.12 would be used. This code replaces the first child node of the last name element with the new text. The code in Figure 5.13 can be used to replace only the text for the node, with the same results.

```
Text lastNameText = xml.createTextNode("Brown");
lastName.replaceChild(lastNameText,
   (Text)lastName.getChildNodes().item(0));
```

Figure 5.12: Replacing a text node.

```
lastName.getChildNodes().item(0).setNodeValue("Brown");
```

Figure 5.13: Replacing the text within a node.

To add or modify attributes of an element, the setAttribute method can be used. The setAttribute method expects the name and value for the attribute. If the attribute already exists, the value will be updated. The line of code in Figure 5.14 is an example of how the *id* field on the customer element can be changed:

```
documentElement.setAttribute("id", "456789");
```

Figure 5.14: Setting an attribute.

SAX

The other major parser for XML is the Simple API for XML (SAX) parser. The SAX parser was the first parser in the Java world. It is, as the name suggests, a simple set of APIs that allow for the parsing and creating of an XML document.

The SAX parser works much differently from the DOM. As described in the preceding section, the DOM parser works by loading the document into a hierarchy in memory. The SAX parser works on an event-based model. As specific key components are encountered, events are sent back (by way of callbacks) to the implementation, which must handle them with the corresponding code.

The SAX parser was created collectively by the members of the XML-DEV mailing list. The specification has been developed and is free to use. Each organization that implements the parser is responsible for the maintenance of its own code. The current version of the SAX specification is Version 2.0.1.

Components of the SAX Parser

DefaultHandler

As described earlier, the SAX parser operates much differently from other parsers. One of the most important classes in the SAX model is the DefaultHandler. This class is the base to which all of the events are sent.

The methods listed in Table 5.10 are part of the DefaultHandler.

Table 5.10: Methods of the SAX DefaultHandler

Method Name	Description
characters	This method receives a notification when there are characters encountered inside an element. The characters are passed into the method inside a character array.
endDocument	The endDocument method is sent a notification when the end of document is encountered.
endElement	This method receives a notification when a previously opened element has ended. Some of the parameters passed in are the URI, the element name, and the qName.
endPrefixMapping	This method is notified when a namespace mapping has ended. The name of the namespace that has ended is passed as a parameter to the method.
error	This method is executed when there is a recoverable error encountered during parsing. A SAXParseException object is passed as a parameter.
fatalError	The fatalError is executed when a fatal error has been encountered. A SAXParseException object is passed as a parameter.
ignorableWhitespace	This method is notified when there is ignorable white space found in an element. The values returned are passed in a character array.
notationDecl	The notationDecl method receives notification when a notation declaration has been encountered.

Table 5.10: Methods of the SAX DefaultHandler, *continued*

Method Name	Description
processing Instruction	The processingInstruction method receives notification when a processing instruction has been encountered in the XML document. The target and the data are passed to the method.
resolveEntity	This method resolves an external entity. The public ID and systemID are passed as parameters.
setDocument-Locator	The setDocumentLocator specifies a locator object for the document events. The locator object is detailed later in the chapter.
skippedEntity	A notification of a skipped entity is sent using this method. Use of a filter, which will be described later, may skip entities.
startDocument	This notification is received when the start of a document is encountered.
startElement	The startElement is executed when the beginning of an element is encountered. The URI, name, the namespace, and any attributes are sent as parameters.
startPrefixMapping	This method is called when the start of a namespace has been encountered. The namespace is passed in as a parameter to this method.
unparsedEntity-Decl	This method is used to notify that a unparsed entity has been encountered. All of the information about the entity is passed to the method.
warning	This method is called when a parsing warning has been encountered. A SAX error is passed to the method.

The DefaultHandler is implemented by the following four core SAX handlers:

- ContentHandler
- DTDHandler
- EntityResolver
- ErrorHandler

For all the various handlers, it is up to the application to store the information returned. The parser will only report when a specific component has been encountered. The values may be stored inside a hash table or in variables for future use.

ContentHandler

The ContentHandler is the most commonly used handler. It is will be used for all types of well-formed documents.

The order in which the events are called is very important to the structure of the XML document. Let's take, for example, Figure 5.15, which contains a simple XML containing some customer information. The SAX parser would read this document by sending the following event information back to the implementation:

```
<?xml version="1.0" ?>
<customer>
   <firstname>Joe</firstname>
   <initial>E.</initial>
   <lastname>Smith</lastname>
</customer>
```

Figure 5.15: Simple customer XML document.

1. Start of the XML document
2. Start of the customer element
3. Start of the firstname element
4. The characters: Joe
5. End of the firstname element
6. Start of the initial element
7. The characters: E.
8. End of the initial element

9. Start of the lastname element
10. The characters: Smith
11. End of the lastname element
12. End of the customer Element
13. End of the XML document

DTDHandler

When an application is in need of information about notations and unparsed entities, the DTDHandler can be used. It returns DTD-specific events so that a DTD document can be parsed and understood. The handler may return items of information in any order, regardless of the order in which they have been declared.

The DTDHandler has an additional two methods to help parse a DTD document; these methods are shown in Table 5.11.

Table 5.11: Methods of the SAX DTDHandler

Method Name	Description
notationDecl	This method receives the notification that a notation has been encountered. The method receives the name, the public ID and the system ID as parameters.
unparsedEntityDecl	This method receives a notification when an entity has been encountered. The name, public ID, the system ID and the notation name are sent as parameters to the method.

ErrorHandler

When errors are encountered during parsing, they can be captured in an ErrorHandler interface. If this interface is not established, parsing errors, warnings, and fatal errors may go undetected. It is the responsibility of the application to report the error and provide custom error handling.

The ErrorHandler interface has three types of events that it can capture:

- Warnings
- Errors
- Fatal Errors

A warning is captured when a noncritical error is encountered (for example, an extra attribute for an element). This may not be a concern for the application, and it may choose to continue. The default behavior is to ignore the warning and continue.

An Error is raised when there is a violation in the XML data (that is, the data is not correct for an attribute or an element). The application *may decide* that it does not want to continue with processing because more data may be invalid.

A fatal error event is raised when there is a problem with the format of the XML document. In that case the XML is not well formed, and processing cannot continue.

An error handler is established by using the setErrorHandler method on the XMLReader class. The error handler must be identified prior to receiving any document events. Figure 5.16 shows how an error handler is set for an XMLReader.

```
XMLReader saxReader = XMLReaderFactory.createXMLReader();
SaxHandler myHandler = new SaxHandler();
saxReader.setContentHandler(myHandler);
saxReader.setErrorHandler(myHandler);
```

Figure 5.16: ErrorHandler set for an XMLReader.

EntityResolver

An entity resolver is referenced when the parser must identify data identified by a URI. The resolver will return either the system ID or an InputSource object to read from. This will allow the application to confirm the entity inside the referenced document. An entity resolver is set on the XMLReader by calling the setEntityResolver method.

Attributes

The attributes interface contains all of the attributes for an element. When an element containing attributes is encountered during processing, an attributes class is passed as a parameter to the method. At that time the values can be extracted from the necessary attributes. The attributes interface implements the methods listed in Table 5.12.

Table 5.12 Methods of the SAX Attributes Interface

Method Name	Description
getIndex	The getIndex method returns the index value for an attribute. The qualified name, or both the URI and the local name, can be used to get the index.
getLength	This method returns the number of attributes returned for the element.
getLocalName	getLocalName returns the local name of the attribute. The index is used to determine which attribute to use.
getQName	The getQName method returns the qualified name for the attribute. The index is used to determine which attribute to use.
getType	This method is used to retrieve the type of attribute. Supplying the index, the qualified name or both the URI and the local name can retrieve the type. The attribute can be one of the following values "CDATA", "ID", "IDREF", "IDREFS", "NMTOKEN", "NMTOKENS", "ENTITY", "ENTITIES", or "NOTATION".
getURI	The getURI method will retrieve the attributes namespace by the index provided.
getValue	The getValue method will retrieve the value of the attribute by supplying the index, the qualified name, or both the URI and the local name.

Locator

The locator interface identifies to the application where it is in the current XML document. It provides the exact line and column the parser is currently processing. This can be useful when debugging a parsing error. It can help provide detailed error information when used in trapping an exception.

To specify a locator, use the setDocumentLocator method on the content handler. To use a locator, you must specify it prior to receiving any events.

XMLFilters

XML Filters are available so that the returned values can be altered or separated prior to being processed by the handler. This allows for values to be modified or ignored based upon a specific need.

The XMLFilter interface extends the XMLReader class. The code is written to perform all the necessary actions prior to the handler receiving the notification. Once completed, the filter is then used to read the document and pass it to the handler. The handler will ultimately see only the actions that the filter allows.

Parsing an XML with SAX

As mentioned, parsing an XML document with the SAX parser is a very different process than parsing using the DOM. The following steps are necessary for parsing using the SAX parser:

1. Create a handler class to accept the incoming events from the XML. This handler can be specific to the XML.
2. Inside an application, create an instance of an XMLReader. It sends the events to the handler.
3. Create an instance of the handler and link it to the XMLReader.
4. Open the XML document.
5. Parse the document.

Given the XML from Figure 5.7, the Java code shown (with line numbers added) in Figure 5.17 could be used to parse it. This code would be responsible for receiving the alerts from the XMLReader.

```
01 import org.xml.sax.*;
02 import org.xml.sax.helpers.*;
03 public class MyHandler extends DefaultHandler
04 {
05        public MyHandler ()
06        {
07           super();
08        }
09        public void startDocument ()
10        {
11           System.out.println(“Start document”);
12        }
13        public void endDocument ()
14        {
15           System.out.println(“End document”);
16        }
17        public void startElement(String uri, String name,String
            qName, Attributes atts)
18        {
19           System.out.println(“Start element: ” + qName);
20        }
21        public void endElement (String uri, String name, String qName)
22        {
23           System.out.println(“End element: ” + qName);
24        }
25        public void characters (char ch[], int start, int length)
26        {
27           System.out.print(“Characters: ”);
28           for (int i = start; i < start + length; i++)
29           {
30           System.out.print(ch[i]);
31           }
32           System.out.println(“”);
33        }
34 }
```

Figure 5.17: SAX handler class.

The handler has some events specifically for the start and the end of the XML document. Lines 09 through 12 have the event code for the start of the XML document, and lines 13 through 16 have the event code for the end of the document.

Probably the most import events are the beginning and end events for an element. These two events contain most of the processing for the XML document. Lines 17 through 20 contain the code for the beginning of an element, and lines 21 through 24 contain the code for the end event.

The last event method captures the character data for the current node. The method receives an array of characters as well as the length and the start value for the array.

```
01 import org.xml.sax.*;
02 import org.xml.sax.helpers.*;
03 import java.io.*;
04 public class SaxRead
05 {
05       public static void main(String args[]) throws Exception
06       {
07          XMLReader xmlReader = XMLReaderFactory.createXMLReader();
08          MyHandler handler = new MyHandler();
09          xmlReader.setContentHandler(handler);
10          xmlReader.setErrorHandler(handler);
11          FileReader fileReader = new FileReader(“customerinforma-
              tion.xml”);
12          xmlReader.parse(new InputSource(fileReader));
13       }
14 }
```

Figure 5.18: Application using the handler.

Figure 5.18 shows the code for the application, which is responsible for pulling all of the classes together. As described, requesting it from the XMLReaderFactory creates the XML reader, as is seen on line 07. The handler that was created in Figure 5.17 is created on line 08 and is set as the content handler and the error handler on lines 09 and 10.

One line 11 the file customerinformation.xml, which was defined in Figure 5.7, is loaded into a File Reader class. It is then used on line 12 with the XML Reader class in the parse method.

The output shown in Figure 5.19 is the results of the parsing.

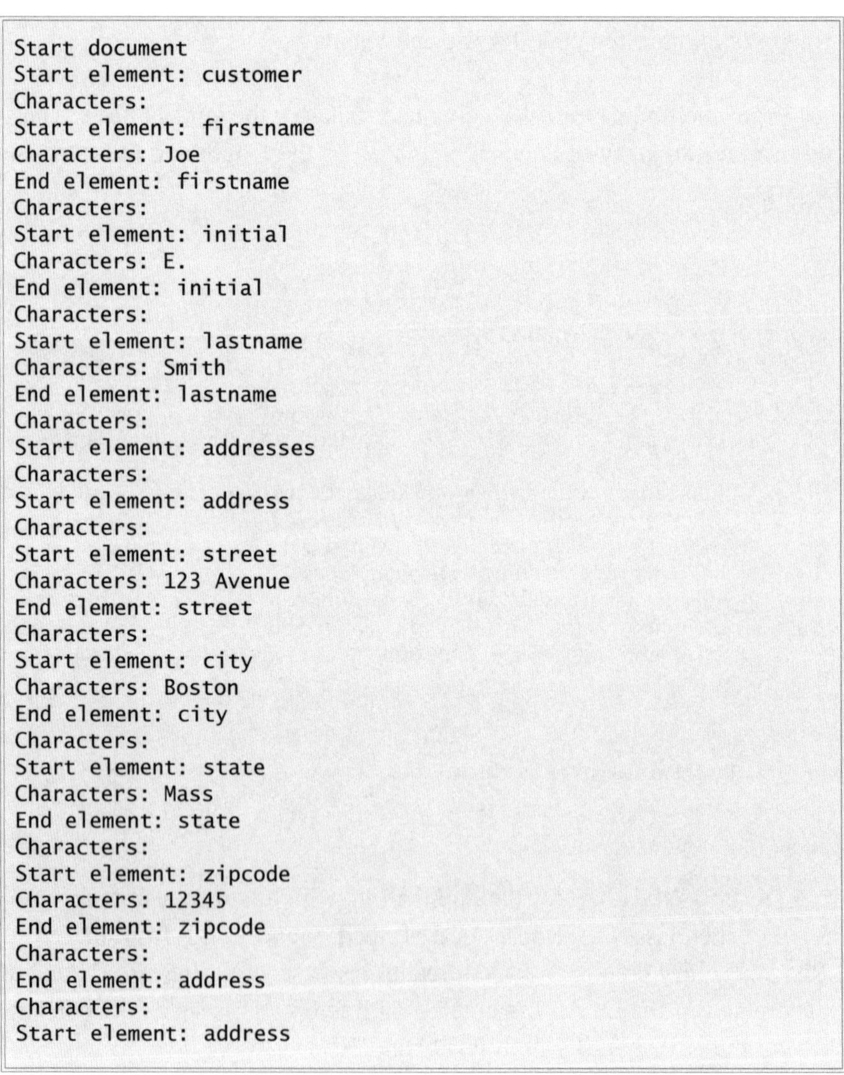

```
Start document
Start element: customer
Characters:
Start element: firstname
Characters: Joe
End element: firstname
Characters:
Start element: initial
Characters: E.
End element: initial
Characters:
Start element: lastname
Characters: Smith
End element: lastname
Characters:
Start element: addresses
Characters:
Start element: address
Characters:
Start element: street
Characters: 123 Avenue
End element: street
Characters:
Start element: city
Characters: Boston
End element: city
Characters:
Start element: state
Characters: Mass
End element: state
Characters:
Start element: zipcode
Characters: 12345
End element: zipcode
Characters:
End element: address
Characters:
Start element: address
```

Figure 5.19: The output of the SAX parser (part 1 of 2).

```
Characters:
Start element: street
Characters: 123 Street
End element: street
Characters:
Start element: city
Characters: Atlanta
End element: city
Characters:
Start element: state
Characters: Georgia
End element: state
Characters:
Start element: zipcode
Characters: 23456
End element: zipcode
Characters:
End element: address
Characters:
End element: addresses
Characters:
End element: customer
End document
```

Figure 5.19: The output of the SAX parser (part 2 of 2).

Parsers for the iSeries

The iSeries comes with a version of the Java Xerces parser. It is located in the following path on the iSeries Model 400 server: */QIBM/proddata/OS400-/xml/lib/xerces103.jar*.

In order to use the parser, it must be added to the CLASSPATH environment variable. If the Java application is packaged in a WAR (Web application archive) file, the jar file may already be included. In this case, the jar inside the WAR file will be used.

Also included on the iSeries is the XML for C++ parser, Version 3.1.0 (XML4C). The parsers can be found in the service program QXML4C310. Contained in the service program QXML4C310 are both the SAX and DOM parsers.

RPG and procedural languages also have an option for a user who wants to work with XML documents. The XML Interface for RPG and Procedural Languages, Version 3.1.0 (XML4PR) is also available for the iSeries. This interface provides RPG, COBOL, and ILE C programs with access to XML documents and data. The interface is a bridge between the XML for the C++ parser and the calling program.

To replace the parser with a new version, in the Java case, simply replace the old file with the new one. Care must be taken when replacing a parser with a new one. There may be deprecated classes or methods that older applications or processes may require. Complete regression testing is recommended when a parser is replaced.

All of these parsers are available within the XML tools for OS/400.

When to Use Which Parser?

Both the DOM and SAX parsers provide unique interfaces to XML data. But when should each be used? The DOM requires a great deal of development effort to read all of the data in an XML document. It contains a vast number of classes and interfaces so that all of the data can be accessed. As seen in the example, it requires specific code to access each node and all of the attributes. This requirement can be rather cumbersome when the XML document is complex and large. Requesting an element with DOM requires the parser to query the entire context. If done incorrectly, this can lead to a great deal of extra overhead.

The SAX parser provides a very simple set of classes that accomplish the same task. Because it alerts the handler when elements and data have been encountered, it does not go through the document multiple times searching for elements. The values as they are encountered are stored in variables and requested when needed. The SAX parser is a much more efficient tool when an XML document needs to be read.

The DOM classes and interfaces indicated earlier not only provide access to the data but also provide the ability to update the data. This provides the means of updating existing XML documents and creating new ones. The SAX parser does not have any means of editing or creating XML files. The events that are defined for the SAX parser are strictly for reading; there are no events that allow for the data to be manipulated. Creating a new XML would require the use of another process such as XSL.

Use the SAX parser when:

- Memory and resources need to be optimized.
- The structure and the order of the elements are important for processing.
- Sections of the XML are required.
- Only reading XML data is necessary.

Use the DOM parser when:

- Complex XML documents are to be built.
- Components are to be added to an XML document.
- Data inside an XML document is to be modified or updated.
- The components needed from the XML are not known.

XML Tools for iSeries

Aside from the XML parsers, there are additional iSeries tools that can assist in XML processing. These range from graphical tools to database interfaces. Each provides a different set of functionality that will assist in implementing an XML solution on the iSeries.

Xeena

Xeena is an XML tool that can generate XML based upon a DTD. The result is the skeleton of the XML document. The XML skeleton will contain all of the elements and attributes necessary to ensure that the XML passes validation. The skeleton can be used in conjunction with the DOM parser to build new XML documents.

Xeena displays the XML graphically in a hierarchical format. By displaying the XML in a treelike format, Xeena makes it easy to understand the structure of the XML document. Xeena ensures that all XML documents that are generated conform to the rules established in the DTD.

This tool can also be used to ensure that an XML document meets the requirements of the DTD document. If there are any problems validating the document, Xeena will identify the problem and the reason why.

To find out more information about Xeena, visit *alphaworks.ibm.com/tech/xeena*.

DB2 XML Extender

The DB2 XML Extender provides new data types so that XML documents can be stored. This toolkit also provides additional functions to work with XML data. XML elements and attributes can be transformed into traditional SQL data types to assist in indexing and querying.

Documents can be generated by using an SQL statement or by the database model. XML data is mapped to database columns by a document access definition (DAD). The DAD can be used to place data into a table, or it can be used to place data into XML elements and attributes.

DB2 XML Extender also contains the following features:

- XML elements and attributes can be inserted into SQL data types.
- SQL data can be transformed into XML documents.
- XML documents can be retrieved, stored, and updated in a single column.
- XML documents can be internationalized.
- DTDs are managed within a repository.
- XML Extender is capable of sending and receiving messages from MQSeries.

- Communication using Web services is carried out using Web Services Object Runtime Framework (WORF) Beta.

To find out more information about DB2 XML Extender, visit *www-306.ibm.com/software/data/db2/extenders/xmlext/index.html* for more information.

XForms

HTML forms have become the norm for Web-based development. They are used in all Web applications and have provided a great deal of functionality for a long time. They have been used in almost every conceivable situation. However, as the expectations of the Internet have increased, the functionality of HTML forms has not. As the need to capture more information grows, so does the development behind the scenes. This has forced developers to become very creative to make complex forms available.

Eventually HTML forms were to have a successor that would provide a rich set of functionality that would remove the need for complex development. The successor had to be able to address the limitations of HTML forms, including the following:

- HTML is unable to adapt to complex and multiple page forms.
- Integration with XML standards is limited.
- Development includes integration into back-end systems.
- Only a limited number of devices are supported.

The W3C has tried to bridge the gap between HTML and XML as well as to extend form functionality by introducing the XForm recommendation. XForms provide a means of generating device-independent forms that work with other XML standards. The key goals to the XForm standard are the following:

- To support multiple devices, including printers and scanners
- To provide a robust user interface to meet today's requirements including support for multiple-page forms and suspend/resume capabilities
- To separate presentation logic from integration logic

Figure 5.20 shows an example of an HTML form. In this example the user is required to submit her or his first name and email address to subscribe to a mailing list. The result of this submission would be the values of *name* and *email* being sent as HTTP parameters. Figure 5.21 shows how the parameters from the form would be requested using Java.

```
<html>
<body>
<form action="http://www.someurl.com/application" method="post">
<p>Full Name:<br />
<input type="text" id="name" name="name" /></p>
<p>Email Addres:<br />
<input type="text" id="email" name="email" /></p>
<p><input type="submit" name="submitButton" value="Submit" /></p>
</form>
</body>
</html>
```

Figure 5.20: HTML Form example.

```
String inName = request.getParameter("name");
String inEmail = request.getParameter("email");
```

Figure 5.21: Obtaining parameters from an HTML form using Java.

```
<head>
<xforms:model>
      <xforms:instance>
          <subscription xmlns="">
             <fullname/>
             <email/>
          </subscription>
      </xforms:instance>
   <xforms:submission action="http://www.someurl.com/
     application" method="post" id="submit" includenamespaceprefixes=""/>
</xforms:model>
```

Figure 5.22: XForm equivalent of the example in Figure 5.20 (part 1 of 2).

```
11 </head>
12 <body>
13    <xforms:input ref="fullname">
14          <xforms:label>Full Name:</xforms:label>
15    </xforms:input>
16       <xforms:input ref="email">
17          <xforms:label>Email:</xforms:label>
18       </xforms:input>
19       <xforms:submit submission="submit">
20          <xforms:label>Submit</xforms:label>
21       </xforms:submit>
22    </body>
```

Figure 5.22: XForm equivalent of the example in Figure 5.20 (part 2 of 2).

The XForms equivalent to the form in Figure 5.20 is shown in Figure 5.22 (with line numbers added). The skeleton of the XML is found on lines 04 through 07. The values are associated with the XML in each of the input tags. In the full name input tag (lines 13 through 15), the XForms code contains a reference to the *fullname* tag. A submission using the example from Figure 5.22 would result in the XML shown in Figure 5.23.

```
<subscription>
   <fullname>Joe Smith</fullname>
   <email>jsmith@someaddress.com</email>
</subscription>
```

Figure 5.23: XML produced by submission of the form in Figure 5.22.

For more information about XForms, visit the following address: *www.w3.org-/MarkUp/Forms/.*

When to Develop

With all of the robust tools and plug-ins available to assist in XML development and processing, when should the solution be to develop or to use an existing tool?

An example would be how to communicate with a Web service using SOAP messages, which will be discussed in detail in Chapter 10. The message can be created with the DOM parser and be sent using a manually established and maintained connection. This approach works when the Web service is an internal resource and there is communication when there has been a change to the request or response. However, when the Web service is an external resource, there may be a change without notice, forcing an immediate change to the code. The choice of developing the communication with a Web service makes maintenance a challenge.

However, when one is dealing with Web services, the Web Service Description Language (WSDL) can be used to generate stub code. The stub code is populated with the necessary parameters and then can open a channel to the Web service, sending the SOAP request. Once the Web service has finished processing, it will send the SOAP response to the stub, which will parse the input and make the values available to the calling application.

In this case the choice is obvious: Use the WSDL to generate the stub code. However, in many cases, using new technologies is not an option. The problem arises when dealing with legacy systems that do not understand but are used to generating XML documents or when dealing with internal or external systems that do not expose Web services and deliver XML data. In this case, there are no tools that can be used to assist in the parsing of the XML. The XML must be parsed and the necessary data extracted by hand-developed code.

The solution is to do some research and decide what is the best approach. The ideal solution should consider the available technologies, development time, maintenance effort, and, most important, resource knowledge base.

Conclusion

The various tools available provide a robust set of features that can be used to develop XML-aware applications for iSeries systems. The SAX and DOM parsers provide a way to read in XML data so that the calling application can understand the message. The DOM parser can also be used to generate new messages, so that the message can be sent to another application for processing.

The DOM model provides a great deal of classes and interfaces: one for each component of an XML document. These provide the necessary components to create, read, and update XML documents. Based on a tree model, the document is loaded into memory and accessed as necessary.

The SAX parser provides an event-based model that sends an alert when an element has been processed. The SAX parser is a very efficient parser that can filter events and uses very little overhead during processing. Combined with XSL, it can be used to generate new XML documents.

The iSeries-specific parsers provide a way to use existing COBOL, ILE C, and RPG programs to generate XML documents. They use both the DOM and SAX models when processing an XML document. This can be extremely useful when complex business logic contained in legacy programs needs to be used to generate XML data.

Tools such as Xeena can be used to ensure that XML documents are properly formatted. They can also be used to generate the skeleton of an XML document. DB2 XML Extender provides an XML interface to DB2 databases. It allows data to be modified based upon the XML.

References
www.w3.org/DOM/DOMTR
xml.apache.org/
www.saxproject.org
alphaworks.ibm.com/tech/xeena
www-306.ibm.com/software/data/db2/extenders/xmlext/index.html
www.w3.org/MarkUp/Forms/

6

What's in a Namespace?

In this chapter you will learn:

- ✓ How to define your own namespaces
- ✓ Some of the namespaces in common use
- ✓ The difference between a URI and a URL
- ✓ How the Resource Directory Description Language describes URIs
- ✓ How to refer to namespaces in your XML documents

The extensible nature of XML makes it possible to create XML vocabularies that describe data for almost any type of applications. This also presents a problem against which you are certain to come up, which is the inevitable collision of names. For example, if one XML document describes a database field element that uses the name *field*, that element's attributes and meaning are totally different from those of a *field* element that might appear in a farm markup language. Namespaces provide a definitive answer to the question: Are we working with the same thing?

You might think that careful planning could obviate the need to use namespaces in your applications. Many of the XML applications deployed today, however, rely on namespaces, which makes it likely that you will have to understand at least the purpose and syntax of namespaces.

Providing a Unique Identity

The stated purpose of namespaces is to provide a simple method for qualifying element and attribute names used in Extensible Markup Language documents by associating them with namespaces identified by Uniform Resource Identifier (URI) references. The formal specification that describes namespaces is "Name-spaces in XML," a W3C recommendation that is available at *www.w3.org/TR/REC-xml-names/.*

Namespaces are an area where the various XML standards have been somewhat contentious. This relatively simple concept has generated quite a bit of debate, centered on the inability to retrofit namespaces to older standards such as DTDs, the way to associate a namespace with a responsible party, and the responsibilities of parsers and applications. After these issues were resolved, further questions centered on what a namespace URI resolves to.

The result of this debate is a simplified way of reusing tags and markup from one XML document in another XML document. Rather than use a DTD to define and declare another XML document's markup and then copying that markup, a namespace provides an easier way of referring to external content along with an extended name to deal with name conflicts.

Another question, "What does a namespace URI resolve to?" (which many felt did not need an answer), resulted in the creation of a new markup based on modularized XHTML. This markup, Resource Directory Description Language (RDDL), combines XHTML Basic, XLink, and one new RDDL element that describes a particular resource.

When Names Collide

In many cases, it is necessary to combine markup from more than one source into a single XML document. For example, in the timber industry, if you are sending information about log payments that combined timber information with payment information, a “log” could be ambiguous. When referring to timber, a log is a tree that has been cut; with payments, a log might be a list of payments. A namespace provides a way to prevent these types of name collisions.

The purpose of a namespace is to provide a way to distinguish the elements and attributes used in one markup from those used in another. To do this, a namespace associates a URI with the elements and attributes defined for a particular markup. The resulting two-part naming system ensures that each element and attribute has a unique name. The first part of the name is the namespace name, the second part is the local name, and together they are the universal name.

A namespace URI is simply a unique identifier. Although these identifiers often look just like regular file URLs, they do not have to point to anything. URIs provide a well-known system for creating unique identifiers.

When you declare a namespace, you can provide a short name used locally to refer to the namespace portion of the two-part name. You refer to elements using the short name, followed by the element name, separated by a colon (:). You can also declare a namespace as the default namespace for an XML document; in that case, the URI part of the two-part name is automatically provided for elements that do not specify a namespace.

Declaring a Namespace

A namespace declaration that surrounds some markup effects all elements enclosed in the namespace declaration. Namespace declarations take two forms. The first form associates a namespace with a prefix, the second form does not have a prefix. If the declaration doesn’t have a prefix, the namespace becomes the default for the part of the document enclosed in the namespace declaration. If the declaration has a prefix, any element enclosed in the declaration that specifies the prefix is associated with the namespace.

```
<log xmlns="http://www.plumcreek.com">
   <species>WESTERN LARCH</species>
   <grade>PEELER</grade>
   <large-end-diameter>15</large-end-diameter>
   <small-end-diameter>12</small-end-diameter>
   <length>32</length>
</log>
```

Figure 6.1: XML log element referring to timber.

The code in Figure 6.1 declares a default namespace for a timber-related *log* element. In this example, a namespace is set up using the URI *www.plumcreek.com*. Remember that this URI does not need to point to anything in particular and simply provides a unique name. Because no prefix was set for this namespace, all of the enclosed elements with no prefix are associated with the namespace declaration. In this case, the *log*, *species*, *grade*, *large-end-diameter*, *small-end-diameter*, and *length* elements are implicitly associated with this namespace.

```
<tml:log xmlns:tml="http://www.plumcreek.com">
   <species>WESTERN LARCH</species>
   <grade>PEELER</grade>
   <large-end-diameter>15</large-end-diameter>
   <small-end-diameter>12</small-end-diameter>
   <length>32</length>
</tml:log>
```

Figure 6.2: Log element with namespace prefix.

The next example, shown in Figure 6.2, uses a prefixed namespace declaration for the same markup: In this example, the prefix *tml* is associated with the namespace declaration. Elements that specify the *tml* prefix are associated with the *tml* namespace. In this case, only the *log* element is associated with the namespace, because it was the only one to specify the *tml* prefix.

The preceding examples have been relatively simple. Often, namespace declarations are part of an XML document's root element and declare several namespaces. Figure 6.3 shows an example that declares two namespaces: one with an *fo* prefix for formatting objects and one for scalable vector graphics (SVG) with an *svg* prefix. Each namespace in this example has a prefix, making it necessary to specify the namespace on all elements. One of these namespaces could have been set as the default so that a prefix would not be required on all elements.

```
<?xml version="1.0" encoding="UTF-8"?>
<?cocoon-format type="text/xslfo"?>

<fo:root xmlns:fo="http://www.w3.org/1999/XSL/Format"
        xmlns:svg="http://www.w3.org/2000/svg">
   <fo:layout-master-set>
      <fo:simple-page-master master-name="one">
         <fo:region-body margin-top=".1in" margin-bottom=".25in"
            margin-left=".25in" margin-right=".25in"/>
      </fo:simple-page-master>
   </fo:layout-master-set>
   <fo:page-sequence master-name="one">
      <fo:flow flow-name="xsl-region-body">
         <fo:block font-size="24pt"
         line-height="28pt" space-before.optimum="12pt"
         space-after.optimum="12pt">Simple SVG Image
      </fo:block>
      <fo:block>
         <fo:instream-foreign-object>
            <svg:svg width="2.5in" height="1.25in">
               <svg:rect x=".5in" y=".5" width="2in"
                  height="1in"/>
               <svg:text x="1in" y=".5in">Text in a Box</svg:text>
            </svg:svg>
         </fo:instream-foreign-object></fo:block>
      <fo:block>The above is an example of an SVG graphic</fo:block>
   </fo:flow>
  </fo:page-sequence>
</fo:root>
```

Figure 6.3: Mixing formatting object and scalable vector graphics.

In case you are curious, Figure 6.4 shows what the output of the document in Figure 6.3 looks like in a browser. I ran this example on my iSeries system using a Java-based, open-source XML publishing engine called Cocoon. Cocoon is a servlet that takes a document such as the one shown and applies transforms and other processes necessary to render the final output. In this case, Cocoon just converted the document to a PDF file by calling an XML-to-PDF utility called FOP. I had to convert the document to a PDF file so that Internet Explorer could display the graphic elements. In the future, browsers should be able to display SVG graphics directly.

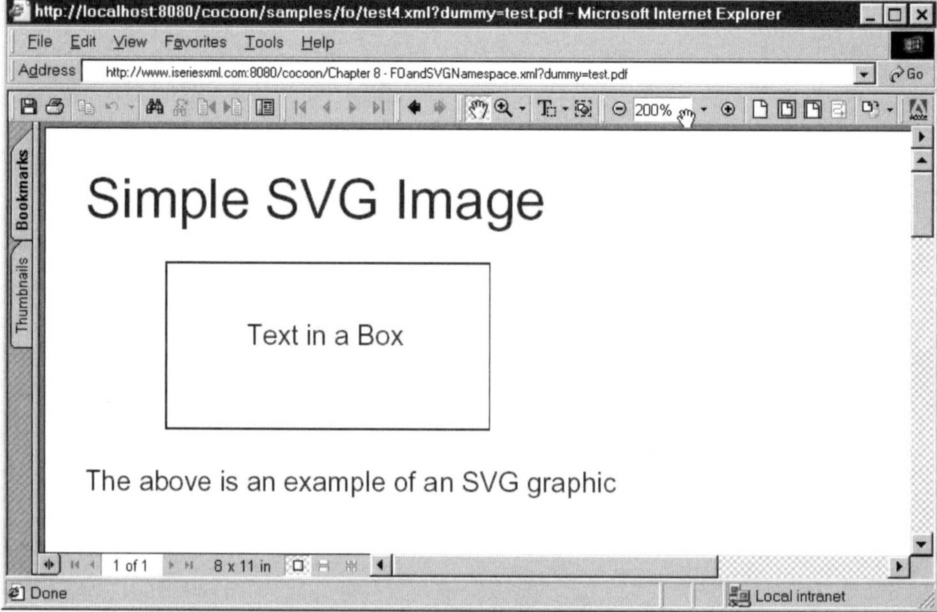

Figure 6.4: The resulting output from the XML document shown in Figure 6.3.

You normally generate this type of document using an XSLT transform that combines a base XML document with formatting object tags. The result of that transformation would be the XML document you see in Figure 6.3. Chapter 8 will describe XSL and XSLT in more detail.

One browser that does support this type of graphic directly is the W3C's Amaya browser. Amaya is available on the W3C Web site at *www.w3.org/Amaya*. The Amaya browser is what the W3C uses to test new XHTML features, so its support of XHTML is very good. Amaya also has a built-in XHTML editor that understands XML's linking languages, MathML, and SVG.

Undoing a Namespace Declaration

It is impossible to undo a namespace declaration made with a prefix. Once you declare a namespace, the name is in effect until the element closes. You can override a namespace declaration to a new URI by embedding a new namespace declaration that uses the same prefix.

You can undo a default namespace declaration. To undo a default namespace declaration, you make a new default namespace declaration and specify a blank URI. The example in Figure 6.5 removes the default namespace for the species element. In this example, the *log*, *grade*, *large-end-diameter*, *small-end-diameter*, and *length* attributes are part of the default namespace, and *grade* is not.

```
<log xmlns="http://www.plumcreek.com">
   <species xmlns="">WESTERN LARCH</species>
   <grade>PEELER</grade>
   <large-end-diameter>15</large-end-diameter>
   <small-end-diameter>12</small-end-diameter>
   <length>32</length>
</log>
```

Figure 6.5: Undoing a default namespace declaration.

Declaring a Namespace in a DTD

A DTD attribute list declaration can associate a namespace with elements and attributes when name collisions are not a concern. The attribute declaration sets the fixed value for the *xmlns* attribute to the appropriate namespace. The following example shows how to associate the SVG namespace with the *svg* element: *<!ATTLIST svg xmlns CDATA #FIXED "http://www.w3.org/2000/svg">*. This attribute declaration allows you to omit the namespace declaration from *svg* elements; it is also one of the few cases in which a fixed attribute list declaration is used. You include this attribute declaration in either an internal or an external DTD.

Declaring a Namespace in a Schema

With a schema, as with a DTD, elements and attributes can be associated with a namespace to avoid collisions. The additional namespaces are identified inside the schema element and will reference the namespace to be used. The example in Figure 6.6 shows how a schema references an additional namespace. To reference the namespace within the schema, code like that in Figure 6.7 would be used. The elements declared in the figure reference the *address* element defined inside the *http://www.example.com/add* namespace.

```
<schema  xmlns="http://www.w3.org/2001/XMLSchema"
         xmlns:add="http://www.example.com/add"
         targetNamespace="http://www.example.com/add">
```

Figure 6.6: Declaring namespaces in a schema.

```
<element name="billingAddress" type="add:Address"/>
<element name="shipToAddress" type="add:Address"/>
```

Figure 6.7: Referencing a namespace in a schema.

Referring to Elements and Attributes Using a Namespace

To associate an element or attribute with a particular namespace, you specify the namespace prefix, or no prefix for the default namespace, on each element. The document in Figure 6.8 contains two namespaces. The first is the XHTML transitional namespace, which is set up as the default namespace. The second is a timber-related namespace used for log markup.

```
<?xml version="1.0" encoding="UTF-8"?>
<!DOCTYPE html PUBLIC
   "-//W3C//DTD XHTML 1.0 Transitional//EN"
   "http://www.w3.org/TR/xhtml1/DTD/xhtml1-transitional.dtd">

<html xmlns="http://www.w3.org/1999/xhtml"
      xmlns:tml="http://www.plumcreek.com">
   <head>
      <title>Deliveries</title>
   </head>
   <body>
      <table border="1">
         <tr>
            <th>Scale Ticket</th>
            <th>Weight</th>
            <th>Delivered Date</th>
         </tr>
         <tr>
            <td><tml:scale-ticket>12345</tml:scale-ticket></td>
            <td><tml:weight>42168 LBS</tml:weight></td>
            <td><tml:delivery-date>10/29/2001</tml:delivery-date></td>
         </tr>
```

Figure 6.8: An XHTML document that incorporates timber-related elements (part 1 of 2).

```
        </table>
        <table border="1">
        <tr>
           <th>Species</th>
           <th>Grade</th>
           <th>Large End Diameter</th>
           <th>Small End Diameter</th>
           <th>Length</th>
        </tr>
        <tr>
           <td><tml:species>WESTERN LARCH</tml:species></td>
           <td><tml:grade>PEELER</tml:grade></td>
           <td><tml:large-end-diameter>15</tml:large-end-diameter></td>
           <td><tml:small-end-diameter>12</tml:small-end-diameter></td>
           <td><tml:length>32</tml:length></td>
        </tr>
        <tr>
           <td><tml:species>WESTERN LARCH</tml:species></td>
           <td><tml:grade>PEELER</tml:grade></td>
           <td><tml:large-end-diameter>13</tml:large-end-diameter></td>
           <td><tml:small-end-diameter>9</tml:small-end-diameter></td>
           <td><tml:length>32</tml:length></td>
        </tr>
      </table>
   </body>
</html>
```

Figure 6.8: An XHTML document that incorporates timber-related elements (part 2 of 2).

One place where namespaces are commonly used is in XHTML documents. The XHTML document in Figure 6.8 shows how to combine XHTML elements with markup from another namespace. The root element contains the namespace declarations, which are in scope for the entire document. In this document, the timber-related markup uses a *tml* prefix, which is associated with the *http://www.plumcreek.com* URI. All elements that do not specify a prefix are part of the XHTML transitional namespace, associated with the *http://www.w3.org/1999/xhtml* URI.

When you use XHTML elements within an XML document, the W3C recommends that you set the XHTML namespace as the default and not specify an XHTML prefix, because many older implementation of XHTML are not namespace aware. Other elements, not part of the XHTML namespace, should specify a namespace.

The Scope of a Namespace

A namespace declaration is in scope for the duration of the declaring element. This means that a namespace declaration is in effect from the opening of the declaring element through the closing of the declaring element. All child elements contained within the declaration are part of the namespace until another namespace declaration.

Often, it is clearest to declare all namespaces used in an XML document on the root element and then prefix all elements with the appropriate namespace. A namespace declared on the root element is in scope through the entire document. This is particularly useful when an XML document has elements from several namespaces interspersed throughout the document.

Attributes and Namespaces

A namespace does not have to apply to an element; it can apply to attributes as well. One example of an attribute that uses a namespace is XLink. XLink uses namespaces, so XLink attributes may appear on elements from other namespaces. The example in Figure 6.9 shows a logo element containing two attributes from the XLink namespace.

```
<iseriesxml:logo xmlns:iseriesxml="http://www.iseriesxml.com"
                 xmlns:xlink = "http://www.w3.org/1999/xlink"
   xlink:type="simple"
   xlink:href="iseriesxml.jpeg"/>
```

Figure 6.9: Attributes associated with a namespace.

Attributes that do not specify a namespace are not actually in a namespace, not even the default namespace. This doesn't really matter to an XML processor, except when an attribute needs to be associated with a specific namespace as in the previous example.

Attributes with no prefix are the norm; the semantics of their associated element defines their use. In contrast, a prefixed attribute derives its semantics from all element types. An XLink link is associated with any element and therefore needs the XLink namespace to derive its meaning.

Defining URIs and URLs

With HTML, a Uniform Resource Locator (URL) provides a mechanism that enables you to type in a string of characters and receive a resource in return. That resource might be an HTML document, a zip file, or an audio clip. Web pages contain references to URLs that point to other resources, making them an essential part of most Web sites. Every URL is unique and assigned to a domain that is responsible for the URL.

The original purpose of a URL was to provide a unique way of identifying a resource on the Internet. Over time, URLs have assumed more responsibility. A standard also exists for Relative Uniform Resource Locators, which use the current location of a resource as part of their location. In 1998, Tim Berners-Lee led an effort to combine these two into a more encompassing standard for identifying resources. The result was the *Uniform Resource Identifier* (URI).

Request for Comments 2396 (RFC 2396) defines a URI as "a compact string of characters for identifying an abstract or physical resource." A URI may be further classified as a locator, a name, or both. A URL becomes a subset of URIs that identifies resources via a representation of their primary access mechanism, rather than identifying the resource by name or by some other attribute of that resource. The term *Uniform Resource Name* (URN) refers to the subset of URIs that are required to remain globally unique and persistent even when the resource ceases to exist or becomes unavailable.

Because URIs borrow so much from existing standards, they are familiar. An absolute URI commonly begins with a protocol such as *http:*, *ftp:*, *mailto:*, *file:*, or *urn:*. When retrieving something, two slashes follow. After this, an optional port, path, and other information that uniquely identifies a resource follows a host computer name.

As you may recall, an XML document is a set of nodes. Every node is associated with a URI, which is its base URI. The base URI of the document node is the URI of the document entity. A relative URI uses the base URI of the current resource as a prefix. Some URI-aware applications provide a way to set the URI base. An absolute URI results from the combination of the relative portion of a URI with its base portion.

Answering the Namespace URI Riddle

During the development of the original namespace specification, several points were fiercely debated. Early in 2001, a new debate resumed over what a namespace URI points to. The "Namespaces in XML" document specifically leaves open the question of what a namespace points to, and it specifically states that it is not a goal for a namespace to point to any schema. One reason the W3C wanted to avoid putting anything at the end of a namespace URI is that there are too many good choices. In some cases, a DTD might make sense; in others a schema or stylesheet.

In most cases, a URI is also a URL, and URLs locate resources. A namespace URI is defined as an identifier and not a locator, but that has been a large source of confusion, because it is difficult to distinguish between a URI and URL. Many people wonder whether parsers and applications use a URI to retrieve information (they don't). This open-ended solution also had some developers worried. The concern was that someone would impose a de facto standard that would remove flexibility from namespace choices.

After seeing this question "What does a namespace URI point to?" asked time and again on various mail lists, the members of the XML-DEV mailing list decided to provide an answer. That answer they came up with is *Resource Directory Description Language* (RDDL), pronounced "riddle" in its abbreviated form.

RDDL provides a way to describe a namespace. The purpose of RDDL is to allow people and software robots to locate resources associated with a particular namespace. Instead of putting one thing at a namespace URI, RDDL puts a document there that lists any number of documents that might be available. Those documents include DTDs, schemas, stylesheets, and specifications.

As of mid-2001, RDDL was still just an unsupported standard, but work was continuing. The RDDL markup borrows heavily from XHTML Basic and XLink and adds one new RDDL element to describe a particular resource.

```
<?xml version="1.0" encoding="UTF-8"?>
<!DOCTYPE html PUBLIC
          "-//XML-DEV//DTD XHTML RDDL 1.0//EN"
          "http://www.rddl.org/rddl-xhtml.dtd">
<html xmlns="http://www.w3.org/1999/xhtml"
      xmlns:xlink="http://www.w3.org/1999/xlink"
      xmlns:rddl="http://www.rddl.org/"
      xml:lang="en">
>
   <head>
      <title>Simple Recipe Resource Directory Description</title>
   </head>
   <body>
      <h1>Simple Recipe Resource Directory Description</h1>
      <rddl:resource
         xlink:href="http://www.iseriesxml.com/xml/dtd/simplerecipe.dtd">
         xlink:title="Simple Recipe Markup">
      />
   </body>
</html>
```

Figure 6.10: A simple RDDL document found at a namespace URI/URL target.

Figure 6.10 shows a simple RDDL document. This RDDL document is understandable by humans (as a Web page) and by software that might use this information to understand more about documents associated with the namespace. If you are interested in finding out more about RDDL, go to the RDDL home page at *www.rddl.org*. This page contains the official standard as well as information about this emerging standard.

Chapter Highlights

- The enclosing element determines the scope of a namespace declaration.
- A namespace may apply to an element's attributes.
- A namespace URI does not point to anything in particular.
- A URL is a type of URI.
- Without a prefix, a namespace becomes the default.
- RDDL attempts to provide something meaningful at a namespace URI.

In this chapter you learned about namespaces and their importance to XML. A namespace provides a way to associate a set of markup with a URI. The combined namespace name and local name provides a universal name that removes any ambiguity related to the source of an element or attribute. In the next chapter I am going to show you how XML's linking languages provide a powerful linking mechanism allowing you to cross-link XML documents.

7

XML's Linking Languages

In this chapter you will learn:

- ✓ About the functionality provided by XPath, XLink, and XPointer
- ✓ How to create links between XML documents
- ✓ The differences between linking in XML and in HTML
- ✓ How to combine XPath and XPointer to identify a location in a document
- ✓ How to refer to a specific XML document node with XPath
- ✓ What a link group is and how it is used

The concept of linked documents has been around for a long time; Vannevar Bush described linked information in his 1945 *The Atlantic Monthly* article, "As We May Think." HTML's success is due to its linking capability, but linking between documents is an area in which XML provides capability that exceeds that of HTML. XML's linking languages allow you to set up a link to a specific point within another XML document without identifying the target.

This chapter covers three parts of XML linking: XML Path Language (XPath), XML Linking Language (XLink), and XML Pointer Language (XPointer). The first of these, XPath, is a language for addressing parts of an XML document used by both Extensible Stylesheet Language Transformations (XSLT) and XPointer. The W3C made XPath a recommendation in November 1999. XPath allows you to write expressions that refer to specific nodes, or sets of nodes, within an XML document.

XLink became a W3C recommendation in June 2001. The XLink specification explains how to use elements that describe links between resources. XLink uses XML syntax to create structures that describe links that are similar to HTML's hyperlinks, as well as more sophisticated links.

XPath is the language used to identify fragments for any URI reference that locates an XML document or application. Based on XPath, XPointer supports addressing into the internal structures of an XML document and allows applications to traverse the internal parts of an XML document. XPointer uses properties such as element type, attribute values, element content, and relative position to address parts of an XML document.

XPointer became a recommendation in March 2003. It contains three parts: XPointer Framework, XPointer element() scheme and XPointer xmlns() scheme.

Rethinking Linking

In order to work with your XML documents, you need to be able to locate them. Once you locate your document, it is likely that you will need to locate some specific information contained in it. The linking support provided by XPath, XPointer, and XLink allows you to locate documents and specific content in a way that is far more powerful than HTML's *href* and anchor tag.

The Uniform Resource Identifier (URI) and its subset, the Uniform Resource Locator (URL), provide the ability to locate a document anywhere on the Internet. The XPath and XPointer languages allow you to identify a specific point within an XML document.

One reason for the success of the Internet is the hyperlink. A hyperlink describes a simple relationship between two points and is embedded at the referring point. XLink goes beyond the hyperlink, allowing bidirectional links and multiple ending points. An XLink can also be stored independently from the documents it links.

Providing a Path with XPath

The XPath language provides a way to identify a specific part of an XML document. Using XPath expressions and XPath functions you can identify parts of an XML document, including elements, attributes, text, comments, processing instructions, and namespaces. You refer to these parts by their position in the XML document hierarchy, relative position, type, or content. The XPath expression language syntax comes in two forms: abbreviated and full. The full syntax is more descriptive and easier to follow, whereas the abbreviated syntax is cryptic and reminiscent of *grep*, which only UNIX programmers seem to appreciate.

Both XSLT and XPointer use XPath expressions. XSLT, which generally combines XML markup from two sources into an output XML document, uses XPath expressions to select parts of an XML document for processing and is the most popular application using XPath.

XPath expressions allow you to return Boolean values, strings, or numbers that allow you to do simple manipulation of data. That manipulation can sum values, number pages, cross-reference elements, combine text, and other feats. An XPath expression can also return null when the result of the expression is nothing.

The Document View

In order to understand how XPath works, you have to understand how an XML document is structured. An XML document is a treelike structure made up of nodes. There are seven types of nodes. In the last chapter, you read that each node has an associated Uniform Resource Identifier (URI), known as its base URI. The following list describes each type of node:

- *Document node:* This node represents the document entity and contains the whole document, including the document declaration, prolog (DTDs), and root element. XPath does not recognize the document node.
- *Root node:* The root node contains the content of an XML document and is at the top of the hierarchy in the XPath data model. The root node is not the same as the root element, which is an element node contained in the root node. The root node includes the processing instructions and comments that come before and after the root element.
- *Element nodes:* These nodes represent the elements, including the root element, of a document. Every element node has a parent node that is another element node, except the root element node, whose parent is the root node.
- *Text nodes:* A text node contains the textual content of an element. Any general entities are resolved to their actual values; therefore *<* is returned as the less than (<) character.
- *Attribute nodes:* The attributes of an element are attribute nodes. An attribute node is not a child of an element node. A node is not created for unspecified attributes with an #IMPLIED default value supplied in a DTD or for namespace attributes.
- *Namespace nodes:* A namespace node keeps track of the set of namespace prefix/URI pairs in effect at any given point. Like attribute nodes, a namespace node is associated with an element node.
- *Processing instruction nodes:* These nodes contain the processing instructions' value as strings.
- *Comment nodes:* The comment nodes represent the document's comments as a strings.

The XPath data model uses these nodes to construct a tree representing an XML document. Figure 7.1 shows a typical XML document used to demonstrate the tree structure of an XML document. Several XPath examples later in this chapter also refer to this example.

```
<?xml version= "1.0" encoding="ISO-8859-1" standalone= "no"?>
<?xml-stylesheet href="deliveries.xsl"
                 type= "text/xsl"?>
<!DOCTYPE deliveries SYSTEM "Deliveries.dtd">

<!-- Sample log delivery XML document -->
<deliveries>
   <load scale-type="DTL">
      <vendor>
         <name>Dave's Trucking</name>
         <address>
            <street>1310 Cameron Lane</street>
            <city>Whitefish</city>
            <state>MT</state>
            <zip>59937</zip>
         </address>
         <url xlink:href="http://www.iseriesxml.com/"/>
      </vendor>
      <scale-ticket>12345</scale-ticket>
      <weight>42168</weight>
      <weight-uom>LBS</weight-uom>
      <scale-uom>US</scale-uom>
      <delivered-date>
         <month>10</month>
         <day>29</day>
         <year>2001</year>
      </delivered-date>
      <log>
         <species>WESTERN LARCH</species>
         <grade>PEELER</grade>
         <large-end-diameter>15</large-end-diameter>
         <small-end-diameter>12</small-end-diameter>
         <length>32</length>
      </log>
      <log>
         <species>WESTERN LARCH</species>
         <grade>PEELER</grade>
         <large-end-diameter>13</large-end-diameter>
         <small-end-diameter>9</small-end-diameter>
         <length>32</length>
      </log>
   </load>
</deliveries>
```

Figure 7.1: XML document for illustrating the tree structure. Several examples refer to this document.

The diagram in Figure 7.2 shows the tree structure of the XML document from Figure 7.1. An elliptical box represents each node from the document. Nodes represented with a repeating backdrop are nodes that may repeat based on the source document's DTD. To keep this document short, I did not include the DTD in this diagram.

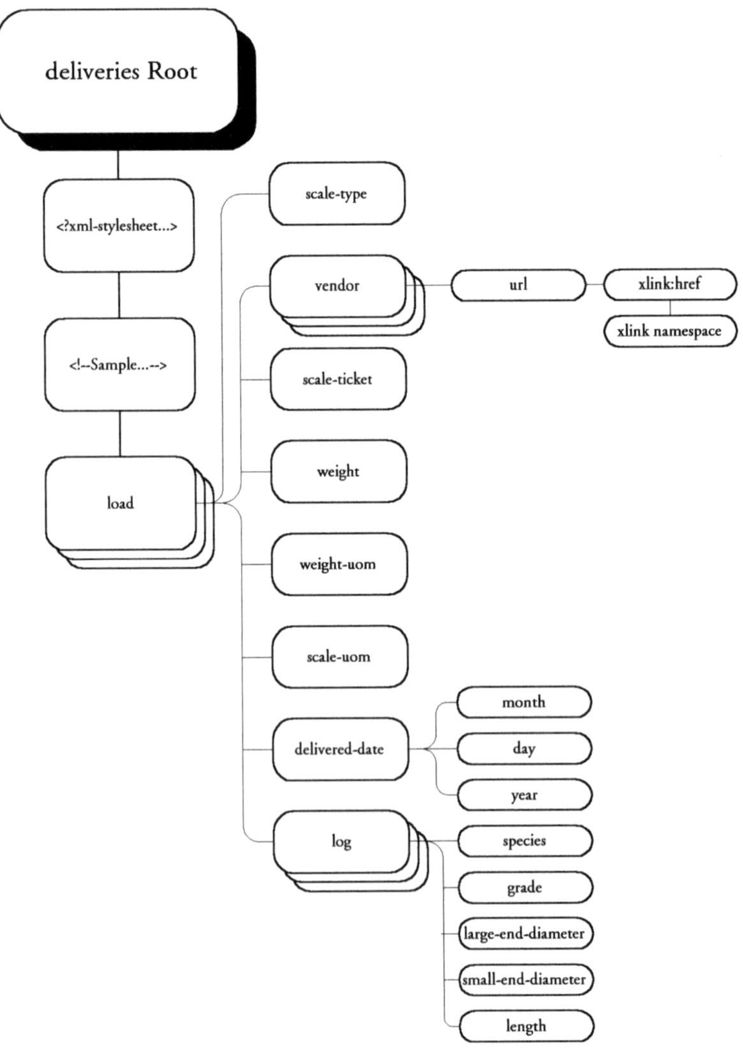

Figure 7.2: The deliveries XML document tree.

It is important to keep in mind a few things about the structure of the XPath data model. First, the root is not the same as the document's root, and it includes processing instructions and comments that occur before the XML document's root element. In this case, the stylesheet reference and comment that precede the root element are part of the root node.

Another thing to remember about the XPath data model is that it does not include the XML document declaration or DTD reference. XPath does use information from the DTD when it parses the document. In this case, the XSLT processor brings in several default attributes from the Deliveries.dtd file.

One more point about the XPath data model is that namespace attributes are not accessible as attribute nodes. They become namespace nodes. One exception to this rule is that older parsers that do not recognize namespaces will treat them as attribute nodes.

Expressions in XPath

Expressions in the XPath language work against the XPath data model, enabling applications to process and manipulate the contents of an XML document. The XPath specifications define several types of expressions. You combine expressions of different types to perform various tasks. Those tasks fall into several categories and use mathematical, string, path, and node manipulation capabilities.

Describing a Location Path

What you describe with XPath is the path between two points within an XML document. The description of this path is an XPath expression. Applications such as XSLT and XPointer use XPath expression to locate and work with the parts of an XML document. The path that XPath describes has a starting point, a route, and a destination.

The starting point of the path is the context node. Most frequently, this is the root node of the XML document, but it can be any node. The route the path takes consists of a direction and steps. XPath separates each step with a forward slash (/) and describes direction using terms such as *child* (forward) and *parent* (back). The names *child* and *parent* are not arbitrary; XPath describes 13 directional terms, called axes. The destination is a node or set of nodes.

A location path expression is a special type of XPath expression that is the most important construct of the XPath language. You use a location path expression to route between the context node and a set of nodes. Every location path makes at least one step, and the resulting node set may be empty, contain one node, or contain multiple nodes.

There are two basic types of location paths: absolute and relative. A relative location path starts at the current context node in an XML document and starts with an axis. An absolute location path starts with the forward slash character (/) and describes a path that starts at an XML document's root element. A single forward slash without anything following selects the document's root node and is the simplest possible location path.

```
axis::nodetest/axis::nodetest/axis::nodetest
              ^              ^
     Step Delimiter Step Delimiter
```

Figure 7.3: Format of a location path.

Figure 7.3 shows the format of a location path. When you describe a location path with XPath, you provide a sequence of steps separated by forward slashes (/). Often a location path consists of a single step. Each step selects set of nodes relative to the current context node. Each selected node becomes a context node for further steps. An axis defines a set of selectable nodes starting from the context node. Some commonly used axis values are *child*, *parent*, and *attribute*. The node test further qualifies the type or name of selectable nodes. Testing for node() selects all nodes; text() selects only text nodes.

XPath Context

An XPath context consists of a node, which is the context node; two integer values, representing the context position and size; a set of variable bindings; a function library; and the namespace declaration in scope for the XPath expression.

The context node is the relative starting point and represents a node in the XPath data model. As XPath expressions are processed, the context node can and usually does change dynamically. There are several ways to refer to the context node. The first is to use the abbreviated form, which uses a period (.) to refer to the current context. You can also refer to the context node using the full-form notation of *self::node()*. The following example shows the abbreviated form: *species[.='WESTERN LARCH']* This example selects a *species* element with the string value of *WESTERN LARCH*. The period says to look at the current context and could have been replaced with the unabbreviated *self::node()*.

The context position is an integer representing the position of a node within the nodes returned by an XPath expression; the context size is the total number of nodes returned. You use the *position()* XPath function to retrieve the context position, and the *last()* function returns the context size. The expression *position()!=last()* will test true for all but the last in a set of nodes. You would use such an expression when the last node is to be processed differently from other nodes. This sort of test is common for converting element values to a string that treats the last element differently.

The most common use for XPath at this time is to support XSLT transformations. XSLT and XPath use different terminology to describe the current position within an XML document. The following paragraphs describe these differences; Chapter 8 describes the use of XPath expressions in XSLT stylesheets more completely.

XPath uses the terms *context node*, *context position*, and *context size*, whereas XSLT uses *current node* and *current node list*. During an XSLT transform, a node becomes current when processed using an *<xsl:apply-templates>* or *<xsl:for-each>* instruction. Another way in which XSLT refers to the current node is to use the *current*() function. When an XPath expression is processed in an XSLT stylesheet, the context node is the same as the current node except in predicates.

The main thing to remember about the other parts of the context is that they do not change during the evaluation of expressions. That means that the variable bindings, function library, and namespace declarations used to evaluate a subexpression are always the same as those used to evaluate the containing expression. In contrast, as stated, the context node, context position, and context size can change. Several kinds of expressions change the context node, and a predicate may change the context position or context size.

Setting a Direction with Axes

There are two directions of travel with XPath: forward and backward (although you can also stand still). An axis describes that direction. The following list describes the available axes; remember that the context node is the starting point:

- *ancestor:* Backward; the nodes before the context node up to and including the root node, also described as the parent node and parent's parent nodes of the context node
- *ancestor-or-self:* Backward; the context node and all ancestor nodes
- *attribute*: The attribute nodes of the context node (if the context node is not an element, this axis is empty)
- *child:* Forward; the direct child nodes of the context node
- *descendant:* Forward; the nodes after the context node (because only child nodes are selected, this will never include namespace or attribute nodes); also described as the child nodes and child's child nodes of the context node
- *descendant-or-self:* Forward; the context node and all descendant nodes
- *following:* Forward; all nodes in the same document as the context node that are after the context node hierarchically in document order, excluding descendant, attribute, and namespace nodes
- *following-sibling:* Forward; all following nodes at the level of the context node
- *namespace:* The namespace nodes of the context node (empty if the context node is not an element node)
- *parent:* Backward; the parent node of the context node (empty for the root node)

- *preceding:* Backward; all nodes in the same document as the context node before the context node hierarchically in document order, excluding ancestor, attribute, and namespace nodes
- *preceding-sibling:* Backward; all preceding nodes at the level of the context node
- *self:* The context node

There are two ways to refer to axes. The first is to use the full axis name as listed. The second is to use an abbreviated form. The abbreviated form allows only access to *child*, *attribute*, *descendant-or-self*, *self*, and *parent*.

Stepping through Nodes

Location path expressions provide a way to access the elements of an XML document. A *location path expression* consists of one or more *location steps*. Each step has three parts:

- An axis, which specifies the relationship between the desired target nodes and the context node
- A node test, which specifies the node type and name of the nodes to be selected by the location step
- One or more optional predicates that specify selection criteria for the location step

An abbreviated syntax can be used to specify location path steps. Most of the time, this abbreviated syntax is adequate. In some cases, however, you will need to access nodes that the abbreviated syntax does not support; in those cases you must use the unabbreviated syntax.

The unabbreviated form of location step, shown in Figure 7.3, uses a double colon (::) to separate the axis from the node test. The unabbreviated format of location step notation combines the axis with the node test. Table 7.1 shows the notation used in abbreviated location path steps.

Table 7.1: Abbreviated Syntax Used to Specify Location Path Steps

Abbreviated Location Path Steps	Unabbreviated Equivalent
	child:: (no symbol indicates a child)
@	attribute::
//	descendant-or-self::node()
.	self::node()
..	parent::node()

These abbreviations are interchangeable with the full location step names. For example, the two location path steps *attribute::scale-type* and *@scale-type* are equivalent, and select the *scale-type* attribute of the current context.

Here are some examples of location path expressions:

1. / selects the root node (not the document element node).
2. */deliveries* selects the deliveries root element.
3. */deliveries/load/log* selects *log* elements that are children of *load* that is a child of *deliveries*.
4. */deliveries/load/** selects all child elements of *load* that is a child of *deliveries*.
5. */deliveries/load[@ scale-type]* selects *load* elements with a *scale-type* attribute.
6. */deliveries/load[@ scale-type="DTL"]* selects load elements with *scale-type* equal to DTL.
7. *//vendor* searches the document to select all *vendor* elements.
8. *//[@*]* searches the document and selects all elements that have any attribute.

9. */deliveries/load/vendor* | */deliveries/load/log* selects all *vendor* or *log* elements that are children of *load* elements that are children of *deliveries*.

Processing of location path expressions starts from the context node. In each of these examples, the starting context is the root of the document. In example 2, the first and only step is to the *deliveries* element node. Further steps are specified with additional forward slashes (/).

At each step, the current context changes. The result of each step is a node set representing the selected nodes for the step. In example 3 the first step returns the *deliveries* element as a node set. That node set (except for duplicates), becomes the current context for the next step. That step selects all load element nodes in the new current context. Processing continues like this until evaluation of the location path expression is complete.

Predicates

A predicate is a special type of qualifying expression used to select a subset of nodes in a node set or step. For example, you may want to select an element's nodes that refer to a child element with a particular value. You would use a predicate in this case that checked for the existence of the child element with the value you specify. The predicate discards nodes that do not match the specified criteria.

To write a predicate, you enclose the qualifying criteria in square brackets ([]). For each predicate, the criterion found between the square brackets is applied against the nodes returned at the step. The result of this test is a Boolean value; a false result discards the node being tested. For example, *//load[@scale-type="DTL"]* is a typical XPath expression with a predicate. This predicate selects any *load* element with a *scale-type* attribute of *DTL*, because the Boolean test performed by the predicate returns true.

In addition to equal (=), predicates may test using other relational operators including less than (<), greater than (>), less than or equal (<=), greater than or equal (>=), and not equal (!=). One thing to be aware of when using a relational operator containing the less than (<)symbol in an XML document is that the symbol will need to be escaped and written as *<*.

There are several types of predicates. The previous example compares the string value of an attribute to a literal value. You can also test for the existence of a node using a location path expression in a predicate. For example, *//load[scale-ticket]* shows a location path expression in a predicate. This predicate returns true for any *load* element that contains a *scale-ticket* element, so this step selects all *load* elements that contain a *scale-ticket* element. In this case each *load* element that meets this selection becomes the current node and is available for processing.

Another way to use a predicate is to select a particular element by its ordinal position. The current context is the set of nodes selected by the previous step. You can select a node by its relative context position. In other words, you can select the *n*th occurrence of a child element. For example, *//load/log[1]* returns the first log element for each load. The predicate in this example uses the shorthand notation, which assumes that the context position is what is specified, but it could have also been written as *[position()=1]*. To select the last log, you would specify the function *last()* for the predicate. To select all log elements except for the first one, you would use *[not(position()=1)]*.

Predicates can be simple like the example in the preceding paragraph, or they can be quite complex. For example, in the logging industry, mills do not generally pay for mixed-species log loads by weight. Selecting all loads containing more than one species in XPath, you might use a location path expression that uses nested predicates, as follows:

```
//load[log/species[.!=string(ancestor::load/log/species[1])]].
```

This expression is much more complex than the previous examples and uses several aspects of the XPath language. If the expression contained in the outermost square brackets, ([) and (]), returns a Boolean true, the *load* is selected. If a location path is used as a predicate and returns a node, it is true. In this case, the predicate returns the species nodes with string values that are not equal to the string value of the first species on the load. The *ancestor* axis backs up from the current context to the *load* element and then goes forward to select the first species element on the load.

Abbreviated and Unabbreviated Location Paths

As discussed, there are two forms of XPath location path expressions: abbreviated and unabbreviated. The abbreviated form is more cryptic and removes some of the redundancy from location path expressions. The unabbreviated form is clearer and in some cases more powerful.

Abbreviated location path expressions combine the axis and node test, eliminating the double colon (::).

The abbreviated form of location path expression is much more common. There are several reasons for this. First, the abbreviated form requires less typing, but the more likely reason that the abbreviated form is more popular is that most of the early examples of location path expressions used the abbreviated form. Another reason that the abbreviated form is more common is that XSLT match patterns can use only abbreviated location paths.

With abbreviated location paths, you use special symbols for each location step. For example, the following location paths are equivalent: *descendant-or-self::species[self::node()='WESTERN LARCH']* and *//species[.= 'WESTERN LARCH']*. These two location path expressions are equivalent. The first uses the unabbreviated form to specify the *descendant-or-self* axis to select all *species* elements and uses a *self* node test in a predicate that selects nodes with the specified value. Applying either of these expressions against the XML document shown in Figure 7.1 selects the two species element nodes with a value of *WESTERN LARCH*.

Unabbreviated location path expressions are more powerful than abbreviated location path expressions because they give access to eight additional axes: *ancestor*, *ancestor-or-self*, *descendant*, *following*, *following-sibling*, *namespace*, *preceding*, and *preceding-sibling*. The following example shows a location path expression that must use the unabbreviated syntax because of the *ancestor-or-self* axis: *descendant-or-self::species[self::node()='WESTERN LARCH']/ancestor-or-self::node()*. This location path expression selects all *species* element nodes with a value of *WESTERN LARCH*. The *ancestor-or-self* step selects the entire hierarchy that precedes the selected species nodes. Applying this location path expression to the XML document in Figure 7.1 selects seven nodes. The seven selected nodes are the document node, the deliveries, load, and two log element nodes, as well as two species element nodes.

Other Expressions

In addition to location paths, which work with node sets, another group of expressions provides the ability to manipulate Boolean values, numbers, and strings. These other expressions cannot be compared directly against a node set or node, but their value can be compared against the value of a particular node.

Boolean Expressions

A Boolean expression tests a condition and returns the value *true* or *false*. The most common way to write a Boolean expression is to separate two values with a relational operator. The relational operators that XPath supports include equal (=), less than (<), greater than (>), less than or equal (<=), greater than or equal (>=), and not equal (!=). You combine tests with the *and* and *or* operators.

When the less than (<,<=) operators are used, they must be quoted, so < becomes *<* and <= becomes *<=*. The XPath expression in Figure 7.4 tests to see whether the value for *large-end-diameter* is less than 12.

```
<xsl:if test="large-end-diameter &lt; 12">
   <!-- do something -->
</xsl:if>
```

Figure 7.4: XPath code to test a condition.

The order of precedence for Boolean operators, lowest first, is as follows:

1. or
2. and
3. =, !=
4. <=, <, >=, >

The operators are left associative, meaning that equivalent operators are evaluated from left to right. So 3 > 2 > 1 is equivalent to (3 > 2) > 1, and both will evaluate to false. This is nonintuitive, because the test could be interpreted as a test to see whether 2 is between 3 and 1. Instead, it compares the Boolean result of testing 3 > 2 with 1.

The most common place for a Boolean tests is in a predicate attached to a location path expression. Often the presence or absence of an element or attribute is tested. For example, *vendor/url[@xlink:href]*, shows a test for an *href* attribute on a *url* element that is a child of *vendor*. This example appears in the source in Figure 7.1.

There are all kinds of uses for Boolean tests. If the value contained in an element is not numeric, you might replace the value with text that indicates the error condition. For example, *string(number(@value))='NaN'* is a Boolean test that checks for a numeric value in a weight element: This Boolean test compares the string value of a node to the special value *NaN*, short for Not a Number. This expression returns true for any node containing a string that does not contain a valid number. The next section on numeric expressions describes the range of numeric values.

Sometimes it is necessary to reverse the result of a Boolean expression. One way to do this is to use the not() function. In the example in the preceding paragraph, you could select only valid numeric nodes with the following test: *not(string(number(avalue))='NaN')*. This test will return true when a string contains a valid numeric value. In this case, adding the *not* is functionally equivalent to changing the = to !=, so that the expression looks like *string(number(avalue))!='NaN'*. You may be wondering why the *not()* function is needed at all. In the earlier example of *vendor/url[@xlink:href]*, which does not contain a relational operator, *not* is the only way to reverse the test.

One more point about Boolean tests is that unlike other languages, XPath provides no reserved word to test conditions like RPG's *ON and *OFF or Java's true and false. For the rare cases where a true or false literal value provides a more expedient solution, you can use the *true()* or *false()* function.

Numeric Expressions

XPath supports several types of numeric expressions that let you add, subtract, multiply, and divide numbers. All numbers in XPath are stored in 64-bit (double-precision) floating-point format and conform to the Standard for Binary Floating-Point Arithmetic (IEEE 754), which is the same format that Java uses for *double* primitives. The IEEE standard defines special values to represent positive and negative infinity as well as a special value for not a number (*NaN*).

Table 7.2 lists the five arithmetic operators. The XPath standard does not specify a precedence order for these operators or rounding rules, although most implementations follow the Java standard.

Table 7.2: The Arithmetic Operators Supported in XPath Expressions

+	Addition
-	Subtraction
*	Multiplication
div	Division
mod	Modulus

In addition to the operators in Table 7.2, XPath provides several functions that you can use with numeric values. The following list describes those functions:

- *boolean()* returns true if a number is not zero and not NaN.
- *ceiling()* converts a number to the next higher integer.
- *floor()* converts a number to the next lower integer.
- *number()* converts a string value to a number.
- *round()* rounds a number to an integer value.

- *string()* converts a number to a string value. A value that is not a number returns *NaN*. Positive and negative infinite values return *Infinity* and *-Infinity*, respectively.
- *sum()* totals a set of nodes.

The arithmetic operators and numeric functions will never return an error. When numeric overflow occurs, you get back one of the special values *Infinity* or *-Infinity*. To refer to positive infinity in an expression, use *1 div 0*; to refer to negative infinity, use *-1 div 0*. As mentioned, when a number cannot represent a value, you get the special value *NaN*, which means not a number. To refer to not a number in an expression, use *number("NaN")*.

When you write an expression that subtracts two numbers, you have to include a space before and after the minus (-) sign. If you do not include the space, *a-b* is interpreted as a hyphenated name, *a-b*, rather than as *a* minus *b*.

String Expressions

A string value in XPath expression consists of one or more Unicode characters. The supported characters are the same as for XML. Single or double quotes enclose a string literal, as in *'string value'* or *"string value"*. You can use character and entity references within a string literal to supply characters that are difficult to enter directly.

The string itself may contain any character except for the enclosing character, so *"Dave's XML Emporium"* and *'he said "XML is Great"'* are both valid string literals. In an XSLT style sheet, you would have to write these as *'"Dave's XML Emporium"'* and *"'he said "XMLis Great"'"* because of the extra set of enclosing quotes.

Testing XPath Expressions

Often, applications will use a series of XPath expressions to produce results. A mistake in any expression within the series can be difficult to locate. While developing applications that rely on XPath expressions, it is often helpful to try out various XPath expressions against an XML document to observe the results. You can do this by running XSLT Transforms against a test XML document, or you can use a specialized XPath testing tool.

The XPath testing tool that I use is available free from FiveSight Technologies and is an open-source Java tool that allows you to enter an XPath expression and view the results. Figure 7.5 shows what the interface to FiveSight's XPath Tester looks like.

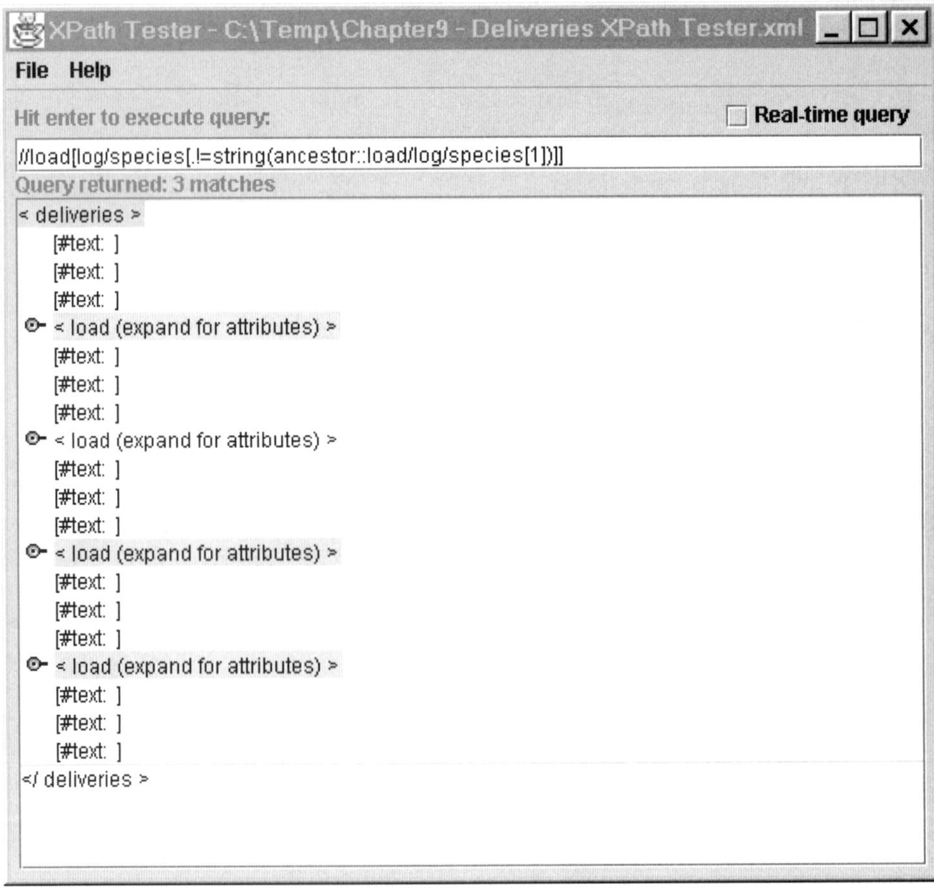

Figure 7.5: FiveSight's Xpath Tester.

Building Links with XLink

One of the biggest reasons for the success of the Web is the ability it provides to hyperlink documents. Links gave users a way to navigate through a Web site and access other resources and applications. Linking also provided a way to access HTTP, HTTPS, Gopher, and FTP resources all from a hyperlink.

Links could be used to connect to various types of files. They can connect HTML pages to other HTML pages, images, PDFs, sound files, movies and many other formats. To link to a file, the URL would be referenced in the *href* attribute. This attribute is available only in a few HTML tags. Frame, anchor, and image tags are capable of providing links to other files. Figure 7.6 shows a few examples of the types of links that would typically be found in an HTML document.

```
<a href="http://www.someurl.com/main.html">Click here to return to the
  main page.</a>

<a href="ftp://ftp.someurl.com/somefile.zip">Zipped File</a>

<img src="http://www.someurl.com/images/main.gif" />
```

Figure 7.6: HTML link examples.

Each one of the anchor (*a*) tags in Figure 7.6 would allow the user to navigate to other pages or files. In these cases the user would click on the hyperlink and would then navigate to the selected resource. In the last example in Figure 7.6, the resource requested is an image. The browser would request the image and display it in the page.

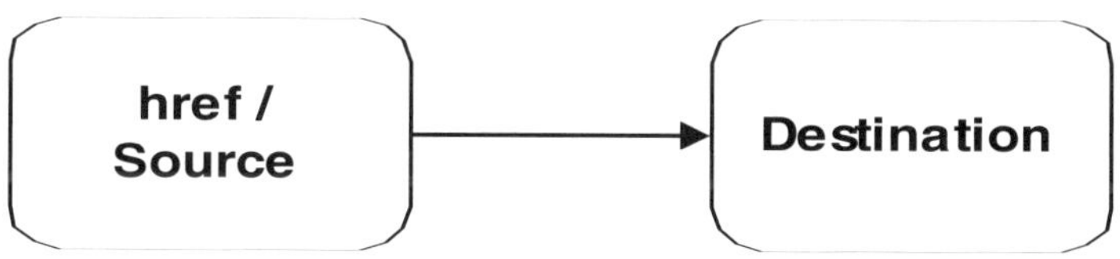

Figure 7.7: HTML source and destination.

In each one of these examples, unless some sort of content management software is used, the path to the resource is static. This poses a serious challenge when URLs or destinations change frequently. HTML linking allows only a single resource to be referenced. In each of the foregoing examples, they reference a single URL. Without the use of some sort of hardware for load balancing, there is no means of pointing the URL to multiple servers. Nor is it possible to route a link to one file based upon a specific role and route to a different file for another role.

With these limitations in mind, the W3 Group developed the Xlink recommendation. The recommendation's main objective is to centralize link information. By placing the link information in external XML documents, the links can be managed and updated in a central location.

The Xlink recommendation goals are the following:

- To use XML syntax
- To make the syntax human readable
- To define the bounds of a link without editing the source document
- To define the direction a link may go
- To ensure that the link is compatible with HTML links

The Xlink recommendation has a few key concepts that are essential to understanding the specification. Table 7.3 shows a list of those key concepts.

Table 7.3: Basic Xlink Concepts

Component	Description
Arc	Information about the connection between two resources is called an arc. This contains information about the direction and possibly application behavior.
Ending Resource	The ending resource is the destination resource in a transversal.

Table 7.3: Basic Xlink Concepts, *continued*

Component	Description
Hyperlink	A hyperlink is an addressable resource meant for human use. It will be used by way of an anchor tag to allow a user to navigate through a site.
Inbound	When the direction of the arc points from an external resource to a local resource, it is called an inbound arc.
Link	A link is an explicit relationship between two or more resources.
Link Bases	Link bases contain a collection of inbound or third-party links.
Linking Element	A linking element is an element that contains the information about a link. The linking element defines the link.
Outbound	When the direction of the arc is pointing from a local resource to an external resource, it is called an outbound arc.
Participate	When a resource is associated with a link, it is said to "participate" with the link.
Remote Resource	A remote resource is any resource that participates in a link. Even if the resource is local, it is still considered remote from the point of view of the link.
Resource	A resource is any addressable unit, including files, images, and programs. A resource is accessed by a URI.
Starting Resource	The starting resource is the resource that has begun a transversal.
Third Party	If the link will not be started or ended within a resource, then the arc is a third-party arc.
Transversal	When a link is used for any purpose, it is known as a transversal.

A simple link works by linking one resource to another. The link associates one resource to another, with an arc connecting the two. Figure 7.8 shows how a simple link works.

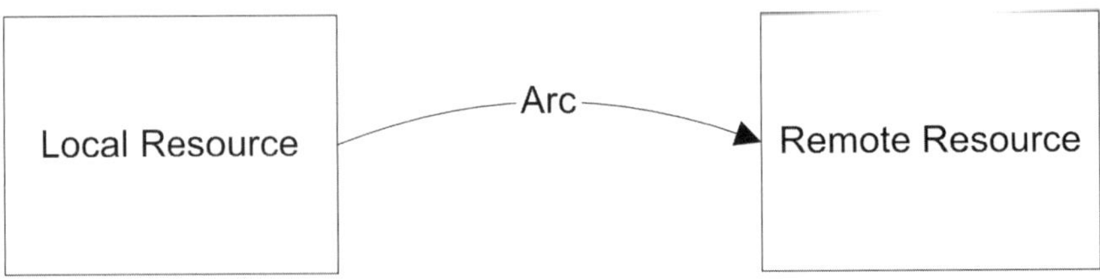

Figure 7.8: A simple link using Xlink.

Xlink works by setting the attributes to the linking element. The linking element has the syntax shown in Figure 7.9. The linking element attributes are provided by the Xlink recommendation. They are listed, grouped by functionality, in Table 7.4.

```
<my_link xmlns:xlink="http://www.w3.org/1999/xlink">
   ...
</my_link>
```

Figure 7.9: Setting Xlink attributes on a linking element.

Table 7.4: Attributes for Linking Elements

Type	Attributes
Identification attribute	type
Locator attribute	href
Semantic attributes	role, arcrole, title
Behavior attributes	show, actuate
Transversal attributes	label, from, to

The *type* attribute identifies what type of link is to be declared. The type attribute will have one of the following values:

- *simple:* A simple link between two resources
- *extended:* An extended, possibly a multiresource, link

- *locator:* A pointer to an external resource
- *resource:* An internal resource
- *arc:* Rule between resources
- *title:* A descriptive title for another linking element

The type attribute defines the role of the element as well as which attributes are required. The type attribute is a required attribute for every linking element. The required and optional attributes for each of the element types are listed in Table 7.5.

Table 7.5: Required and Optional Attributes for Each Linking Element Type

	simple	extended	locator	arc	resource	title
type	*	*	*	*	*	*
href	+		*			
role	+	+	+		+	
arcrole	+			+		
title	+	+	+	+	+	
show	+			+		
actuate	+			+		
label			+		+	
from				+		
to				+		

(* indicates required, + indicates optional)

```
01 <example
02    xmlns:xlink="http://www.w3.org/1999/xlink"
03    xlink:type="simple"
04    xlink:href="http://www.someurl.com/somefile.xml"
05    xlink:title="Example List">
06       List of Examples
07 </example>
```

Figure 7.10: Simple Xlink example.

Figure 7.10 shows (with line numbers added) an example of a link specified through Xlink. On line 3 in Figure 7.10, the type is a *simple* element. The page to which this link will navigate is defined on line 4, which points to *http://www.someurl.com/somefile.xml.*

To use Xlink, the first thing that will be needed is an Xlink processor. There are a few organizations that have developed implementations of the Xlink specification. Fijitsu and XlinkFilter (available at *www.simonstl.com/projects/xlinkfilter/*) have Xlink implementations. To get more information about Xlink, visit *www.w3.org/TR/xlink.*

Giving Pointers with XPointer

Hyperlinks in HTML give users a means of navigating throughout the Internet without the need to worry about long, convoluted URLs. This has been extremely useful since the early stages of the Internet, when URLs were not as well known as they are now. Hyperlinks provide a simple means to connect one HTML document to other HTML documents as well as other file formats. By simply using the <*a*> tag, a document can be linked to another document.

One of the current uses of HTML hyperlinks is linking to a particular place on a page. For example, a page can have a listing of all of the available sections at the top of the page, each with a link to the start of that section. This allows users to examine the contents of the page before navigating to the desired section. Using this feature requires the HTML document to have anchor tags with an *id* attribute rather than an *href.* These tags must be placed at the beginning of each section. The link to the section must have an anchor tag with a reference to the section as its *href* attribute, as shown in Figure 7.11.

```
<a href="chapter7.html#XPointer">Giving Pointers with
  Xpointer</a>
...
<a id="Xpointer" name="XPointer" />
Giving Pointers with Xpointer
```

Figure 7.11: Section linking in HTML.

If the document being referenced were an XML document, this approach would pose some problems, because the *id* attribute would have to be added to the sections. As the first problem in that process, if there were a DTD or schema associated with the XML, the *id* attribute would have to be declared there. This may not be a problem if there isn't already an *id* attribute, but if there is an existing attribute with the name *id*, it may not be compatible. Simply adding this attribute to the DTD or schema may not be a simple task. Changing the structure of an existing XML document should always be done with caution.

The second problem, which also relates to the HTML linking, is how to deal with a change to how the document is being linked. A simple example would be sorting a listing of agents by state rather than by last name. With HTML, if a server-side process generated the page, the code would need to be updated. If the HTML is static, then the HTML would need to be updated to reflect the changes.

With XML, these types of changes would include some possible development effort. If there were server-side code that generated the XML, it would have to be updated to supply the new ID attribute. If there were a DTD or a Schema associated with the XML, it would also need to be updated so that the XML is valid.

The W3 group has addressed these issues with XML linking and proposed the XPointer recommendation. With XML documents, XPointer provides a means of executing a query on an XML document, returning only the relevant elements. XPointer recommendation takes advantage of XPath expressions to query the XML document.

The XPointer recommendation uses XPath to address the necessary elements inside the XML document. When the resource is requested, the XPointer information is placed in the URL. The server responds with the requested resource; however, it does not process the XPointer portion. The client will receive the response, recognize the XPointer information in the URL, and process the XML.

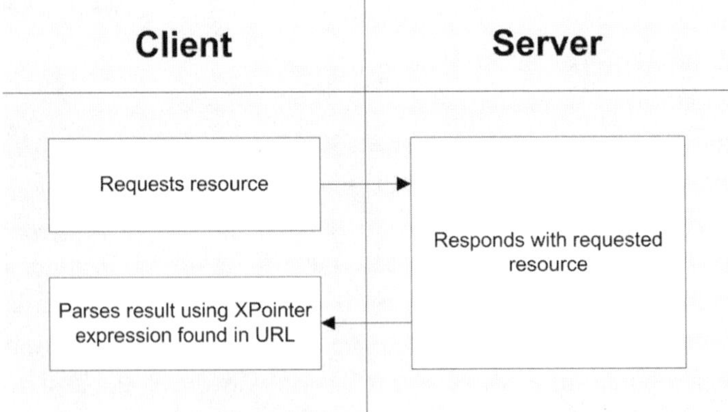

Figure 7.12: XPointer transactions.

An advantage of using XPointer is that any element or attribute in the XML document can be referenced. Because any component of the XML document can be used, no alterations are required so that it can be used with XPointer. If the linking requirements change, there is no need to update the XML, providing that the information is present. The link is the only component that needs to change.

XPointer uses XPath expressions, so, as seen in the section on XPath, it provides a robust set of features. XPointer can be used to return subsets of data, ranges, as well as specific queries for elements. Once the results have been returned, they can be used with XSL so that a browser or the device can present the data. XSL will be discussed in detail in the next chapter.

XPointer Terminology

Below are some of the key terms used in working with XPointer.

Location

A location is a single unit that is contained by a location-set. A location is the point to a single node.

Location-set

A location-set is an unordered set of locations produced by an XPath expression. This is a set of points to the nodes that are the results of the query.

Point

A point is the position in the XML document in which an item is found. Points are identified by a number convention based on the hierarchy of the elements found in the XML. Figure 7.13 contains an XML document that has a single element and contains a single text node. Figure 7.14 shows how this XML document will be assigned its points. Point 1.0 in the figure is just inside the root element. Point 1/1.0 begins the element named *e1*. Between points 1/1/1.0 and 1/1/1.5 is the text found inside the *e1* element.

```
<root>
   <e1>hello</e1>
</root>
```

Figure 7.13: Simple XML document.

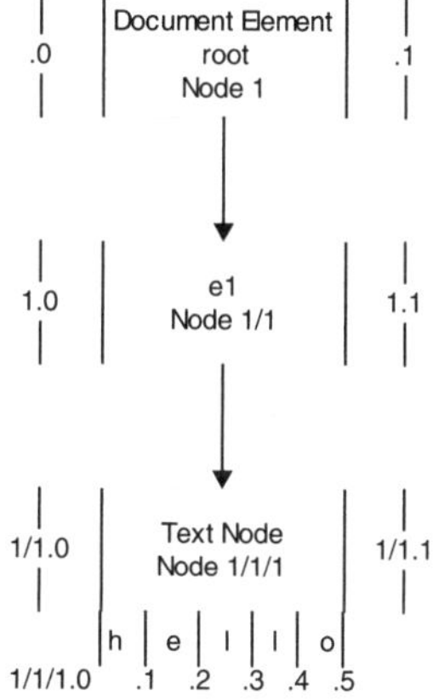

Figure 7.14: Points in the example document in Figure 7.13.

Range

A range of data is returned when the results are found between two conditions; for example, if X is between 3 and 9. This type of functionality is helpful when a set of data needs to be returned. An example would be to show chapters 4 through 6 of a book. There are a few functions that assist with the range capabilities:

- *range-to* returns all of the items from the beginning of the context to the value supplied.
- *string-range* returns all of the items that fall between the two values supplied.
- *covering-range* and *range-inside* return all of the items that are found inside the context in which it is searched.
- *start-point* and *end-point* return the starting and ending element, respectively, found in the current context.

Each of these functions returns a location-set as its result.

XPointer Syntax

An XPointer contains the keyword *xpointer*. It is followed by the XPath expression that will be used to evaluate the XML document, *xpointer(xpath-expression)*.

Figure 7.15 contains an XML document containing a list of recording artists. The Xlink in Figure 7.16 will send the user directly to the artist with an ID of 1. In the *href* attribute, the XPath will search through the list of artists for the *id* equal to 1.

```
<?xml version="1.0"?>
<artists>
   <artist id="1">
      <firstname>Bob</firstname>
      <lastname>Dylan</lastname>
   </artist>
   <artist id="2">
      <firstname>Bruce</firstname>
      <lastname>Springsteen</lastname>
```

Figure 7.15: Recording artists XML (part 1 of 2).

```
    </artist>
    <artist id="3">
        <firstname>Celine</firstname>
        <lastname>Dion</lastname>
    </artist>
</artists>
```

Figure 7.15: Recording artists XML (part 2 of 2).

```
<item xmlns:xlink="http://www.w3.org/1999/xlink"
    xlink:type="simple"
    xlink:href="artists.xml#xpointer(//artists/artist
      [@id='1'])">Bob Dylan</item>
```

Figure 7.16: XLink example using XPointer.

XPointer is currently limited because of the implementations of client-based software. There are few client applications that currently support XPointer. A list of all of the implementations is available on the W3 Web site at *www.w3.org/XML/Linking*.

Chapter Highlights

- XPath expressions can be used to filter an XML document.
- XPath is used with XSL and XPointer specifications.
- Linking between XML documents is done using XLink and XPointer.

Resources
www.w3.org/TR/xpath
www.w3.org/TR/xlink
www.w3.org/TR/xptr/
xpointerlib.mozdev.org/

8

Applying Style to XML: XSL

In this chapter you will learn:

- ✓ What XSL is
- ✓ The components of XSL
- ✓ How XSL works
- ✓ Elements of XSLT
- ✓ How to transform an XML document

Now that you have an XML document, what do you do with it? How do you ready it for presentation? These are a few questions most people have when using XML. Without some means to formatting the data, there is no benefit to using XML.

A few years ago the presentation may have been done pragmatically. This would require an extension to your application that would read the XML document and then format it for the client. That's right—more coding. Any XML parser could have assisted in getting the data out. Then a server-side application such as a servlet or a JSP page would help in presenting the data and would have served for your browser. And if there were any additional client/server interactions or an intranet application, you would have had to do it again; readying it for the next client application—that is, if you couldn't reuse the code. There would have definitely been multiple client interfaces created, all written using the server-side application.

Doesn't it seem a little odd that you would have to write more and more code for each of your client types? Where is the benefit to using XML when you have to do the same or more work? Isn't XML supposed to make life easier? Most people would not have used XML and would have directly communicated with their databases and tried to get some reuse of code inside their stored procedures. But now, when applications are tiered and componentized, this approach is not feasible.

Now the answer is simple: Use XSL to prepare your XML for presentation. XSL provides all the means to format the data or render an XML document for a wide variety of formats. One of the biggest advantages about using XSL is that you have full control over how the formatting gets completed.

Introducing XSL

As developers began to deliver these rich XML documents, it was obvious something had to be developed to complement these structures. As described before, a great deal of programming could be involved to format the XML, but there had to be an easier way. XSL (eXtensible Stylesheet Language) made this transformation possible. Applying an XSL template to the XML transformed the data into other client-specific formats or prepared the data for document rendering. Essentially, the same XML document can be used to present data to many clients using a variety of custom XSL documents. This is not only a time saver during the development stage; it also readies environments for future clients.

XSL is intended to be a platform- and media-independent language, and it has the ability to produce a wide variety of formats. Usually, XSL is considered to be specific to the Web, but its strongest features have to do with document rendering. An XSL document does contain some logic, but it does not require a great deal of programming knowledge to write. It contains some simple logic, using if and loop capabilities, but it does not have a typical programming syntax.

This means that you do not need to use your experienced developers to design XSL documents. A base foundation of XSL and some knowledge of the output format (e.g., HTML) are all that is required. These specifics of the formatting will be discussed in greater detail later in the chapter.

The XSL Originators

In August 1997, the first formal proposal for XSLT was written and developed by the XSL Working Group. This includes key resources from Adobe Systems, Arbortext, Bell Labs, Bitstream, Datalogics, Enigma, IBM, Interleaf, Lotus, Microsoft, Novell, Oracle, O'Reilly & Associates, RivCom, SoftQuad Inc., Software AG, Sun Microsystems, and the University of Edinburgh. This proposal can be found at *www.w3.org/TR/NOTE-XSL.html*. The proposal was loosely based upon DSSSL (Document Style Semantics and Specification Language), an ISO standard for formatting print and online rendering.

The XSL Working Group wanted to create a new specification because of usability on the Internet. DSSSL specification did not provide Web-based functionality, and so the group decided to diverge. At the time, the potential of the Internet was becoming increasingly obvious, and so were the possibilities of using it with XML. Probably one of the goals of the group's development was to make the XSL documents as simple as possible but provide a great deal of functionality. This always seems to be one of the most difficult goals of development.

During the development of the proposal, Microsoft had a concern regarding the complexity of the proposal. Its concern was that most people would use this only to format the XML into HTML documents. Microsoft felt that what it was creating was too complicated and that nobody would use it. So after what I'm sure was a great deal of deliberation, the final specification was designed into three parts:

- XML Stylesheet Language for Transformations (XSLT)
- XML Stylesheet Language Formatting Objects (XSL-FO)
- XML Path Language (XPath), which is shared with XML Linking specification

XSLT was the result of Microsoft's concern and probably is the most-used component of the XSL proposal, so we have Microsoft to thank for this separation. Designed with HTML in mind, even though it can be used for other formats. XSLT allowed you to format the XML document and produce another format. Just by simply embedding some HTML tags, it produces HTML output. Or, by placing other, custom tags, it can transform the document into another XML document.

XSL-FO is what the proposal was originally intended for: the ability to transform an XML document into many formats, including printable documents or even audible format. These formats tend to have much more precise print areas and cannot tolerate the flexibility of HTML. An example of a printable format is a Portable Document Format (PDF), or Acrobat, document. HTML will not put a header or footer on each of the pages in the document. This makes it very difficult to produce print-quality material. Even when Cascading Style Sheets (CSS) are used inside the HTML document, the results are unable to produce consistent and high-quality print material.

XPath, described in Chapter 7, is an expression language used by XSL to access data in XML documents. One of the many uses of XPath is for node matching. An XPath expression can be used for numerical calculations or string manipulations as well as testing Boolean conditions. Its most characteristic use is to identify parts of the input document to be processed. This is how the XSL document knows how and what to apply to the XML document.

XSLT and XSL-FO: What's the Difference?

The biggest difference between XSLT and XSL-FO is one's ability to render and the other's ability to format. XSLT will transform the XML into a new format. It will find the nodes it needs and embed HTML, XML, or other tags or delimiters into the output. The results are in a new format, ready to be sent directly to the client. The way this works is quite simple; but working with the new tags takes some getting used to.

XSL-FO works very similarly in the way it processes all the nodes it needs to and produces a new format. Actually, it uses the exact same language syntax as

XSLT. The difference is what it produces. Using XSLT, specific tags and characters are embedded for the output for the client. With XSL-FO, on the other hand, the results are in a new interpreted language. The results contain all of the formatting necessary for the desired output, including font size, table size, and borders, and so forth. The output file is then passed to a rendering engine, which then creates the desired format.

When Do I Use XSLT and XSL-FO?

XSLT's main purpose is to transform the XML into another format, which will be its final format. Typically, little tends to be done to the results of the transformation. So, when you produce an HTML document, you will send it directly to the client browser, and of course it would be interpreted. XSLT can produce dynamic HTML (DHTML), other XML documents, comma- or space-delimited files, or other uniquely formatted files.

XSL-FO documents are transformed into a format that requires an engine to make the final format. Typically these formats tend to be much more complex than anything that can be created using HTML plus CSS. Such formats include PDF and Rich Text Format (RTF).

Indications for using XSLT and XSL-FO are summarized in Table 8.1.

Table 8.1: When to Use XSLT and When to Use XSL-FO

Use XSLT when...	Use XSLFO when...
The results are HTML, XML, comma-delimited	The results are PDFs, Rich Text Format, audible format
The results can be sent directly to its final location	The final format requires a rendering engine to produce the result
There is no need for a precise output format	The output has a very distinct output format
Your device is a Web or Wireless Application Protocol (WAP) browser	The output device can interpret the rendered document

Why Use XSL?

With the use of tiered architectures comes the ability to update and maintain components without affecting the operation of the other components. This is where XSL fits perfectly into the tiered application paradigm. The XSLT processor handles the transformation of the XML based upon the XSL stylesheet. When updates to any one of these components are necessary, they can be done without impacting the system.

Here is an example of how all of this could come together in a Web-based Java architecture:

1. The client device sends a request to a servlet. The device can be an HTML browser, a PDA, or a WAP device.
2. The servlet accepts the request and determines what action the user is trying to perform.
3. Based upon the action type, the servlet performs some simple validation on the data. An example of the type of validation the servlet performs might be ensuring that all of the incoming parameters are present and are of the correct data type. This validation reduces the number of conversations to the back-end systems.
4. The information is then passed in XML form to the integration layer. Some sort of messaging engine could be inserted here. The messaging engine would ensure delivery of the XML message and could be used in a load-balancing environment.
5. The integration layer parses the incoming request and performs all necessary operations. This layer communicates with all the back-end systems and databases. Most companies have their data distributed over many systems and databases. This layer ensures that the data, no matter where it is, gets updated.
6. Once completed, the integration layer returns the results in XML format back to the servlet.
7. The resulting XML is applied to the proper XSL stylesheet based upon the incoming request type and the client device type. As an alternative to

the XSL stylesheet, a compiled XSL stylesheet (XSLTC), which will be discussed later in the chapter, can be applied. The results are exactly the same.

8. The results of the transformation are sent directly to the client.

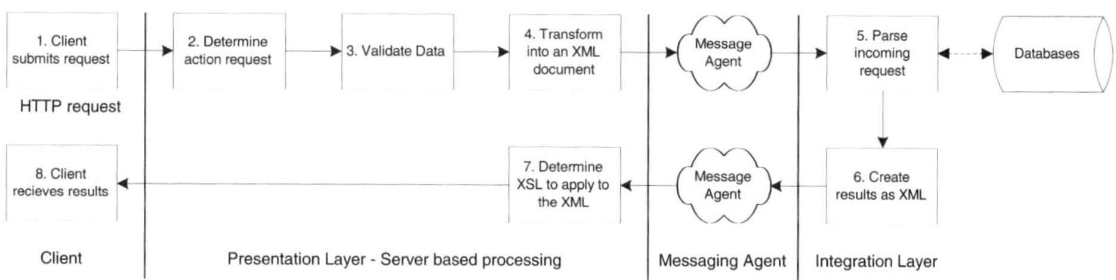

Figure 8.1: Example of a Web-based architecture.

Figure 8.1 shows the steps just described and how they can be separated in an architecture. Web-based architectures allow for many variations to this type of processing. This is not the only way to perform Web processing. This is one of the more simple ways of processing incoming requests.

The advantage of any type of Web-based architecture is that it allows for a matrix-style approach to handling the requests for various clients. Some of the factors that could determine these requests are device, action type, and language. For each one of these combinations, there would be an XSL document that would format the results.

This matrix approach allows the Web architecture to add devices or languages without invasive development. A common pitfall in the development of Web architectures is that they are pretty short-sighted. When a new technology or a new organizational direction arises, the architecture is ill equipped to handle change.

How Does It Work?

As described earlier, there are three components to XSL: XSLT, XSL-FO, and XPath. XSLT and XSL-FO work simply by going through each node and trying to find a template to apply to it. If the XSLT or XSL-FO processor finds a match, it processes the template. XPath is used to help find these nodes and apply templates. Note that not every node must be transformed. Some nodes may be present only to help with any logic inside the XSL.

XSLT

The XSLT process works very simply. The process tries to match XSL templates to nodes found in the XML and then transforms the nodes to the new format. Inside the template are HTML tags, a new XML format, or some new text format—each with XSLT elements. The XSLT elements provide a means for the data to be placed into the output. Once the process is completed, the results are then returned.

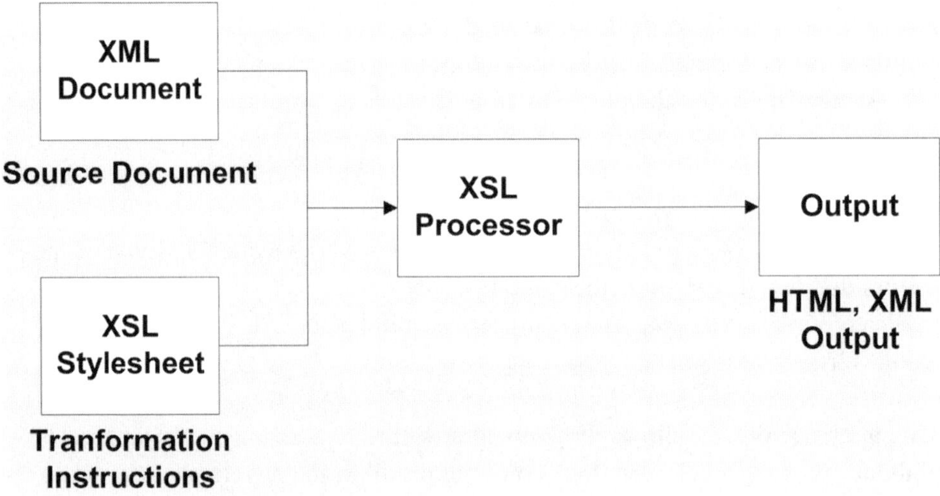

Figure 8.2: Simple XSLT transformation.

Figure 8.2 shows the XML document and the XSL stylesheet being sent to the XSLT processor. The processor sending these two documents to the XSL processor can be done pragmatically, by command line, or referenced in the XML for client processing. Each of these will be discussed further in the chapter. Note that there can be additional parameters sent to the XSL processor to aid in the processing. The results of the transformation will be sent to the client.

When XSLT is used to produce HTML, the option is available to perform the transformation on either the client or the server. On the server side, an XSLT processor would receive the XML and XSL and then perform the transformation. The results would then be returned to the browser. On the client side, the XML would be sent to the browser with a URL reference to the XSLT template. The browser would request the XSLT template and then perform the transformation.

Processing the transformation on the server does have its advantages. It ensures that the transformation has been completed properly. If an error occurs, it can be handled properly and a message can be returned. Also, server-based processing ensures that clients that are too old or are incapable of handling the transformation get something. Processing on the client side, however, does have its own unique advantages as well. Having the client perform the transformation takes some processing away from the server. An intranet environment would be ideal for client-side processing because the software configuration of the clients would be known, thus ensuring that there would be no problems for the transformation.

Let's take a look at the XML document in Figure 8.3. The document contains some simple customer information: ID, first name, initial, and last name.

```
<?xml version="1.0" ?>
<customer>
   <id>123456</id>
   <firstname>Joe</firstname>
   <initial>E.</initial>
   <lastname>Smith</lastname>
</customer>
```

Figure 8.3: Simple customer XML document.

Now let's apply the stylesheet shown in Figure 8.4 to the document in Figure 8.3. Before we look at the results, an explanation of some of the components is needed. First, the *xml* element identifies the version of XML used in the document and the character encoding. Next, the XSL environment is established for the XSL translation by using the *xsl:stylesheet* element, which is always the document element. There is only one *xsl:stylesheet* declared in any XSL template, and it is a requirement for XSLT transformations. Inside the *xsl:template* element is where the output format, an HTML document, begins. The *template* element gets called when the *customer* node is matched to the XSL template, as specified by the *match* attribute on the *xsl:template* element. Once the template is executed, the values of the XML elements in the customer document are placed into the results. The values are referenced directly by the *select* clause of the *xsl:value-of* tag.

```
<?xml version="1.0" encoding="UTF-8"?>
<xsl:stylesheet version="1.0"
 xmlns:xsl="http://www.w3.org/1999/XSL/Transform">

<xsl:template match="customer">
<html>
   <body>
   Customer Information: <br />
   <table border="1">
      <tr><td>ID:</td>
         <td><xsl:value-of select="id" /></td>
      </tr>
      <tr><td>First name:</td>
         <td><xsl:value-of select="firstname" /></td>
      </tr>
      <tr><td>Middle initial:</td>
         <td><xsl:value-of select="initial" /></td>
      </tr>
      <tr><td>Last name:</td>
         <td><xsl:value-of select="lastname" /></td>
      </tr>
   </table>
   </body>
</html>
</xsl:template>

</xsl:stylesheet>
```

Figure 8.4: XSL stylesheet for customer XML.

The one thing to note before we look at the results is the formatting of the HTML code, specifically the table cells. In the past, HTML code was often written with closing tags missing. Today's browsers will make assumptions and will compensate for these missing tags, and it is these accommodations that make it difficult to develop Web applications that work for all the various browsers. Because an XSL document must be well formed, it cannot contain this type of code. Here are two examples: one with missing HTML tags (Figure 8.5) and one that is well formed (Figure 8.6).

```
<table>
<tr>
<td>Blah blah blah
<td>Blah blah blah
</tr>
</table>
```

Figure 8.5: Example of HTML with missing tags.

```
<table>
<tr>
<td>Blah blah blah</td>
<td>Blah blah blah</td>
</tr>
</table>
```

Figure 8.6: Example of well-formed HTML.

As you can see, in the first example a few closing tags are missing. The second example contains all of the necessary tags. These two examples will produce the same results when they reach a browser. As we look to the future, however, when specifications such as XHTML as well as new devices will be generally accepted, we must take care when writing HTML code. The example in Figure 8.5 will not work when used with the new generation of specifications and devices. As a note, XHTML is a fairly new standard that will ensure that HTML is well formed and will even go to the lengths of using a DTD to validate the code.

The results of applying the stylesheet in Figure 8.4 to the XML document in Figure 8.3 are shown in Figure 8.7. As you can see, the customer data has been placed inside the HTML and is well formed.

```
html>
<body>
Customer Information:<br/>
```

Figure 8.7: XSL transformation results (part 1 of 2).

```
<table border="1">
<tr><td>ID:</td>
<td>123456</td>
</tr>
<tr><td>First name:</td>
<td>Joe</td>
</tr>
<tr><td>Middle initial:</td>
<td>E.</td>
</tr>
<tr><td>Last name:</td>
<td>Smith</td>
</tr>
</table>
</body>
</html>
```

Figure 8.7: XSL transformation results (part 2 of 2).

XSL-FO

XSL-FO is a vocabulary for formatting XML documents. The XSL-FO process works similarly to the XSLT transformation but with some obvious differences. Like XSLT, it attempts to match templates to the nodes found in the XML document. The difference is in what it produces. The result is a very specific language of sorts: XSL-FO. It contains all of the specifics regarding the formatting of the document and then substitutes values from the XML document into it. The results are then sent to a rendering engine that produces the final format.

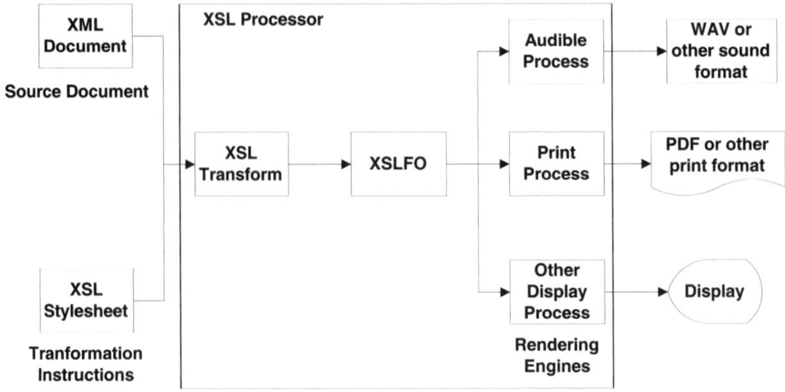

Figure 8.8: XSL-FO rendering process.

Figure 8.8 shows the XML document and the XSL stylesheet being sent to the XSL Processor as in the XSLT process. The results are an XSL-FO document, which is then sent to the rendering engine, which produces the final format.

XSL-FO provides a more sophisticated and intelligent visual layout model than HTML + CSS. XSL-FO is based on rectangular boxes called *areas*. Each area can contain text, images, blank space, or other formatting objects. Each area can contain its own border and padding on each of its sides. The XSL processor reads the formatting objects and determines the position of each in the document. It is intelligent enough to determine page breaks and will ensure that text that may be longer than a page wraps properly to the next page.

Another difference is the types of documents XSL-FO produces. XSLT can produce HTML, XML, or text files, whereas XSL-FO produces PDFs, WAV audio files, or other print-ready documents.

Basic XSLT Components

There are two types of elements in the XSLT world: instruction elements and top-level elements. Top-level elements typically are almost as they sound, top-level: child elements of either the *xsl:stylesheet* or *xsl:transform* element. Inside top-level elements are instruction elements. Instruction elements provide the processing of the XML document.

The xsl:stylesheet and xsl:transform Elements

The *xsl:stylesheet* or *xsl:transform* element indicates the environment in which the XSL environment will operate. One or the other of these elements is always the document element of the XSL document. This element will contain many top-level elements.

Top-Level Elements

The following are top-level elements.

xsl:attribute-set

The *xsl:attribute-set* element groups attributes so that they can be applied to a tag together. Grouping the attributes together makes the code much cleaner and easier to update and allows the same group to be referenced in multiple locations. This element also allows other attribute sets to be included in the current attribute set. This approach reduces the need for coding when there are similar sets to include.

xsl:decimal-format

The *xsl:decimal-format* element provides the instructions to format numeric data. Once declared, it will provide the same number formatting throughout the entire XSL document. This works well when there is a single XSL per language. The decimal format can be initialized with the proper formatting for each language. Once the format is declared, the *format-number* function will format the number.

xsl:import

The *xsl:import* element allows elements declared inside other documents to be included in the current document. This feature permits elements to be reused in multiple locations, thus saving development time. In the event that there are duplicate templates, the templates in the imported file will have a lower priority. Priorities are assigned to a template and determine which template will be executed in the event that there are multiple instances.

xsl:include

The *xsl:include* element works almost exactly the same as the *xsl:import* element. The difference is in how it handles priorities. The external templates referenced using the *xsl:import* will always have a lower priority than the current document, but when *xsl:include* is used, the templates will always maintain their priorities.

xsl:key

The *xsl:key* element allows you to specify a name for a group of nodes by defining a pattern. This capability enables you to call upon this set of nodes throughout the processing.

xsl:namespace-alias

The *xsl:namespace-alias* element allows an alias to be identified for a specific namespace. This is used when the XML is being transformed into another XML format, not when it is being transformed into HTML, text, or other type of non-XML output.

xsl:output

The *xsl:output* element provides instructions to the processor on how to format the results, such as indentation, what type the results will be, whether to include the XML header, the version of the XSLT translation, and whether this XSL document is a stand-alone document.

xsl:param

The *xsl:param* element is used when parameters are needed for a template or a sytlesheet. The *xsl:param* element allows the parameters to be placed into variables so that they can be referenced in the template when this element is used with the stylesheet to aid in the processing of the document. The value is passed when the document is to be transformed and is used to direct the processing.

xsl:preserve-space

The *xsl:preserve-space* function allows spacing to be preserved for the elements specified. This ensures that intentional spaces are saved, as some spacing is necessary. Multiple elements can be identified, so the element does not need to be called more than once.

xsl:strip-space

The *xsl:strip-space* element works very similar to the *xsl:preserve-space* element, but instead of saving the space, it strips all the spacing from the specified nodes. Multiple elements can be identified, so this function does not need to be called more than once.

xsl:template

The *xsl:template* element is the most important element in XSLT transformations. It is the key to matching the patterns from the XML so that a set of actions can be performed upon the information in the document. In addition to matching patterns, the *xml:template* element can also be used for declaring subroutines. Parameters can be passed into the template to aid in the processing, using the *xsl:param* element.

In XSLT transformations there can be only one set of transformations done to a match in any mode. This can be a problem when there is more than one template matching the element in the XML document. It can be difficult to determine which template will be executed. In the event that this occurs, the *priority* attribute will determine which template will be applied.

xsl:variable

The *xsl:variable* element allows values to be stored in "place-holders" so that they can be referenced later in the processing. The scope of a variable depends on where it was declared. When a parent declares a variable, all of its children can reference the same variable. A child node may even declare a variable with the same name; in that case the variable declared by the child applies within the child and its children. However, no two variables can be declared with the same name in the same scope.

Instruction Elements

The following are instruction level elements.

xsl:apply-imports

The *xsl:apply-imports* element does almost exactly what it sounds like: It applies templates from another, imported XSL document. This feature allows two templates to process the same node.

xsl:apply-templates

The *xsl:apply-template* element copies the contents of the current position of the XML tree to the output, matching any templates it can to the elements found in the tree. By using the *select* attribute of the *xsl:apply-template* element, specific nodes of the XML can be affected.

xsl:attribute

The *xsl:attribute* element simply allows an attribute to be added to a tag. This capability is very handy when you are trying to apply a dynamic value to an attribute of an HTML tag. As an example, the URL (*href*) for an anchor tag could be inserted during processing, allowing the URL to be dynamically generated.

xsl:call-template

The *xsl:call-template* is used to call and execute a template when there is no match. It behaves somewhat like a subroutine or a function call in a procedural language. Instead of using a match, the template is referenced by name. This element can be used with the *xsl:with-param* element when there are parameters to pass into the template.

xsl:choose

In some ways the *xsl:choose* element is similar to a set of nested *if* statements or a *switch* statement in a procedural language. It allows multiple conditions to be tested. If they match, the instructions inside the element are executed. If there is no match, the *xsl:otherwise* element will be executed. This is the catch-all for the statement, and will always ensure that something is executed.

xsl:comment

When typical comment tags (between <!-- and -->) are entered into an XSL document, they are ignored by the processor and therefore are not passed to the output. The *xsl:comment* element gets around that problem. It instructs the XSL processor to add the contents to the output as a comment.

xsl:copy

The *xsl:copy* element copies the current node to the output. This is particularly handy when the result of the transformation is another XML document. When the item to copy is an element, the item is copied as an element, and if it is an attribute, it is copied as an attribute.

xsl:copy-of

The *xsl:copy-of* element works very similar to the *xsl:value-of* element in that it takes the requested nodes and puts them into the output. However, the *xsl:value-of* element converts the results to a string, which can cause problems when the results contain a set of nested elements you wish to put to the output as such.

xsl:element

The *xsl:element* element constructs a new element for the results. It uses the instructions inside the element to process the contents. This feature allows elements to be created when the name of the element is unknown until execution.

xsl:fallback

When there is no document element found in the XML, the instructions found inside the *xsl:fallback* element are executed.

xsl:for-each

The *xsl:for-each* element repeats the same set of instructions for a group of nodes. The group of nodes is identified using XPath. An example of this is processing an HTML table. Each row in a table contains the same set of formatting, borders, and so forth, with the exception of the contents of each cell.

The *xsl:sort* element can be used with this element so that the nodes to be processed are in a specific order.

xsl:if

The *xsl:if* element provides some simple conditional processing. If the value of the test statement is correct, the contents of the element are processed. The *xsl:if* element does not have any sort of *else* processing. If there is a requirement for such processing, the *xsl:choose* element with *xsl:otherwise* can be used instead. The *xsl:if* element, like *if* statements in other languages, allows 'or' and 'and' operators as well as decimal and aggregate XSL functions to be used in its condition.

xsl:message

The *xsl:message* element logs a message to the console when an error has been detected. This message does not get passed along to the results. In the event of a fatal error, this element provides the ability to halt execution.

xsl:number

The *xsl:number* element is used to provide a means of numbering nodes so that it can aid the generation of the results. This element provides instructions on how to format the number, where to start, and how to group the numbering, as well as indicating the language to use. When used with the *xsl:for-each* element, it could be used to output the current position in the node list. This is particularly useful for HTML numbered lists or a table of contents-like page.

xsl:processing-instruction

The *xsl:processing-instruction* element is used to return the result of a processing instruction. This places the instruction into the input using the name and the contents for the instruction.

xsl:text

The *xsl:text* element is used to write text to the output. The effect is similar to that of the *xsl:value-of* element, but with the *xsl:value-of* element the results are escaped for special characters. The *xsl:text* element will preserve the space and send the content to the result with no escaping unless it is specified in the disable-output-escaping flag.

xsl:value-of

The *xsl:value-of* element changes the result of the given XPath expression into a string and sends the result to the output. In the event that there are multiple nodes returned, it will process each and concatenate the strings. This element also provides a means of enabling and disabling escaping the results.

In the event that the value of an element or attribute needs to be inserted into a tag, the { } around the element or attribute will provide the same functionality as the *xsl:value-of* element.

xsl:variable

The *xsl:variable* element stores the result of an XPath expression into a variable so that it can be referenced at a later time during processing. The variable is visible only to itself and all of its siblings. As in other programming languages, there can be no two variables declared with same name within the same scope.

Basic XSL-FO Concepts

XSL-FO uses all of the XSL elements just described to produce an FO document. It will process the XML document using the template match and transform the document similarly to the XSLT process, but the result will have some distinct components compared to the XSLT result.

An XSL-FO document contains the following components: regions, block areas, line areas, and inline areas. All of these together provide the building blocks for an XSL-FO document.

Regions

Regions are the highest level in XSL-FO documents. These areas contain the instructions on how pages are formatted. A region would describe what to include in the header and the footer as well as the page size and margin information. These instructions can be applied to the first page, to odd or even pages, or to the last page (whether odd or even).

Block Areas

Areas are typically stacked in a part of the body of a page. Two types of areas that are used are *block* areas and *inline* areas. Block areas are paragraphs, tables, and list items. They are usually stacked on a page either vertically or horizontally. Block areas can contain other areas, as described in the following paragraph. Inline areas are text chunks and inline images. Inline areas are placed inside other inline areas or inside line areas.

Each block area is categorized as one of the following: block, table, list, or block container. A block container can contain multiple block areas. The block container can contain any number of blocks, tables, and lists.

Blocks

A block contains the instructions on how a paragraph is to be formatted. It contains the instructions for font characteristics, indenting, paragraph spacing, line spacing, border spacing, and character spacing. It also allows for images and background images to be inserted into the area.

Tables

XSL-FO provides greater ability to control how a table is formatted than HTML does. An HTML table can sometimes be unpredictable, but with XSL-FO this becomes a problem of the past, because the output is formatted for a specific page. As with a block, an XSL-FO table allows the area to be formatted specifically for the contents in the cell.

Lists

XSL-FO lists are relatively straightforward. The syntax contains the list label and the text. The caption can be a predetermined text or can be used in conjunction with the *xsl:number* element.

Inline Areas

Inline areas provide for formatting of text inside a block. An inline area provides the means of italicizing, bolding, or subscripting a piece of text. Inline areas also place images inside blocks and provide the instructions on how to align the image with the text.

Line Areas

Line areas are a unique type of block area. A line area is a line of text inside a block area. There is no formatting applied to a line area; instead, the block area in which it is contained determines the formatting.

XPath Functionality

In addition to the elements described previously, there are other functions that can be applied to an XML. These functions are also provided by XPath specification. They are grouped in the following categories: node-set, string, boolean, and number functions. These functions include counting of items in a node-set, string manipulation, and number range functions.

Transforming XML Documents

Command-Line Transformation

XSL transformations can be carried out at the command line. The command in Figure 8.9 transforms an XML document. This command would apply transform.xsl to source.xml. The results of the transformation would be put into outputfile.html.

```
java org.apache.xalan.xslt.Process -in source.xml -xsl
  transform.xsl -out outputfile.html
```

Figure 8.9: XSL transformation at the command line.

The XSL Processor for Java, invoked by the command in Figure 8.9, is a JAR file (xalan101.jar, Version 1.0.1). It is located in the following AS/400 directory: /QIBM/proddata/OS400/xml/lib. New versions can be placed in this directory.

This method of transforming the XML is not really a practical way of using XSLT. It would be very difficult to use this method in an application. This method would be used to test the XSL transformation.

Programmatic Transformation

The most common method of transforming is programmatically. An application is used to generate the XML and determines which XSL to apply. The Java code shown in Figure 8.10 performs a translation. This code applies the transformation in transform.xsl to the source.xml document. The results would then be placed into outputfile.html. This method allows different XSLs to be applied to the XML based upon values in the XML, device, or language.

```
// 1. Instantiate a TransformerFactory.
javax.xml.transform.TransformerFactory FACTORY =
javax.xml.transform.TransformerFactory.newInstance();

// 2. Use the TransformerFactory to process the stylesheet Source and
// generate a Transformer.
javax.xml.transform.Transformer TRANSFORMER = FACTORY.newTransformer
(new javax.xml.transform.stream.StreamSource("transform.xsl");

// 3. Use the Transformer to transform an XML Source and send the
// output to a Result object.
TRANSFORMER.transform
(new javax.xml.transform.stream.StreamSource("source.xml"),
new javax.xml.transform.stream.StreamResult(
new java.io.FileOutputStream("outputfile.html")));
```

Figure 8.10: XSL Transformation using Java.

A problem with this method of transformation is overhead associated with the file input/output. Constant access to the disk may lead to poor performance. A solution to this problem is to compile the XSL stylesheet into Java using the XSLT Compiler (XSLTC). XSLTC provides a compiler and a run-time processor. The compiler transforms the XSL stylesheet into a set of Java classes known as *translets*. The translets are then applied to the XML document using the XSLTC run-time processor and produces the results.

A stylesheet would be compiled and placed into a JAR file using the following command: java org.apache.xalan.xsltc.cmdline. Compile -j transform.jar transform.xsl (note that the package information can also be specified using the *-p* flag followed by the package path).

A translet can also be generated at run time. Once generated, it is be used to transform the XML. Figure 8.11 shows an example of this process.

```
// Instantiate the TransformerFactory
// Use it with a StreamSource XSL stylesheet to create a translet as a
// Templates object.
TransformerFactory FACTORY = TransformerFactory.newInstance();
Templates TRANSLET =
FACTORY.newTemplates(new StreamSource("transform.xsl"));

// For each thread, instantiate a new Transformer, and perform the
// transformations on that thread from a StreamSource to a
// StreamResult;
Transformer TRANSFORMER = TRANSLET.newTransformer();
TRANSFORMER.transform(new StreamSource("source.xml"),
      new StreamResult(
new FileOutputStream("outputfile.html")));
```

Figure 8.11: XSL transformation using XSLTC.

Conclusion

The purpose of XSL is to assist in the transformation of XML data. Whether the XML document is to be transformed into another XML document, an HTML document, a rendered document such as a PDF file, or some other format; XSL is a versatile language that can transform an XML document into almost any format.

There is no longer any need to have developers spend a great deal of their time creating JSP pages or applications that translate documents into other formats. XSL templates allow developers to do what they do best: write code. Programmers can focus on the development of the application, while XSL authors write the various templates for the final format. This capability eliminates the need to have your programmers spending time writing the HTML or XML format.

In addition, XSL provides a means to create device- and language-specific formats for the XML document. There is no need to recreate the same application for each item; the device and language specificity issues can be addressed by developing a template for each combination.

Essentially, XSL templates can greatly simplify any application. XSL separates the presentation of the data from your application and places the transformation into a separate set of instructions that can be referenced by the file structure or compiled code.

References
www.w3.org
www.apache.org

9

XML Security

In this chapter you will learn:

- ✓ How security fits into XML
- ✓ The importance of security
- ✓ What types of security are available
- ✓ How XML is used on the iSeries (formerly AS/400) platform
- ✓ How to implement security with XML

Security has been an important topic for a long time, especially since the emergence of the Internet. It became painfully obvious to many organizations that they could not rely solely on physical and network security to protect their data. The data in transit also had to be protected.

Any transaction that has no security essentially has no integrity. Organizations that do not use security measures cannot guarantee that transactions have not been compromised. Without security, transaction information may be collected or altered in transit. Transaction integrity also ensures the identity for recipient and the sender. When there is no integrity, transactions can be sent or received by unauthorized parties who, either with malicious intent or accidentally, have gained access to execute commands they should not be permitted to execute.

Now that XML has emerged as an accepted technology, the data must be secure. As seen from many of the examples in this book, XML is in plain text. Passing this type of information across an unsecured HTTP channel poses some serious risks, especially when it may contain sensitive information.

There have been efforts to create a single solution for all security concerns. This was a difficult idea, because each organization had its own unique requirements and environments. Whether it is the languages used to develop applications, software, operating systems, hardware, or general network infrastructure, no single security recommendation can encompass all of these elements. A set of standards had to emerge that could adapt to the changing technologies as well as work together so that they collectively can create a complete suite of security features.

To meet the concerns regarding security and the emergence of XML, a set of XML security standards has been created to address security for XML documents, thus ensuring the data is protected from compromise.

Vulnerabilities Associated with XML Technologies

If you build it, they will hack it… It was just a matter of time before they found something that can be exposed with XML technologies. With XML technologies, it is the parser that provides many of the exposures. In many cases, parsers may have been incorrectly used, which can lead to unexpected exposure. An application may be coerced to open arbitrary files or execute files that may open TCP connections.

Buffer overflow attacks are another type of problem associated with the parser. This is when the amount of data sent exceeds the data expected, thus resulting in unexpected results. They can range from system crashes to the execution of unauthorized applications. These types of problems occur when an application that is exposed on the Internet accepts XML input from suspect sources.

Another vulnerability of XML is the fact that the document is in plain text. There are two problems with using plain text documents: the visibility of the data while in transit and having access to the document on the file system or in another application. Care must be taken when handling XML data so that these two vulnerabilities do not become a problem.

The Importance of Security

The reality of technology is that nothing is perfect. And with increased exposure to systems, whether the Internet, an intranet, or secure channels, these imperfections are exposed. To limit the exposure, security standards are necessary. Some basic security fundamentals include

- Ensuring identity
- Protecting data
- Key management
- User validation and rules

The unfortunate reality is that only once the threat has been identified can it be understood. Once it has been understood, a solution can be delivered. Usually, before it is understood, it leaves a mess to clean up, possibly resulting in damage to the reputation of the organization or in the release of critical information.

Securing corporate data ensures the integrity of the data as well as the reputation of the organization storing the data. The earlier security measures are put in place, the lower the cost and the likelihood of compromise. One way to determine how vulnerable a system is to have an external audit performed. Auditors will assess the exposed systems using the latest techniques as well as old ones. This type of analysis will provide a starting point in deciding which technologies to adopt.

What is XML Security?

XML Security is a common framework that can be shared among applications. It defines the vocabulary and the processing rules to address XML security concerns. To meet today's security requirements, it provides a flexible and practical solution.

Each XML Security standard uses existing technologies to protect XML data. Instead of creating a set of new complex components, it reuses existing concepts, technologies, and algorithms. This allows for support in a large range of environments and infrastructures.

Like many other XML standards it is based on XML, thus eliminating another syntax to learn. These technologies can be implemented within new and existing applications without major reconstruction. The minimal amount of work involved in implementing some of these types of security is well worth the effort.

The core XML standards that will be discussed in this chapter include the following technologies:

- XML Digital Signature (XML DigSig)
- XML Encryption (XML Enc)
- XML Key Management Specification (XKMS)
- Security Assertion Markup Language (SAML)
- XML Access Control Markup Language (XACML)

Additional security standards that will also be discussed in this chapter include

- eXtensible rights Markup Language (XrML)
- Platform for Privacy Preferences (P3P)

An advantage of using these technologies is that they do not require each other to work. Each one of these can be deployed individually or together. They have all been designed to work with each other as well as many other XML technologies, including XPath and SOAP, among others.

Core XML Security Standards

XML Digital Signature (XML DigSig)

One of the concerns when XML data is being delivered, whether over the Internet, over an intranet, or by a secure connection, is the possibility of the data being changed. Once the XML document has been sent, neither the sender nor the receiver can ensure that the data is correct. The recipient does not ask the sender whether each of the values are correct; it assumes that the data is valid and will continue with its processing.

Needless to say, tampering with data can be disastrous. Shipping addresses could be altered to have merchandise delivered to another location. Amounts in financial transactions could be altered, causing a financial inconvenience to their clients. Steps must be taken to ensure the integrity of the data.

Another potential problem with the Internet is the identity of the sending party. When you purchase merchandise at a store with a credit card, the signature on the back of the card will be used to ensure that it is the same on the receipt, thus ensuring the identity of the purchaser to the vendor. This step also assures the card holder that her signature is required to use that card. This practice thus validates the identity of the purchaser to the business as well protecting the card owner. When a message is delivered on the Internet, however, there are a lot of assumptions, one of them being the origination of a message.

These risks are addressed in the XML Digital Signature recommendation. It guarantees the authenticity of data so that it is confirmed to be identical in form when it is received as when it was sent. Use of the digital signature also guarantees the identity of the signer. The recommendation is a joint effort between the W3C Group and the Internet Engineering Task Force (IETF). It provides the rules and syntax so that data of any type can have integrity and authentication.

Digital signatures work by generating a "digest" for the data to be signed. A digest is a unique, fixed-length value that has been generated from the original content by the use of a cryptographic technique. It is extremely difficult to modify the data without detection once a digest has been created. The signature will be valid as long as the contents have not changed since the document was signed. With that, care must be taken in intermediate steps, because the XML document cannot change in any way; otherwise it will not be valid. This constraint includes modifications that would still leave the data identical and keep the document well formed. An example would be additional white space at the end of the document or re-arranging the order of attributes. A parser may automatically do these steps just by simply opening the document.

An XML signature may be applied to many pieces of content. The signature may be handled in three different ways. In the first two, the signature is located in the root of the XML; such a signature can be an enveloped or an enveloping signature. The difference between the two types is where the signed content is located. When an enveloping signature is used, the content being signed is located in the signature. When an enveloped signature is used, the signature is added as a child to the XML element being signed, as shown in Figure 9.1. In some cases it may be useful to have the signed content inside the signature. The third method places the signature in a separate document. This is known as a detached signature.

```
<?xml version="1.0" ?>
<customer>
   <id>123456</id>
   <firstname>Joe</firstname>
   <initial>E.</initial>
   <lastname>Smith</lastname>
<Signature xmlns="http://www.w3.org/2000/09/xmldsig#">
...
</Signature>
</customer>
```

Figure 9.1: Signed customer data using an enveloped signature.

An XML digital signature may contain the following components:

- The encrypted hash value for the XML
- The algorithms used to generate the hash value

- Information on the public key info (PKI) directory
- The Public Key Certificate

Following are the descriptions of the components of the signature element shown (with added line numbers) in Figure 9.2. They describe what each element contains and its purpose.

```
01 <Signature ID="" xmlns="">
02    <SignedInfo>
03       <CanonicalizationMethod Algorithm="" />
04       <SignatureMethod Algorithm="" />
05       <Reference URI="" >
06          <Transforms>
07          <DigestMethod>
08          <DigestValue>
09       </Reference>
10    </SignedInfo>
11    <SignatureValue>
12    <KeyInfo>
13    <Object ID>
14 </Signature>
```

Figure 9.2: Components of a digital signature (line numbers added).

Line 1: The *ID* attribute indicates the unique name for the signature. This allows multiple signatures to be implemented in the same XML. The *xmlns* attribute indicates the namespace for the signature.

Lines 2 through 10: These are required portions of the signature, containing the instructions of how the XML is signed. The necessary information regarding the generation of the digest is inside this section.

Line 4: This line specifies the algorithm used to generate the signature value for line 11. This line will be used to generate a digest of the SignedInfo element. This digest will be compared to the signature supplied with the document to ensure that the signed info information has not changed along with the data. It adds an extra layer of complexity to the signature.

Lines 5 through 9: Each element that will be signed will have its own reference element. This element contains the methods used to create the digest as well as the digested value.

Line 11: The *SignatureValue* contains the digest for the *SignedInfo* element. The algorithm specified on line 4 is used to generate this value.

Line 12: The *KeyInfo* element indicates the key used to validate the signature. KeyInfo can include key names, certificates, key algorithms, and information. This information is not required for the signature, because the signer may not want this type of information revealed.

To find out more information about XML Digital Signatures, visit *www.w3.org/Signature/.*

Confidentiality with XML Encryption

Secure Sockets Layer (SSL) is well known as the encryption technology for the Internet world. SSL protects data by encrypting it into a format that is readable only for the sender and the receiver and is unreadable for anyone else. The sender and the receiver use public-key cryptography to communicate.

SSL works very well for HTTPS requests, but how does it work with XML? Just as for the HTTP requests, it would work well while it is in transit. The application would not require any special tuning to send or receive information, because SSL is a very common standard. However, what if the XML is placed in a queue or is saved onto the file system? The data is in plain text and can be viewed by anyone who has access to the queue or to the system. This exposes the data to those who have access, especially if the XML contains sensitive data.

The XML Encryption Standard

The XML Encryption standard was developed to provide a means of encrypting XML data. It defines the framework and syntax for encrypting and decrypting

XML data. The recommendation was developed by the W3C Group. The recommendation used in this book is the December 10, 2002, recommendation.

With the recommendation comes a great deal of flexibility in what can be encrypted. To begin, both XML and non-XML data may be encrypted. This gives the recommendation a greater use than just for XML documents. Any number of components of the XML document can be encrypted, enabling certain sensitive data to be secured while other, “safe” data does not need to be. However, to be on the safe side, the entire document can also be encrypted.

In encrypting XML data, there are two choices available for what can be encrypted. The data alone can be encrypted, or the data and the element tags may be encrypted. This allows the document to be readable, but it does indicate what type of information is encrypted. The choice of how to encrypt the data must be made to ensure the least amount of exposure.

The recommendation supports a wide variety of encryption algorithms and technologies. It includes block encryption, stream encryption, key transport, key agreement, symmetric key wrap, message digest, message authentication, and canonicalization and encoding. A complete list of the supported algorithms is available on the W3C XML Encryption recommendation page.

Encryption Examples

```
<?xml version=“1.0”?>
<customer>
   <id>123456</id>
   <firstname>Joe</firstname>
   <initial>E.</initial>
   <lastname>Smith</lastname>
   <creditcardinfo>
      <cardnumber>123456789012</cardnumber>
      <cardtype>Visa</cardtype>
      <expirydate>10/2005</expirydate>
   </creditcardinfo>
</customer>
```

Figure 9.3: Customer data with sensitive information.

Having the XML file shown (with line numbers added) in Figure 9.3 available on the file system or visible in a queue can be extremely dangerous because of the risk of that information getting into the wrong hands. The *creditcardinfo* element, located on lines 7 through 11, would need to be encrypted to ensure that it does not get exposed.

```
01 <?xml version="1.0"?>
02 <customer>
03    <id>123456</id>
04    <firstname>Joe</firstname>
05    <initial>E.</initial>
06    <lastname>Smith</lastname>
07    <EncryptedData Type="http://www.w3.org/2001/04/xmlenc#Element"
        xmlns="http://www.w3.org/2001/04/xmlenc#">
08       <CipherData>
09          <CipherValue>...</CipherValue>
10       </CipherData>
11    </EncryptedData>
12 </customer>
```

Figure 9.4: XML document with encrypted credit card information element.

Figure 9.4 shows how the credit card information has been made no longer visible to someone viewing the XML. The *creditcardinfo* element has been replaced with the *EncryptedData* element located on lines 7 through 11. This element tag contains the information about what has been encrypted. In this example the *Type* attribute on line 7 indicates that an element has been encrypted. This allows the name of the element to be hidden from any eyes that may see the document. Line 9 contains the encrypted value for the element tags and the element value.

```
<?xml version="1.0"?>
<customer>
   <id>123456</id>
   <firstname>Joe</firstname>
   <initial>E.</initial>
   <lastname>Smith</lastname>
   <creditcardinfo>
```

Figure 9.5: Encrypted content inside an element (part 1 of 2).

```
08       <EncryptedData xmlns="http://www.w3.org/2001/04/
           xmlenc#" Type="http://www.w3.org/2001/04/xmlenc#Content">
09          <CipherData>
10             <CipherValue>...</CipherValue>
11          </CipherData>
12       </EncryptedData>
13    </creditcardinfo>
14 </customer>
```

Figure 9.5: Encrypted content inside an element (part 2 of 2).

Figure 9.5 is very similar to Figure 9.4, with one exception: It leaves the element tags unencrypted in the XML. Lines 8 through 12 show that there is encrypted data inside the XML. The *Type* attribute on line 8 shows that the type of data is content rather than the element itself.

Care must be taken when deciding what method is used for encryption. If only the content is encrypted, the name of the attribute will still be in plain text. Any person reading the file in Figure 9.5, for example, knows that the encrypted data consists of credit card information. This makes it easier to break the encryption, because the elements may be known from the schema definition.

Encryption and Digital Signatures

XML encryption can be used in conjunction with XML Digital Signatures to provide a great deal of protection for the data inside an XML document. The signature ensures that the data has not been changed and identifies the sender, and the encryption ensures that sensitive information is not available for viewing.

One item to note regarding the use of both of these technologies is what happens first: the decrypting of the data or the verification of the signature. Recall that the document cannot be altered, because altering it makes the signature invalid. The XML Encryption Transform recommendation recommends that the signer must identify what encrypted elements have been used during the signing. This allows the recipient to know what to do first.

To find out more information regarding XML Encryption, visit the following address: *www.w3.org/Encryption/2001/*.

XML Key Management Specification (XKMS)

To use XML encryption and XML digital signatures, there must be some means of managing the various keys. Key management deals with the generation, storage, distribution, selection, destruction, and archiving of the key variables. All these are essential to encryption and signature technologies.

One of the difficulties with an enterprise-wide PKI infrastructure is the complexity associated with its development. A successful implementation requires strong skills in a wide range of technologies. After implementation, another challenge is integrating the infrastructure with other applications. Each application may have some unique requirements and may have incompatibilities with certain infrastructures.

To alleviate some of the burdens of the development and deployment of the management of keys, the XML Key Management Specification (XKMS) was developed. At the time of this chapter, the specification was still in draft state. Microsoft, VeriSign, webMethods, W3C, Citicorp, Identrus, Motorola, Baltimore, Bank of America, Nokia, Treasury Board of Canada Secretariat, Geotrust, and RSA were all involved in the development of the specification.

XKMS provides a simple way to integrate digital signatures and data encryption into e-commerce applications. It supports the full lifecycle of the certification/key process, including the creation of the key pair and the binding of the pair with identity and other attributes. XKMS takes away the complexities of the underlying technologies and provides a framework for deploying key technology. It defines an XML vocabulary to request and receive information from the server.

XKMS provides a Web service interface to the public key infrastructure. SOAP requests are used to request information from the management system, making it easy for applications to interface with the manager. This interface allows a variety of applications and technologies to communicate with XKMS. Because a Web service is the front end for XKMS, the underlying technology can change without any changes to the client applications, enabling future technologies to be incorporated into the infrastructure.

The following functions provide all the features necessary for maintaining, distributing, and validating keys:

- *Registers:* This feature is responsible for the general maintenance of keys, including issuing, reissuing, and revoking keys.
- *Locate:* This function is responsible for returning the requested key information.
- *Validate:* The purpose of this function is to locate key information and validate the key pair.

The XKMS also defines two specifications that are essential for key management: XML Key Registration Services Specification (XKRSS) and XML Key Information Services Specification (XKISS). These specifications provide the request and response SOAP messages for all the various functions of the XKMS specification.

The first of the two subspecifications, XML Key Registration Service Specification (XKRSS), provides the protocols for the registration of a key pair, as shown in Figure 9.6. The specification's main purpose is the complete maintenance of keys. This includes the following key maintenance:

- Registration
- Reissue
- Invalidate
- Revocation

The registration includes the binding of information (name, identification tags, and other necessary information) to a key pair.

Once the key has been registered, it now can be queried. The query language for keys is XML Key Information Service Specification (XKISS). XKISS defines the protocol for requesting and receiving key information, as shown in Figure 9.7. It removes the complexities of the underlying technologies and

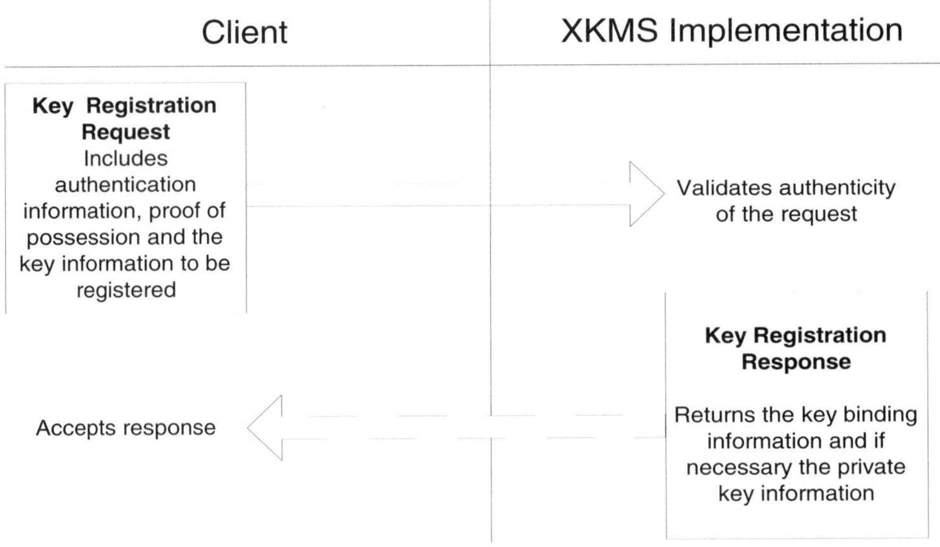

Figure 9.6: XKRSS key registration.

provides a SOAP interface for querying. The underlying architecture and technology may be changed without affecting the incoming requests. XKISS is used to identify, verify, and bind the public key information.

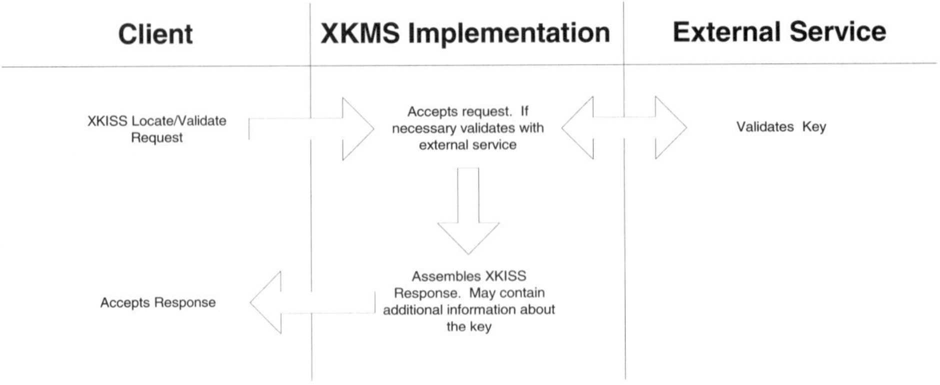

Figure 9.7: XKISS communication example.

To find out more information about the XML Key Management Specification, visit the following address: *www.w3.org/2001/XKMS/*.

Security Assertion Markup Language (SAML)

With XML Digital Certificates comes identity protection and XML integrity; XML Encryption ensures information is secure; and the management of keys is protected with XML Key Management Specification. So what is left? The most obvious choice would be to constrain what actions a user can perform.

Ensuring user security tends to require a great deal of development. Almost always it requires customized development that usually starts with the right intentions but ends up with a complicated mess that becomes more and more complex as time goes on. Typically, application security is tightly woven into custom applications and is very difficult to manage.

Security becomes ever more and more difficult to manage when many applications and Web sites have to be combined to appear seamless. For Web-based systems this is a difficult challenge. The last thing a user would like to do is to register and log into each system. The necessity of doing so makes systems unusable and extremely complex to maintain. As discussed before, a tempting option would be to write some custom code to make interaction with multiple security systems seamless to the user. As well as such code might work, the questions arise of how well it scales and how flexible it is. A solution with a short-sighted scope may be easy to develop but would leave you unable to scale, yet a far-sighted scope may take a great deal of effort to develop.

Fortunately, the Organization for the Advancement of Structured Information Standards (OASIS) group has developed an XML-based framework for dealing with shared security. Based on SOAP messaging, SAML provides a complete and flexible means of establishing rules for actions and resources. It is designed to work with industry-standard transport protocols such as HTTP and SMTP with XML exchange frameworks such as SOAP, BizTalk, and ebXML.

Time and money are saved when there is a single source for authentication. Instead of having many expensive security systems, they can be reduced to a single system using SAML. Often multiple systems have duplicate and inaccurate settings, leading to conflicting and unexpected results. By having a single system, resources that used to be dedicated to administering these systems can have their efforts placed elsewhere.

When the security is built into an application, the effort usually is short-sighted and has little or no ability to accommodate future changes. This results in a greater effort to expand the security so that it can accomplish the new functions. Having the security external to the application allows the development to focus solely on the business logic. In the event that a major reorganization to the security occurs, it will have no effect on the code. The SOAP request for access, which uses XML Access Control Markup Language (XACML), will not change, so the security change will have no effect on the rest of the system. XACML will be discussed in the next section of this chapter.

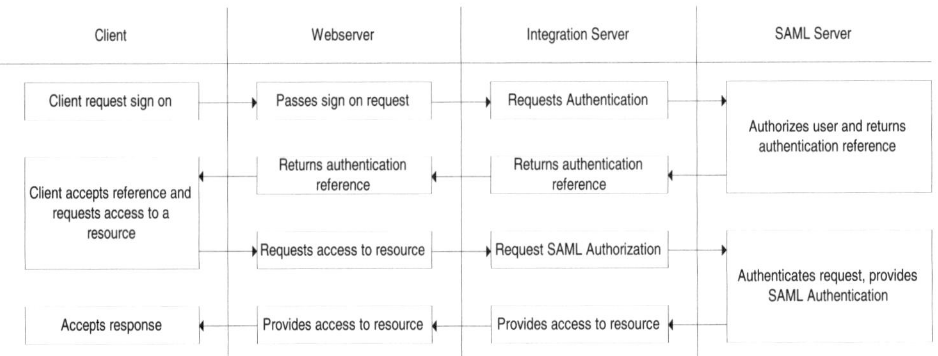

Figure 9.8: Web client example of SAML.

The following steps in login and authentication are shown in Figure 9.8:

1. Client requests a signon.
2. The Web server passes the request to the integration server.
3. The integration server formats the request in the form of a SAML authentication request.
4. The SAML server authorizes the user and returns an authentication reference.

5. The integration server returns the authentication reference to the Web server.
6. The Web server returns the authentication reference to the client.
7. The client accepts the reference and stores it in a session variable. The client requests a resource, and with that request it sends its authentication reference.
8. The Web server will do some minor validation of the incoming request. If everything is okay, it will pass the request to the integration server.
9. The integration server will format the SAML authorization and pass it to the SAML server.
10. The SAML server will authenticate the request and provide access to the resource.
11. The integration server will provide the requested information.
12. The Web server will format the response and send it back to the client.
13. The client accepts the response.

To find out more information about SAML, visit the following address: *www.oasis-open.org/specs/index.php#samlv1.1*.

XML Access Control Markup Language (XACML)

As seen in the previous section, SAML provides the framework to validate and authorize users for a resource. Rules and policies can be established to determine when and how the same user can access the resource. The rules and policies are written in an XML vocabulary called XML Access Control Markup Language (XACML). The OASIS group has written this standard along with SAML. It uses messages that are sent in a request/response XML format.

The XACML request contains the information about the resource being accessed as well as information about the user who is making the request. Typical user information may include the network address the user is requesting from, the time the request is being made, the department, what type of resource, and so forth. The request is essentially a query that contains all necessary information used to determine whether access should be granted to the resource.

The response will always contain an answer to the request. The answer will be one of the following responses:

- Permit
- Deny
- Indeterminate
- Not Applicable

Permit indicates that access has been allowed to the resource, and *Deny* indicates that access has not been allowed to the resource. Both of these indicate that a defined rule has been used to determine access to the resource. *Indeterminate* also indicates that access has not been granted, but for another reason: usually that there has been an error such as an invalid request or a required parameter missing. *Not Applicable* indicates that the service was unable to evaluate the request, perhaps because of invalid parameters, indicating access to a system or user not defined.

There are three basic components to XACML:

- Policies and policy sets
- Targets and rules
- Attributes

The highest level in XACML includes policies and policy sets. A typical policy is a single action; for example, a login and logout would each be a policy. Policies can be combined together to make a policy set.

Targets and rules are on the next level down from policies. Targets are the components of a rule. There are three different types of targets, known as subjects, resources, and actions. Resources are the services, data, or component being accessed. Actions are operations that can be performed on a resource. Subjects are participants or users that are performing an action upon a resource.

Attributes, on the lowest level, are characteristics of a subject, a resource, an action, or the environment in which the action is performed. Attributes focus a rule so that it applies to a smaller group. For example, a rule can be set up for a specific user against a certain resource. A constraint can be placed against a particular resource as well to allow access only during business hours.

```
<Rule RuleId=“Rule1” Effect=“Permit”>
   <Description>Description of the rule</Description>
   <Target>
   <Subjects>
      <Subject>
      <SubjectMatch
        MatchId=“urn:oasis:names:tc:xacml:1.0:function:
        rfc822Name-match”>
         <SubjectAttributeDesignator
           AttributeId=“urn:oasis:names:tc:xacml:1.0:
           subject:department”
           DataType=“urn:oasis:names:tc:xacml:1.0:
           data-type:rfc822Name”/>
      <AttributeValue
         DataType=“urn:oasis:names:tc:xacml:1.0:
           datatype:rfc822Name”>
           Sales
         </AttributeValue>
      </SubjectMatch>
   </Subject>
   </Subjects>
   <Resources>
      <ResourceMatch MatchId=“urn:oasis:names:tc:xacml:1.0:
        function:string-equal”>
         <AttributeValue
            DataType=“http://www.w3.org/2001/
              XMLSchema#string”>
              SalesSystem
         </AttributeValue>
      <ResourceAttributeDesignator
            DataType=“http://www.w3.org/2001/
              XMLSchema#string”
```

Figure 9.9: Example of a rule in XACML (part 1 of 2).

```
              AttributeId="urn:oasis:names:tc:xacml:1.0:
                resource:resource-id"/>
16          </ResourceMatch>
17        </Resources>
18        <Actions>
19          <AnyAction/>
20        </Actions>
21     </Target>
22     <Condition FunctionId="urn:oasis:names:tc:xacml:1.0:function:and">
23        <Apply
            FunctionId="urn:oasis:names:tc:xacml:1.0:function:
              time-greater-than-or-equal">
24        <Apply FunctionId="urn:oasis:names:tc:xacml:1.0:
            function:time-one-and-only">
25          <EnvironmentAttributeSelector DataType=
              "http://www.w3.org/2001/XMLSchema#time"
                AttributeId="urn:oasis:names:tc:xacml:1.0:
                  environment:current-time"/>
26        </Apply>
27        <AttributeValue
            DataType="http://www.w3.org/2001/XMLSchema#time">
            08:00:00</AttributeValue>
28     </Apply>
29     <Apply FunctionId="urn:oasis:names:tc:xacml:1.0:
         function:time-less-than-or-equal">
30        <Apply FunctionId="urn:oasis:names:tc:xacml:1.0:
            function:time-one-and-only">
31          <EnvironmentAttributeSelector DataType=
              "http://www.w3.org/2001/XMLSchema#time"
                AttributeId="urn:oasis:names:tc:xacml:1.0:
                  environment:current-time"/>
32        </Apply>
33        <AttributeValue
            DataType="http://www.w3.org/2001/XMLSchema#time">
              18:00:00</AttributeValue>
34        </Apply>
35     </Condition>
36  </Rule>
```

Figure 9.9: Example of a rule in XACML (part 2 of 2).

Figure 9.9 defines a rule that allows the Sales department access to the SalesSystem during the hours of 8:00 a.m. to 6:00 p.m. Lines 4 through 11 indicate the subjects for the rule. In this example, the rule looks for the request to have the department name equal to *Sales*. Lines 12 through 17 indicate the resource to which the rule will grant access. It will look for a *resource-id* equal to *SalesSystem*. The condition element in lines 22 through 35 describes an additional constraint, defining the allowed time during which the Sales department can access the SalesSystem. The condition will ensure that the *current-time* is greater than or equal to 8:00 a.m and less than or equal to 6:00 p.m.

Platform for Privacy Preferences (P3P)

Most of the standards listed in the preceding sections have been aimed at ensuring the integrity of the XML data, ensuring that sensitive data has not been compromised, and that the issuer is who he says he is. All of these features deal with the direct transfer of data. However, there is nothing indicating how collected information is being used on the Internet.

The W3C group and many of the major organizations associated with the Internet have worked together and created a standard to deal with Internet privacy. That standard is called Platform for Privacy Preferences (P3P). Its goal is to inform users of the organization's privacy practices. It allows users to obtain this information easily and learn how the organization is going to use information they transmit to their site. The ultimate goal is to gain some of the lost trust in Internet privacy. This specification is not meant to eliminate or control cookies, a capability that is currently available in cookie-blocking software.

The recommendation is currently version 1.0. It has taken a great deal of time to get to this stage with the specification. The development effort began in 1998 and became a recommendation in April 2002. The long lead time is due partly to the number of participants in the specification. It was also stalled as it was awaiting the completion of two other specifications: RDF and XML Schemas. Resource Description Framework (RDF) is an XML application that is used for metadata. The original version of P3P was going to use RDF; the current version does not. The privacy policy is written in XML format and is a human-readable document.

Policies indicate a great deal about what information is gathered and the practices of an organization. They also detail how the information will be used. Some of the information that is included in a P3P policy is the following:

- What type of information is being collected (for example, name, address, city)
- How long the information is being stored
- How much access a customer has to the collected data
- How complaints are resolved (for example, internally, within the legal department, or by an external organization)
- Why the information has been collected (for example, research and development, Web administration, reporting, Web tracking, later user contacting such as telemarketing)
- Whom the information is shared with (for example, agents for the organization, delivery services, other organizations, or users of other forums such as bulletin boards or CD-ROMs)
- Types of information stored within cookies

A single policy can be used for an entire site, or multiple policies can be used for different sections on a single site. This allows transaction sections of a site to have a different policy than a visitor site. A visitor site may not be collecting any information and will have a completely different policy.

Now that the organization has identified its privacy standard, a P3P-compliant browser can make decisions based upon the policy. Users can set their browsers to trust only sites that have policies or custom policies that are to their liking. Most new browsers support the P3P standard. If a client enters a site and it does not match the user's settings, the user will be alerted and can decide whether she wishes to proceed.

On any given page there can be many items coming from many areas of a Web site. There can be multiple policies in effect for the entire page: for example, one for images and another for the HTML page. If any of the policies do not agree with the browser's settings, then the user is alerted.

Figure 9.10 shows a section of a P3P policy. In this policy the organization indicates that a user's name and home information (lines 8 through 11) will be

```
01 <STATEMENT>
02     <EXTENSION optional="yes">
03         <GROUP-INFO
             xmlns="http://www.software.ibm.com/P3P/editor/extension-
             1.0.html"
             name="User Information"/>
04     </EXTENSION>
05     <PURPOSE><contact/><individual-analysis/><individual-
         decision/><telemarketing/></PURPOSE>
06     <RECIPIENT><ours/><same required="opt-out"/></RECIPIENT>
07     <RETENTION><business-practices/></RETENTION>
08     <DATA-GROUP>
09     <DATA ref="#user.name"/>
10     <DATA ref="#user.home-info"/>
11     </DATA-GROUP>
12 </STATEMENT>
```

Figure 9.10: P3P example.

collected for the purpose of contacting the client for telemarketing and analysis (line 5). The reason this information is being collected is because it is part of the organization's business practices (line 7).

What happens if an organization lies or does not follow the practices of its policy? It is very easy to put a policy on the Web site that does not reflect the practices of the organization. These policies are not monitored by any organization. However, any false statement on a privacy policy posted on a Web site would violate privacy or antifraud laws in their region.

To find out more information about the P3P standard, please visit *ww.w3.org /P3P/*. To obtain a free P3P editor, visit *www.alphaworks.ibm.com/tech/p3peditor*.

eXtensible rights Markup Language (XrML) 2.0

One of the hardest things to do over the Internet is protect your digital assets. The Internet has enabled the free exchange of various types of assets. At present, the most obvious is recorded music. Exchange of files like those facilitated by Napster have cost the various industries millions upon millions of dollars in lost revenue. Many attempts have been made to thwart illegal access to assets, but most have failed.

Extensible Rights Markup Language (XrML) is an XML vocabulary that is designed to protect digital assets. It can be used to protect assets such as movies, music, books, software, images, documents, and other electronic media.

XrML is based upon Digital Property Rights Language (DPRL), which was developed at the Xerox Palo Alto Research Center (PARC). Written in LISP, DPRL was first introduced in 1996. In 1999 ContentGuard, along with Xerox and Microsoft, ported the DPRL functionality to XML, yielding XrML. The 1999 version of the standard was largely based on DTDs. When version 2.0 was released in 2001, it used XML Schemas.

XrML defines a comprehensive framework for defining rights and conditions to protect content. Content can be restricted to a single use or a limited number of repeated uses as well as restricted to use only by the signer. As described earlier, XrML can protect a wide variety of content.

An XrML document begins with a license. The license is the most important component in XrML. It specifies who can use the resource, what resource the license is for, as well as who has issued the license, and any additional conditions. An inventory can also be used to grant access to multiple assets.

Access is given to a resource by the way of a grant. A grant contains all of the information required to protect the content. The grant contains the following components:

- Principal
- Resource
- Right
- Condition

The Principal is the party who has been issued the grant. The Principal declares only one party for the grant, so this grant cannot be shared or duplicated.

The Resource is what the Principal has been given rights to. A resource can be a movie, a document, a music file, books, software, images, or any other form of digital media. The resource can also be services, such as e-mail or B2B transaction services.

Within the grant a Principal will have Rights to the Resource. A right indicates what type of actions a Principal can perform on the resources. For example, if the resource were a movie or an audio file, the Principal would have play rights, which gives the Principal access to listen to the sound clip or watch the movie. If the resource were a book or a document, the Principal would have print rights, which allow the Principal to print the document.

A Condition defines any special terms and conditions that have been established for the Right. An example of a condition would be a specific time frame in which the resource may be accessed or the number of times a resource may be accessed.

```
01 <grant>
02    <keyHolder licensePartId="Principal">
03       <!-- contains a digital signitature for the Principal -->
04    </keyHolder>
05    <mx:play/>
06    <digitalResource>
07       <nonSecureIndirect URI="http://www.someurl.com/somesong.mp3"/>
08    </digitalResource>
09    <validityInterval>
10       <notBefore>2004-01-01T00:00:00</notBefore>
11       <notAfter>2004-03-31T23:59:59</notAfter>
12    </validityInterval>
13 </grant>
```

Figure 9.11: Grant to an MP3 example.

In Figure 9.11 the Principal is given access to the *play* rights (line 5) for the music file somesong.mp3 (line 7). There is one condition for the access: It is valid only between January 1, 2004, and March 31, 2004 (lines 9 through 12).

XrML can also be used with an XML Digital Signature to ensure that the license has not been altered and to validate the identity of the issuer. XML Encryption may also be used to encrypt the license to ensure that it is kept confidential.

There is no fee to obtain the XrML specification and schema. To find out more about XrML, visit *www.xrml.com.*

In Conclusion

Each one of the XML Security standards provides a unique piece of technology that helps secure corporate data. Together or individually, each provides a unique piece of security that is essential to any organization using XML as its core technology.

There are many obvious reasons to use security. Protecting corporate assets from threats becomes ever more important, especially as new technologies introduce more vulnerability. Hackers have been able to find the smallest compromise and have been able to exploit it. As attacks become more sophisticated, it is becoming more important to protect the data in as many ways as possible.

The importance of these technologies becomes more obvious as attacks are attempted from the inside. The data, no matter where it resides, must be secure so that it cannot be compromised by a virus, a worm, or even an employee.

The XML Security Standards provide a complete suite of technologies that can protect data at any stage of the process. Each one of the following identifies a unique stage in which XML data must be protected:

- XML Digital Signatures ensure that data has not changed while in transit as well as identifying the sender of the message.
- XML Encryption protects the data if it is placed on a file system or while it is in a queue, so that sensitive data cannot be compromised.
- XML Key Management ensures that digital keys are managed properly.

- SAML and XACML together provide a way to provide single-signon authentication as well as identifying access rights to resources.
- XrML protects digital assets by assigning rights and conditions to an asset so that a principal can use it.
- P3P clearly identifies an organization's privacy standards so that users can determine for themselves what they would like the organization to see.

Each one of these standards has been carefully designed. They all work together or individually to provide a complete set of security features.

References
www.w3.org/Signature/
www.w3.org/Encryption/
www.w3.org/2001/xkms/
www.oasis-open.org/specs/index.php#samlv1.1
www.oasis-open.org/committees/tc_home.php?wg_abbrev=xacml
www.w3.org/t3/p3p
www.alphaworks.ibm.com/tech/xmlsecuritysuite
www.xrml.com

10

Web Services

In this chapter you will learn:

- ✓ What are Web services?
- ✓ What can they be used for?
- ✓ The components of a Web service
- ✓ Learn about other Web service technologies: SOAP, WSDL, UDDI
- ✓ The iSeries and Web services

Technologies such as Remote Procedure Calls (RPC), Remote Method Invocation (RMI), and the Distributed Component Object Model (DCOM) make services and features available for remote applications to access. They expose services so that remote systems and applications can access resources. These technologies are widely used within secure networks, but when applied to the Internet the have had limited use. Exposing these services to external organizations have become a challenge requiring many workarounds to meet.

Each of these technologies requires specific network configuration to work with the Internet. The challenge comes in making these technologies work through firewalls and proxy servers. Each of them uses specific communication protocols that are usually denied. Opening channels to allow the necessary communication through a firewall can expose the organization to additional and unwanted threats.

Another limitation of RPC, RMI, and DCOM is that they each require a specific language or platform for communication. DCOM requires Windows-based applications and platforms, RMI requires Java-based applications, and RPCs require a similar system to communicate with. This limits the clients that the system can communicate with.

With the advent of XML, it became obvious that existing technologies could be used to leverage services on the Internet. XML provided a versatile messaging format that can be structured using XML Schemas and DTDs. Internet communication technologies such as HTTP, FTP, and SMTP can also provide the transport mechanism for Internet servicing. The communication protocols are well established and have well-documented security instructions. They can be restricted by firewalls without limiting their capabilities.

These concepts are the foundation on which the Web Services specification was created. Web services use a technology best-of-breed to solve the Internet servicing problem.

What Are Web Services?

A Web service is a business interface that is exposed over the Internet. Web services use a format of XML called SOAP (originally an acronym for Simple Object Access Protocol)_as the message format and use existing technologies such as HTTP, HTTPS, FTP, and SMTP for communication. In a simple example, shown in Figure 10.1, a client makes a request to a Web service by sending a SOAP request. The SOAP message contains all of the parameters necessary to process the request. The Web service performs all the necessary actions. Once it has completed processing, the Web service generates a SOAP response and returns it to the client.

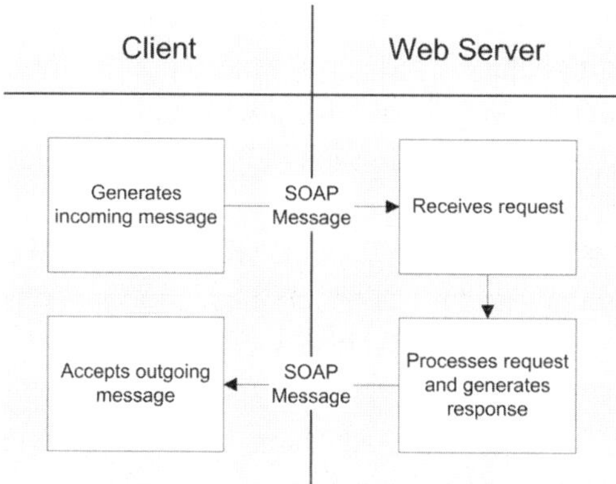

Figure 10.1: Simple Web service request.

As described, this is a simple version of a Web service. Web services can be configured to handle a few different methods of communication. They can be configured for client requests only with no response, request/response, Web service request with no remote response, and Web service request with remote response. These various types of communication provide a wide variety of functionality and potential usage.

Why Use Web Services?

One of the most common pitfalls in developing applications is locking into a technology. Committing components to specific technologies may force other components to join into the same technology group. This commitment may limit future expansion and upgrade capabilities of the infrastructure. With Web services, organizations are not trapped into a specific technology. The services can be removed and replaced without difficulty. They can be easily integrated with a great many other technologies and with very little effort. Most common development tools, such as .NET, WebSphere Studio Application Developer, and JBuilder, all provide a means to integrate code with Web services.

Web services provide a simple way to expose business commands on the Internet. With Universal Description, Discovery, and Integration (UDDI), which will be described later, Web services can permit organizations to expand their markets by adding their services into a registry. New customers using various filters can search the registry to find services to meet their needs. Once the service has been found, the application knows how to establish communication with it as by referencing a description file known as a WSDL file.

Let's not forget the potential internal use of Web services. Web services can be deployed inside architectures for use as an integration layer. The presentation layer can send SOAP messages to Web services, which can provide access to all of the necessary back-end systems. Web services can also be used in clusters to ensure that there is high availability for them. Hardware solutions can also be used to ensure that there is high availability.

Because Web services use Internet communication technologies, common and well-established security measures can be used to protect the data. Internet technologies use known ports and can be secured with the various methods as follows:

- Web servers can prevent access by IP.
- Hardware security such as firewalls and routers can prevent access based upon address, request type, and network location.
- Software solutions, such as operating systems and proxy servers, can prevent access by address.
- XML security standards can be used with Web services. They prevent unauthorized access during transmission, ensure the integrity of the message, and confirm the identity of the sender, as described in Chapter 9.

Web services provide a great deal of functionality and versatility, primarily because of the technologies that they have adopted.

How Web Services Work

Web services are not difficult to create. The process of creating and deploying a Web service contains the following steps:

1. Code and develop the service and supporting classes.

2. Package the Web service.
3. Deploy the package.

The first step is, of course, the development of the Web service. The code for a Web service can be written in any of various languages, including Java, C++, C#, and Visual Basic.Net. A Web service can expose multiple methods so that logically grouped features can be combined inside a single service.

```
package com.example.webservice;

public class CreditLimitService
{
   private double customer1Limit = 1000;
   private double customer2Limit = 2000;
   private double customer3Limit = 1500;

   public double getCreditLimit(String customerNumber)
   {
   // returns the customers credit limit
      if (customerNumber.equals("1"))
         return customer1Limit;
      if (customerNumber.equals("2"))
         return customer2Limit;
      if (customerNumber.equals("3"))
         return customer2Limit;
      return 0;
   }

   public void setLimit(String customerNumber, double newLimit)
   {
   // Sets the customers limit to the value passed in
      if (customerNumber.equals("1"))
         customer1Limit = newLimit;
      if (customerNumber.equals("2"))
         customer2Limit = newLimit;
      if (customerNumber.equals("3"))
         customer3Limit = newLimit;
   }

   public void increaseLimit(String customerNumber,
    double increaseAmount)
   {
   // increases the customers Limit by
```

Figure 10.2: Simple Java Web service example (part 1 of 2).

```
        if (customerNumber.equals("1"))
            customer1Limit += increaseAmount;
        if (customerNumber.equals("2"))
            customer2Limit += increaseAmount;
        if (customerNumber.equals("3"))
            customer3Limit += increaseAmount;
    }
}
```

Figure 10.2: Simple Java Web service example (part 2 of 2).

The Web service example class shown in Figure 10.2 looks no different from any other Java class. That is because it isn't. The class is built no differently from other Java classes and has no additional components. However, there are ways of developing this example more efficiently specifically for a Web service implementation.

The example code exposes three methods: getCustomerLimit, setLimit, and increaseLimit. Each of these expects the customerNumber as a parameter, and the setLimit and increaseLimit methods expect an amount.

Once the application has been developed, the classes must be packaged. Most IDEs provide a means of packaging Web services. WebSphere Studio Application Developer provides the ability to export a Web project to a WAR file (Web application archive). This process automatically includes all of the necessary packages and creates the necessary metadata for the services. Other utilities such as Apache Ant and wscompile can be used to compile the project and to generate the metadata. Each of these compiles the classes and generates information about the Web service, such as the end point and the WSDL files.

The deployment of the Web service depends greatly upon the application server being used. Each server provides a unique method of deploying the Web services. As different as each deployment procedure will be, all will end with the service being exposed. There are additional tools, such as Ant and wsdeploy, that can be used to deploy Web services. They use the information generated during the packaging to determine the available services and provide an interface in which requests can be communicated.

How Do Web Services Differ from Other Technologies?

Why use Web service technology to communicate with other applications? The answer is obvious: Web services are made for application-to-application communication. Web services have been designed specifically to enable one application to access a Web service and have specific and effective language for communication.

Other technologies, such as JavaServer Pages (JSP), servlets, Microsoft Active Server Pages (ASPs), and CGI applications, are made specifically for human interaction. These technologies use forms to submit information to a server-side application for processing. A user enters information on an HTML form and submits it. The results are processed and presented to the user in HTML format. This works well for users, but for other computers such output means little.

There are ways to use these technologies to produce an output for applications rather than human eyes. One way is to have an application submit a form by using URL parameters and have the server-side application produce XML. The calling application would parse the results and continue with its processing. However, this does not make valuable use of developers' time. The time and effort required to generate this type of functionality can be used more effectively elsewhere. And why should developers spend their time inventing something when it already exists with Web services?

Web services have a well-documented language specifically for their own use. Web services use the SOAP specification for communication. (SOAP messages will be discussed in detail in the next section.) SOAP messages are structured specifically for Web service communication.

Communicating with a Web Service

In the past, applications would communicate with each other across a network using Remote Procedure Calls (RPC). RPC technology spans back to the mid-1970s and since then has provided the infrastructure for clients to communicate with servers. The server listens and waits for an incoming request. Once the server accepts a request, it performs any necessary processing and sends a response back to the client.

RPCs have worked very well, but they have some limitations that have become obvious as other technologies have evolved. As long as RPCs communicate with applications on the same or a similar system, they work well. Communication and compatibility issues arise when different systems try to communicate. The results are unpredictable, and a great deal of time has been spent repairing the problem.

Another limitation with RPCs became evident when advanced network hardware or software was implemented. RPCs have difficulties accessing resources through firewalls or proxy servers, because those devices act as an intermediate step in the network communication. To make RPCs work with these technologies required extra channels to be opened up, or patch solutions were used to correct the problem. Rarely has there been a simple solution to allow for this type of communication. As these fixes were implemented, the network became less secure.

With the adoption of the Internet, it was clear that a new technology had to emerge that would allow communication between any combination of hardware and software. The W3C group had come together with many industry leaders and developed a specification that would provide communication of this type. The technology, SOAP, is a communication protocol that uses XML as the language and HTTP as the transport mechanism. It is the ideal method for application-to-application communication over the Internet.

What is SOAP?

SOAP is simply a communication protocol specifically for communication between two applications over the Internet. SOAP messages are used to invoke services, methods, objects, components, and servers.

The difference between SOAP and other RPC-like methods is that SOAP is platform- and technology-independent. Because SOAP messages are in XML and use HTTP as the transport mechanism, the requirements for sending and receiving SOAP messages are available on almost every platform.

SOAP is a stateless, one-way messaging framework. The protocol provides the description of how a SOAP message will be processed and all the required actions that must be taken by a step in the processing. Although SOAP has been defined as a one-way messaging framework, more complex interaction patterns can be implemented in request/response and request/multiple responses scenarios.

The SOAP Recommendation

After a great deal of work, UserLand, Ariba, Commerce One, Compaq, Developmentor, HP, IBM, IONA, Lotus, Microsoft, and SAP proposed the SOAP standard to the W3C group in May 2000. The current recommendation is version 1.2, which was released on June 24, 2003. This book will focus on version 1.2.

The recommendation is broken into three parts: Part 0 (the Primer), Part 1 (Messaging Framework), and Part 2 (Adjuncts).

Part 0: The Primer

The Primer is a less-technical document meant as an introduction to the specification. It is an example-based tutorial that describes the basics of the standard. For developers who will be using SOAP in their applications, it is the best place to start. When the details are required, the other two parts should be referenced.

The Primer can be found at *www.w3.org/TR/soap12-part0/.*

Part 1: Messaging Framework

Part 1 of the specification defines the framework in which each SOAP message is processed. It includes the following aspects:

- Features and concepts of SOAP
- The syntax of a SOAP message
- The SOAP processing model
- The SOAP Protocol-binding framework

SOAP Message Exchange Patterns (MEPs) are among the features and concepts defined in the specification. MEPs define how messages are exchanged between SOAP nodes.

Within the specification are the instructions for how to structure the SOAP message. The specification defines the entire syntax for the SOAP envelope, header, body, and fault elements. This part of the specification defines all of the allowable elements, attributes, and required namespaces for the entire SOAP message.

This section of the specification also defines how a SOAP receiver processes a single SOAP message, also known as the *SOAP processing model.* The SOAP processing model is stateless and does not have any dependencies or knowledge of any other message. SOAP messages can be processed in a distributed model where many systems can aid in the processing before the message is sent to the *ultimate SOAP receiver.* These systems are known as *SOAP intermediaries.*

One of the many features of SOAP is the ability to exchange SOAP messages using a wide variety of protocols. The set rules that define how the message is transferred with or on top of another protocol is known as a binding. The SOAP Protocol Binding framework defines the rules as well as the relationship between the bindings and the SOAP nodes.

The Messaging Framework section can be found at *www.w3.org/TR/soap12-part1/.*

Part 2: Adjuncts

Part 2 of the specification defines the additional components that may be used with the messaging framework. Some of the adjuncts available are

- SOAP Data Model
- SOAP Encoding
- SOAP RPC Representation
- A convention for describing features and bindings

- SOAP-supplied Message Exchange Patterns and features
- SOAP Web Method
- SOAP HTTP Binding

Each one of these items is optional for the SOAP specification. They may be included when the specification needs to be extended to meet some need. For example, if SOAP messages are to be used over HTTP, the SOAP HTTP Binding will be used, because the exchange requires the use of the HTTP protocol.

The Adjuncts section can be viewed at *www.w3.org/TR/soap12-part2/*.

Components of a SOAP Message

There are four main sections to a SOAP message: the envelope, the header, the body, and the fault. The SOAP envelope is the document element for the SOAP message. It identifies the XML document as a SOAP message. The children of the SOAP envelope are the header, body, and fault elements. The envelope element requires a namespace reference to *http://www.w3.org/2003/05/soap-envelope*.

The SOAP header element contains application-specific information related to the processing of the message. The header is an optional element and does not contain any of the essential message data. Typically, information inside the header is intended for the SOAP intermediaries, which are processes that, depending on the application, may need to be executed before the message is sent to the ultimate SOAP receiver.

The SOAP Body is a required part of the message. It contains the primary contents intended for the ultimate endpoint. The data found inside this element will be used in the processing of the request and will be unique for the specific request being executed.

In the event that there is an error in the processing of the SOAP message, the SOAP *fault* element will provide the necessary information for the exception processing. The fault element is not required in order for the message to be processed.

```
01    <ns:getCreditLimit xmlns:ns="http://example.com/CreditLimitService">
02        <p0 i:type="d:string">1</p0>
03    </ns:getCreditLimit >
```

Figure 10.3: Example of a SOAP request.

The SOAP request example shown (with added line numbers) in Figure 10.3 can be used to communicate with the Web service shown in Figure 10.2. Specifically, the code in Figure 10.3 is included inside the SOAP body element. On line 1, the method that has been requested from the Web service is *getCreditLimit*. The parameter for the execution (line 2) is defined as a string and contains the value of 1.

```
01    <ns:getCreditLimitResponse
          xmlns:ns="http://example.com/CreditLimitService">
02            <response i:type="d:double">1000</response>
03    </ns:getCreditLimitResponse>
```

Figure 10.4: Example of a SOAP response.

The response to the request in Figure 10.3 is shown (again with added line numbers) in Figure 10.4. Like the request in Figure 10.3, this content would be found inside the SOAP body element. Line 1 indicates that the message is a response of the *getCreditLimit* method, and the value of the response is found on line 2.

Describing Web Services

Web Services Description Language (WSDL) describes how a requestor communicates with a Web service. The WSDL provides a model, in XML format, describing the exposed components of a Web service. This includes the exposed routines and their parameters as well as how to call the Web service. The input and output messages are also defined with the intent that another application will know how to communicate with the Web service.

Traditional Web-based applications present a user a form that should have a set of instructions describing its use. These instructions enable a user to take his input and enter it in the proper form fields. Once completed, the user submits the form and awaits the response. The HTTP server processes the request, and the results are generated in HTML format and sent back to the user.

What if the user cannot understand the instructions or the language the instructions were written in? The answer is simple: The user cannot submit the form. The user does not know where to place his information and is unable to complete the form. Now, what if the user is not a human being (who might be able to puzzle the form out) but another application, trying to communicate to another application using a Web service? How does the application know where to put its data? Again the answer is simple: It doesn't.

One solution would be to generate the SOAP request inside client code. This way works when the Web service is well known—for example, if the Web service is an internal resource. When changes are made to the Web service, they will typically be developed alongside updates in the custom code that generates the SOAP message. This approach, however, is not as simple when the Web service is external and changes happen without notice or if you have just found out the service exists.

Solving this problem is the purpose of WSDL: how to provide another application with the instructions on how to communicate with a Web service. WSDL describes the structure of the SOAP message to a Web service.

WSDL Essentials

A WSDL document is an XML document that details how a *requestor*, or a calling application, can communicate with a *provider*, which is a Web service. The WSDL document defines the requests and the responses for the Web service. The request and responses are the SOAP messages used to perform an action on the Web service.

The WSDL specification has defined the description of a Web service with two different types of definitions: abstract and concrete. An abstract definition defines the components of the incoming and outgoing messages. It defines the following type of information for a Web service:

- The requested service
- Incoming/outgoing parameters
- Data types for each of the parameters using XML Schemas

Concrete definitions identify the attributes of the service: Components such as the URL of the service as well as how to bind the parameters to the service are examples of concrete definitions. Binding information provides a mapping between the defined message and the Web service.

A note is necessary regarding WSDL: It is not really intended for human eyes. It is readable, and sense can be made out of its syntax, but it is intended for applications to understand how to interact with a Web service. The definitions are precise and do not contain any human-readable components.

The WSDL specification was developed by Ariba, IBM, and Microsoft and is a W3C note. For this book, the WSDL 1.1 specification will be used. For more information about this specification, visit *www.w3.org/TR/wsdl*.

Advantages of WSDL

There are a few possible approaches to accessing a Web service from an application. One approach is to write the connection and communication to the Web service. This would include the generation of the SOAP request message, establishment of a connection to the Web service, transfer of the request, acceptance of the response, and parsing of the incoming values. During this development, exception handling would have to be developed in the event that the service is unavailable or there is some error involving the connection, data typing, or some unknown condition. This is not the best use of developers' time and consumes very large amounts of it. It becomes quite difficult to manage this type of code when many or complicated Web services are involved.

One of the advantages of using WSDL is that it can be used to generate a stub or skeleton code for a Web service. This stub exposes the incoming and outgoing parameters as methods and provides some sort of an *execute* command. The stub handles the connection to and from the Web service as well all of the exception handling for the communication. Stubs can be generated for any language, including Java and .NET.

WSDLs can be used for applications that are not familiar with the Web service to communicate with it. Applications that do not have custom written code or stubs can examine the WSDL and understand how to generate the SOAP request. This is used in conjunction with UDDI so that applications can automatically find Web services exposed by other organizations that suit their needs. This would allow organizations to automatically find shipping companies to transport merchandise across the country. This process would be transparent to the company, because the application would make the request to the shipping company. UDDI will be described in the next section of this chapter.

Components of WSDL

As described earlier, there are two types of definitions for Web services using WSDL: abstract and concrete. These elements provide the building blocks for defining a Web service. The abstract elements provide the elements that expose the means of communicating with a Web service, and the concrete elements provide for binding the message to the Web service.

Abstract Elements

Abstract definitions include elements that describe the incoming and outgoing messages. There are three abstract elements that are used to describe the messages: *portType*, *message*, and *types*. These three elements define the components of the incoming and outgoing messages.

Types

The *types* element defines the structure of the SOAP message. The structure is determined by the XML schemas that have been declared inside the *types* element. The schemas can be either referenced externally or declared inside the *types* section. Referencing the schema externally allows for greater flexibility when the structure of the data changes.

```
<definitions>
<types>
  <schema xmlns:xs="http://www.w3.org/2001/XMLSchema">
    <complexType name="nameType">
      <sequence>
        <element name="firstname" type="xs:string"/>
        <element name="initial" type="xs:string"/>
        <element name="lastname" type="xs:string"/>
      </sequence>
    </complexType>
    <complexType name="addressType">
      <sequence>
        <element name="address" type="xs:string"/>
        <element name="city" type="xs:string"/>
        <element name="state" type="xs:string"/>
        <element name="zipcode" type="xs:string"/>
        <element name="country" type="xs:string"/>
      </sequence>
    </complexType>
    <complexType name="customerType">
      <sequence>
        <element name="name" type="xs:nameType"
         minOccurs="1" maxOccurs="1"/>
        <element name="address" type="xs:addressType"
         minOccurs="1" maxOccurs="2"/>
      </sequence>
    </complexType>
    <element name="limit" type="xs:decimal" />
  </schema>
  . . .
</types>
</definitions>
```

Figure 10.5: Customer schema in WSDL types *element.*

The types element shown in Figure 10.5 defines the structure of the customer information by explicitly declaring the schema. The structure defined in this schema will be used to generate the SOAP message.

Message

The *message* element defines the components of the SOAP message by referencing the types or elements defined in the *types* element of the WSDL document. The *message* element contains one or more logical structures that build the message.

```
<definitions>
   . . .
   <message name="customerInformation">
      <part name="customer" type="xs:customerType" />
   </message>
   <message name="resultMessage">
      <part name="result" element="xs:limit" />
   </message>
   . . .
</definitions>
```

Figure 10.6: Messages defined using the schemas in the types *element of Figure 10.4.*

The *message* element contains one or more *part* elements, which refer to SOAP structures defined inside a schema. The WSDL code in Figure 10.6 defines the part of the SOAP message named *customerInformation* and references the *customerType* defined in the schema described in Figure 10.5. The second message, named *resultMessage*, defines a message that references an element (also defined in the schema) rather than a type.

Port Types

The *portType* element defines the connection point to the Web service. This information identifies the service, the operation type that can be executed, and the parameters used by the operation. It will be used with the binding element to bind the Web service parameters to the values in the SOAP message.

WSDL allows for four different types of transmissions, otherwise known as operations. The four types of operations are one-way, request/response, solicit/response, and notification. One-way transmissions are performed when a client requests an operation from a Web service. In this type of transmission the client does not expect a response from the Web service. Only input parameters are used in this transmission. This type of transmission would be used in a queue environment.

Notification transmissions are very similar to one-way transmissions. They are used when the Web service sends a message and does not expect a response. Output parameters would be the only types defined in the operation. This type of transmission would be the response used in a queue environment.

Request/response or two-way transmissions define transmissions in which the client sends a SOAP request and the Web service responds with a SOAP response. Both input and output parameters are used to define a request/response transmission. In the solicit/response transmission, the opposite of the request/response transmission, the Web service sends a message and receives a response.

In both of these latter types there are input and output parameters. How these two types of transmissions are differentiated are by the order of the parameters. In request/response transmissions the input parameters are defined first and then the request parameters. The solicit/response transmissions have the opposite definitions.

```
01 <definitions>
02    . . .
03    <portType name=“getCustomerLimitType”>
04       <operation name=“getCustomerLimit”>
05          <input message=“ns:customerInformation”/>
06          <output message=“ns:Result”/>
07       </operation>
08    </portType>
09    . . .
10 <definitions>
```

Figure 10.7: portType *element describing the two-way* getCustomerLimit *operation.*

In Figure 10.7, the *portType* element beginning on line 3 describes the port *getCustomerLimitType*. Inside this element is the definition for the *getCustomerLimit* operation, located on lines 04 through to 08.

The *operation* element also defines the parameters that will be exchanged in the communication. The example in Figure 10.7 is a request/response transmission. On line 5 and 6, the input parameter is defined before the output parameter. The *input* element on line 5 describes the value being sent to the Web service, in this example the *customerInformation* type from the namespace *ns* will be used. The namespace defines the type of data that will be used. The *output* parameter defined on line 4 is named *ns:Result* and will be part of the response. The XML schema can reference another file, or the WSDL can include the schema definition.

Concrete Elements

A concrete element pulls together the abstract elements that have defined the message and binds the SOAP message to the Web service. The concrete elements define where the messages are placed in the SOAP message, what the transport mechanism is, and where it gets sent. There are two main elements to concrete elements: binding elements and service elements.

Binding

The *binding* element maps the message and port type defined for using the abstract elements to the outgoing SOAP message and the transport mechanism. For each port type defined there will be a binding definition.

The binding information begins with the declaration of the *binding* element with a name and the port type it will be mapping. Inside the binding node is the SOAP transport mechanism. In this chapter we will be focusing mainly on HTTP transportation, but there are other transportation methods available, including HTTPS, SMTP, and FTP. When files are sent via SMTP, the SOAP message can be sent as an attachment or as part of the e-mail body.

For each message that is sent or received for an operation, the binding element maps the components to the various sections of the SOAP message. The components of the message can be placed in the SOAP body or header.

```
<definitions
   xmlns=“http://schemas.xmlsoap.org/wsdl/”
   xmlns:soap=“http://schemas.xmlsoap.org/wsdl/soap/”>
   . . .
   <binding name=“GetCustomerLimitSOAP” type=“getCustomerLimitType”>
      <soap:binding style=“rpc”
        transport=“http://schemas.xmlsoap.org/soap/http”/>
```

Figure 10.8: Binding information for the GetCustomerLimit operation (part 1 of 2).

```
05        <operation name="getCustomerLimit">
06           <input>
07              <soap:body parts="customer" use="literal"/>
08           </input>
09           <output>
10              <soap:body parts="result" use="literal"/>
11           </output>
12        </operation>
13     </binding>
14   . . .
15 </definitions>
```

Figure 10.8: Binding information for the GetCustomerLimit operation (part 2 of 2).

Figure 10.8 describes how the *getCustomerLimitType* port type is bound to the Web service messages. In the *binding* element on line 3, the *getCustomerLimitType* is the referenced port type. Line 4 defines the transportation method as HTTP. For the operation *getCustomerLimit* (line 5), there are two messages defined: one as the *input* message and the other as the *output*. The *input* message (lines 6 through 8) maps the *customer* message to the SOAP body. When the SOAP message is generated, the Web service will expect the *customer* element inside of the SOAP body. When the Web service has completed its processing, it will return the result element in the SOAP body element of the response (lines 9 through 11). If there were a need to have elements inside the SOAP header, the following would be used inside either the *input* or *output* operation components: *<soap:header part="name" use="literal" />*.

Services

The final component to a WSDL definition is the *services* element. Services map the SOAP message described in the binding definition to the transport mechanism parameters. The service element defines the final destinations, known as ports, for the message. There can be several ports for a message. None of the ports is dependent on any other, and they are not inputs for other ports.

```
<definitions>
   . . .
   <service name="GetCustomerLimitService">
```

Figure 10.9: WSDL service example (part 1 of 2).

```
      <port name="CustomerLimitPort"
       binding="ns:GetCustomerLimitSOAP ">
            <soap:address location="http://somesite/someservice"/>
      </port>
    </service>
    . . .
</definitions>
```

Figure 10.9: WSDL service example (part 2 of 2).

Uses for WSDL

One advantage of WSDL is the ability to generate stub code, a generated interface to a Web service that exposes all of the operations that are available. The code handles all of the communication and data marshalling. This eliminates the need to develop a communication code with a Web service. Most IDEs that support Web services have a process of generating stub code.

Another use, which will be discussed in the next section, is UDDI. Without giving too much away from the next section, UDDI allows for the automatic discovery of Web services and, with the use of WSDL, provides all of the information for communication with a service.

Finding Web Services

Imagine a world without a phone book, specifically the Yellow Pages. There would be no means of finding restaurants for dinner or taxicab companies to get a ride to and from the airport. Or imagine the Internet without search engines. How would users search for Web sites without knowing the sites were there? The user would have to know the address to every Web site.

This is one of the issues when it comes to Web services: How can you find a service without knowing about it first? The Internet provides an unlimited range in communication. It can span any geographical or organizational size to provide useful features and information. If there is no way to discover the services that are available, however, then how can they be used?

The Universal Description, Discovery, and Integration (UDDI) specification defines the framework to register and find Web services. With a simple query, a result of all of the companies who ship with refrigerated trailers in New York and Michigan can be easily found. UDDI provides the framework to reach new customers and find organizations that may provide services.

UDDI provides the functionality to register and discover Web services on the Internet. UDDI defines how organizations can place Web services on the Internet. The registry contains information about the exposed Web service and the business that exposes them. The following are examples of the information available in the registry:

- Business name
- Business mailing addresses
- Contact names
- Contact phone numbers
- Web services offered
- Meta-data describing the Web services

Version 2 of the specification for UDDI was approved by the OASIS Group in April 2003. The leading organizations that developed the specification included Accenture, Ariba, Commerce One, Fujitsu, Hewlett-Packard, i2 Technologies, Intel, IBM, Microsoft, Oracle, SAP AG, Sun Microsystems, Inc., and VeriSign.

UDDI is intended to extend organizations with B2B communications. It exposes services to new and existing customers. Because the Internet is widely accepted, UDDI will open organizations to unexpected customer bases as well as resources. UDDI helps find organizations that may have been impossible to find without prior knowledge. When one is searching for organizations, the UDDI registry helps filter through the masses to help find useful services. Once the service has been found, the instructions are clear on how to communicate with the available Web service.

Why register with UDDI? UDDI will expose Web services so that they can be discovered by organizations with which they are not (yet) doing business. By registering Web services, organizations will see easier integration with new and old partners who have also adopted UDDI.

How to Register Using UDDI?

A few items must be identified before a Web service can be published. First, a service provider must be registered. A service provider registration contains information about the organization that will assist in the discovery process. Multiple providers can be registered under the same organization. When multiple providers are registered, a relationship between the providers must be set up.

The following information must be complete in order to register a service provider/Web service:

1. *General Provider Information:* This contains general information about the provider including the owner, provider name, and descriptions.
2. *Contact information:* This contains a list of contacts for the provider. The contacts can be categorized so that technical and nontechnical contacts may be available for a provider.
3. *Category:* Categories will assist during the discovery process. Categories can be filtered to provide a specific search. A wide selection of categorization types is available, including UDDI Types, Standard Industrial Classification (SIC) codes, North American Industry Classification System (NAICS), and Web Service Search Categorization, to mention a few.
4. *Identifier:* This is a unique reference that identifies a provider within an organization. An identifier may be a cost code or a geographic location identifier.
5. *Discovery URLs:* This is a URL pointing to additional technical or descriptive information about the provider.

6. *Relationships:* When more than one provider is identified for an organization, a relationship must be identified between the providers. If there is only one provider, this section is optional.
7. *Services:* The available Web services can be registered using the WSDL file. This provides all of the information necessary to register the Web service. As described in the previous section, it contains all of the incoming and outgoing parameters and, most importantly, the access point for the Web service. Descriptions in many languages can also be associated with a Web service. WSDL provides a short (up to 255-character) description of the access point.

A *tModel* can be used to describe a Web service. This is usually a WSDL file with associated categories and identifiers. tModels can be shared between providers so that the information does not need to be duplicated.

To register a Web service requires a person with some technical knowledge of the Web services. After the information has been registered, only users with the proper login credentials can change the information. There is no charge to register with the Ariba, IBM, and Microsoft UDDI Business Registries (UBR).

How to Inquire About a Web Service

Searching for a Web service requires knowing what you want to search for. Let's take as an example an organization that needs to transport vehicles to another state. There are few options, so the organization decides to use rail to ship the vehicles. This focuses the search on a specific category and allows a user or an application to search a UDDI registry.

Once the results have been found for the search, the user or the application can use the information to make contact with the Web service. If an application is making contact, it can automatically establish communication with the Web service. The WSDL will provide the framework for establishing communication as well as mapping parameters into and out of the SOAP messages.

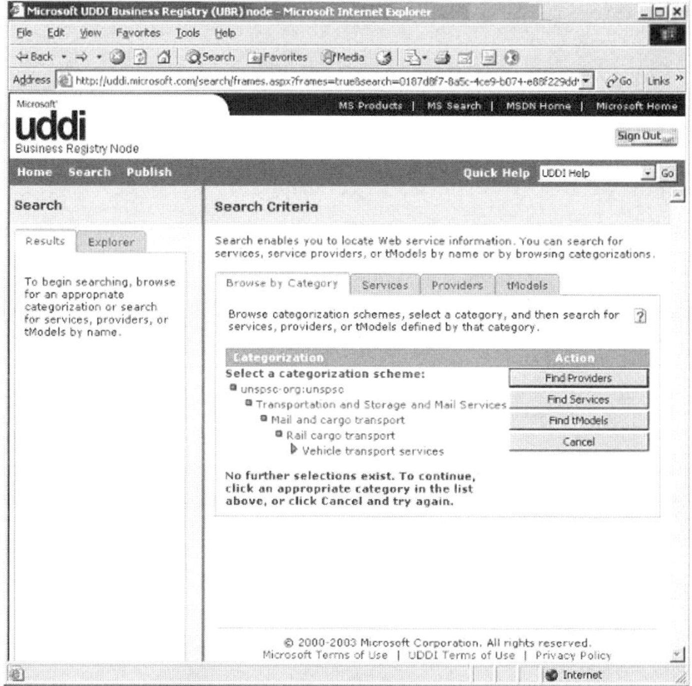

Figure 10.10: Business registry search for vehicle transportation using rail.

To find out more information about UDDI, visit *www.uddi.org*.

Pulling It All Together

Each of these technologies can be used as a specific piece of the communication puzzle. When UDDI is used to find a Web service, the following steps are followed:

1. The Web service has been developed and deployed on the Internet.
2. Using a UDDI Business Node, the Web service has been registered. During the registration, the WSDL for the service was identified so that calling applications can reference the file during the discovery.
3. The client application makes an inquiry to the registry using a filter. The results are returned, and a Web service is selected.

4. The WSDL is requested by the client application.
5. The SOAP request is generated by the client and sent to the Web service.
6. The Web service accepts the request and performs all necessary actions.
7. The resulting SOAP response is generated by the Web service and sent to the client.

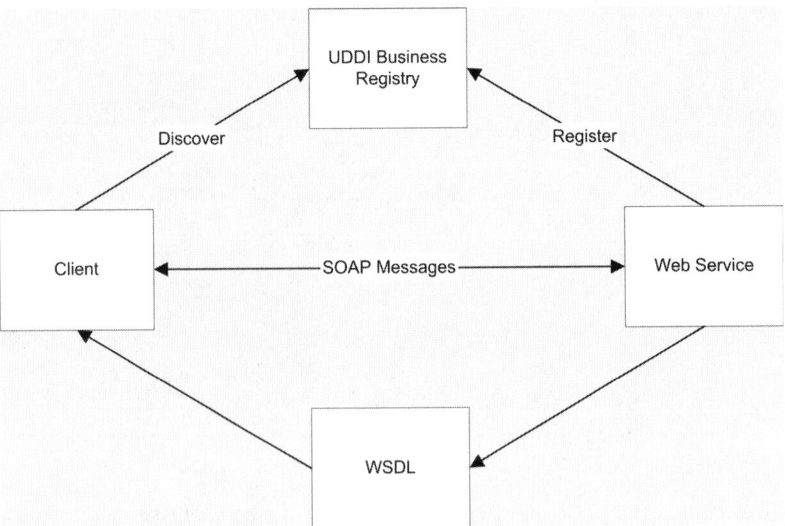

Figure 10.11: How the Web service technologies fit together.

If UDDI is not used to find the Web service, only steps 5 through 7 will be used. This approach is common when the Web service is known to the organization. Stub classes can be used to assist in the integration of a Web service. As described earlier, the WSDL is used to generate the stub code.

Web Services and the iSeries

Now how do all these Web service technologies apply to the iSeries? Almost all of these technologies are required for Web service development on the iSeries. Each of these is an integral component of the Web Services foundation.

However, some additional technologies, not yet mentioned, may be necessary for the iSeries:

1. WebSphere Application Server
2. An iSeries program (for example, an RPG program)
3. IBM Toolbox for Java

WebSphere Application Server is the HTTP server that will accept the incoming requests for the Web service. It also acts as the Java application server, which will process the Java code. WebSphere also can be configured to use an SSL key if the channel is required to be secure. A Java Web service will be configured to access iSeries resources through a set of Java classes.

The second item that is required is a resource to access. When deciding how to access iSeries resources, you can choose to use an existing iSeries program or to access the databases directly using a JDBC driver. There are some advantages to using existing iSeries programs. The business logic has already been developed and may be reused to expand its usage.

There are two ways to call iSeries programs from Java: PCML or RMI. The IBM Toolbox for Java provides Program Call Markup Language (PCML), which is an XML representation of the instructions on how to communicate with an iSeries application. PCML can easily be used to create JavaBeans that will access an application. PCML is discussed in Chapter 11.

There are few limitations to using PCML with RPG programs. RPG programs are not by default thread-safe, so they may cause unexpected results when multiple requests are made to the same RPG application. To alleviate this problem, there is a way to make RPG programs serializable. The option *THREAD(*SERIALIZE)* can be added to the *H* spec to ensure that this problem does not occur. Once it has been added, however, there is a potential for performance problems. If the execution takes a significant amount of time because the program is serialized, it may cause some applications to time out.

Java Remote Method Invocation (RMI) provides a way for objects running on one Java Virtual Machine (JVM) to invoke methods on another JVM (on the same or a different computer). By using RMI on the iSeries, various types of iSeries programs can be accessed.

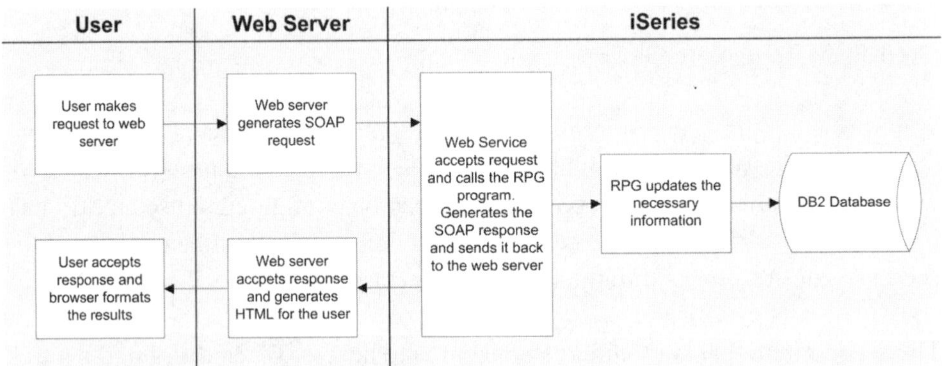

Figure 10.12: Web service implementation with the iSeries.

Figure 10.12 shows a potential implementation of Web services with the iSeries. In this example, the Web service is separate from the iSeries system. For all intents and purposes, it can be on the same system. To limit the exposure the iSeries server has to the Internet, however, the Web server can be placed on another system, and communication between the two systems can be limited.

The Future of Web Services

Are Web services just hype, or does the concept contain enough substance to convince organizations to begin to adopt them? With technologies such as Java, .NET, SOAP, XML, WSDL, and UDDI in its corner, there is a great deal of potential, not to mention the organizations that support Web services, such as IBM, Apache, Sun, and Microsoft, to name a few.

SOAP provides the messaging protocol to and from the Web service. Built on XML technology, SOAP messages are used as the message format for the requests and responses. SOAP provides a technology-independent messaging format that can be transmitted through most hardware technologies built for restricted access.

The description language, WSDL, provides applications the information necessary to communicate with a Web service. WSDL files are used to generate stub code so that developers do not have to waste time generating SOAP messages; the stub code does it for them. As well, it handles the communication with the Web service.

Coupled with WSDL, UDDI provides the means of publishing a Web service into a registry. An organization can query this registry to find the services it requires. The WSDL is referenced, and the application knows exactly how to format the SOAP message.

Web services extend the use of existing RPG and other iSeries applications. By using Web services to expose existing applications, you can provide a new interface to your back-end systems and resources. This approach provides a new way to architect applications and give a new role to the iSeries. Various applications, platforms, and development languages can use stub code or SOAP messages to communicate with iSeries Web services.

Web services provide a technology-independent interface to back-end resources. Using available tools and existing technologies, Web services can be easily implemented in most organizations to provide immediate benefits.

References
www.w3.org/TR/soap12-part0/
www.w3.org/TR/wsdl
www.uddi.org/
ant.apache.org/

11

Beyond the Web

In this chapter you will learn:

- ✓ How XML and its technologies are not limited to the Internet
- ✓ How XML can fit in an organization
- ✓ How XML can communicate with iSeries programs
- ✓ Various products that can be used with XML and the iSeries

It is obvious by now how powerful XML has become. XML itself has the capability of storing any format of data. An XML document can be structured in any format, with the structure enforced by the use of DTDs or XML schemas. XML can be used with XSLT to produce HTML pages, PDF documents, new XML documents, and other presentations simply by applying an XSL stylesheet. XSLT provides a means of transforming XML documents into other formats. When Web services are exposed, they allow other organizations to access core business systems remotely by sending SOAP messages with HTTP or HTTPS. XPointer and XLink provide a scalable and reliable linking solution. By using XPath, XPointer can limit the results returned to a client for an XML document. Coupled with XLink, the management of the links is centralized. To cap it off,

XML Security can be applied to all of these areas to ensure that the integrity of the message and the participants is maintained.

These technologies provide the building blocks for developing a comprehensive and scalable solution for the Web, each of these providing a key part to an XML-based solution. Not all of these components are required in developing a solution. One of advantages of these standards and recommendations is that there are no interdependencies.

The Internet is not the only use for XML technologies, however. To this point, this book has had a slight trend in content towards the Internet. This is because the primary use for most of these technologies is for the Internet. As these technologies evolved, however, new uses were conceived and eventually implemented. XML technologies can provide a great deal of functionality in many places within an organization.

A recent consideration has been to use XML and its technologies within an application framework. The core of the framework should use XML as the message format. By using XML, it would enable any XML data structure to be transmitted through an architecture.

The ideal solution would promote reuse and a simple means of communicating with the architecture. With XML as the message format, any application that can generate an XML document can communicate with any back-end system connected to the application framework.

The "XML" in Architecture

How do XML technologies fit inside an application architecture? Simply, they fit everywhere. The XML technologies provide a great deal of functionality that can be spread throughout an entire architecture.

Many project efforts can be led into "silo" development, in which the development is focused on the tasks at hand and does not consider the efforts used in other projects. This heads-down approach typically ends with duplicate development and integration to back-end systems.

In typical application architectures, the system is divided into separate, distinct sections, thus allowing any component to be updated or replaced without affecting the other components. The layers found in an application architecture would include the following:

- Presentation layer
- Transportation (optional)
- Business logic
- Integration layer
- Data components

The listed components could be connected similarly to Figure 11.1.

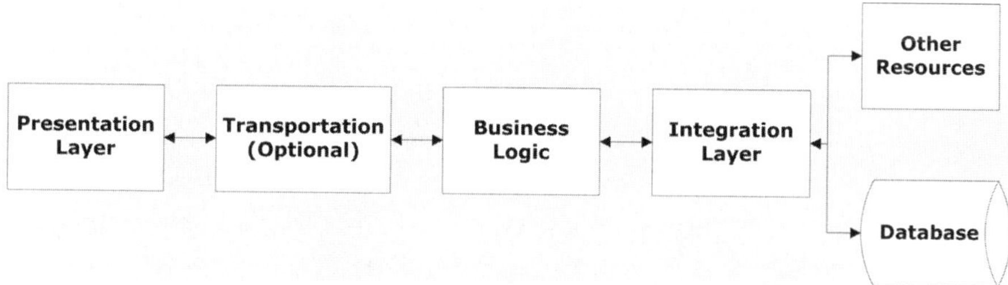

Figure 11.1: A typical application framework.

An architecture provides a standard approach to developing an application. It places separate and distinct components within a system, allowing components to be updated and replaced without disturbing other components. This capability is very important as technology matures. As new technologies emerge, the consideration to replace existing technologies with new is always a challenge. Knowing that a component can be replaced more easily will allow an organization to take advantage of newer technologies without lagging behind.

Another advantage to using an architecture is that it allows for many interfaces into a system. The end result is that the same business logic is executed for many different interfaces. This is a challenge for operations that require updating to many systems. Figure 11.1 shows the presentation layer communicating with the business logic by way of a transportation mechanism. In the event that a presentation layer is not required (for example, for non-Web-based commands from the console), another interface may generate the same message to be sent along the transportation mechanism. This approach would allow other systems besides the presentation layer to communicate with the business logic.

Presentation Layer

The presentation layer accepts incoming requests from a client and readies them for transportation. It can perform some basic validation on the incoming data. For example, it can ensure that all required values are present. It will not perform complex data validation, such as ensuring that shipping dates do not fall on holidays.

The presentation layer submits the request to either the transportation or the business logic layer. If it sends the request to a messaging system such as WebSphere MQ, the request will be formatted within an XML message and placed in a queue. Other options will be discussed later in this chapter.

The last thing that the presentation layer will do is ready the results for presentation to the user. This step is the final preparation of the results prior to responding to the user's request. It is in this step that technologies such as JSP or XSL may be used. Another option available is to use PDML, which defines the layout of an iSeries user interface. It will be discussed later in this section.

XSL

As already mentioned in Chapter 8, XSL can be used to generate the final preparation of the response for the client. From an architecture standpoint, there may be a few factors to consider when deciding which XSL to apply. The device that the client uses will decide which XSL to apply. The formatting for a browser will be much different from that for a handheld device or a cell phone. Another factor may be language. Where multiple languages are to be supported, a separate XSL for each language will determine how to format the results.

JSP

JavaServer Pages (JSPs) can also be used to display the results. In this case, the results will be substituted and placed in key locations on the page. JSPs are equivalent to XSL stylesheets. In the event that different languages and devices need to be supported, a JSP for each will have to be generated.

Speech Recognition

Another interesting technology that may be used when formulating the response is Speech Recognition Grammar Specification (SRGS) Version 1.0. This specification details the format of an XML message that will communicate with a speech recognizer. The speech recognizer will read the XML document and use the clear text found in the XML to generate words and patterns of words to be listened for. This capability can be used in conjunction with other technologies such as XSL. To find out more information regarding the Speech Recognition Grammar Specification, please see the W3 site at *www.w3.org/Voice/.*

Struts

Many existing architectures can be used as a starting point for development. The Struts architecture is a widely accepted and adopted presentation framework for Web development. The architecture, developed by the Apache group and based on Java, uses standard technologies such as servlets, JavaBeans, ResourceBundles, and, of course, XML. The Struts architecture is based on a Model-View-Controller (MVC) paradigm.

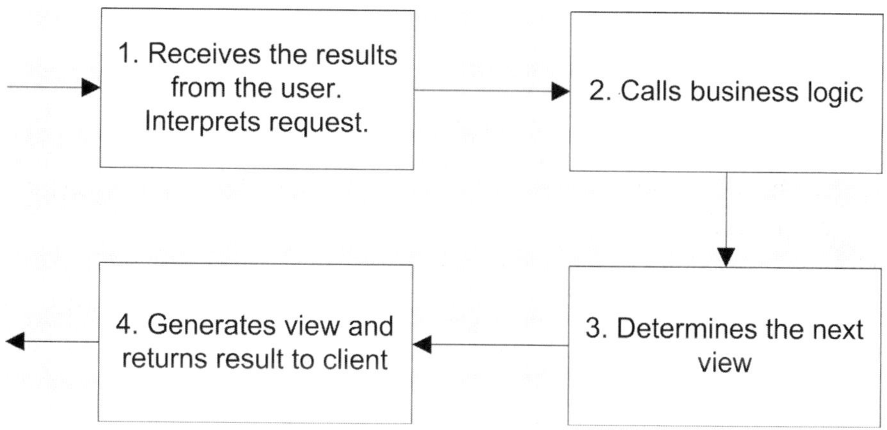

Figure 11.2: MVC request process.

Figure 11.2 shows how MVC handles a simple request. In step 1, the application receives the request from the user. The Controller interprets the request and, in step 2, calls the necessary business logic (the Model). Once the business logic has completed processing, the Controller determines the next View as seen in step 3. Finally, in step 4, the results are generated and returned back to the user.

For more information about the Struts framework, please visit *jakarta.apache.org/struts/index.html*.

PDML

Panel Definition Markup Language (PDML) is a markup language used to define graphical user interfaces (GUIs) for iSeries applications. PDML is a platform-independent language, based on XML syntax, used to define the layout of a user interface.

PDML files are generated using the Graphical Toolbox, which provides a user interface that allows users to create new interfaces and connect them to JavaBeans. Custom help files can be generated along with the interface.

The end result of using PDML is less work to develop an interface, whether for a Java application or for an applet running inside a browser. Because PDML is platform independent, any Java environment can use the file and access iSeries resources.

When PDML is required to run as an applet via the browser, a Java plug-in must be installed and enabled. Sun's Java plug-in is recommended. PDML requires the following components when used with a Java application on the client:

- Graphical Toolbox Jar files
- JVM 1.1.7 or higher

The iSeries system requires V4R2 or later and option 11 from the licensed program menu installed. Option 11 is 5769JC1 - AS/400 Toolbox for Java.

Transportation

The transportation layer component is used to deliver messages between the presentation and business layers. The message format used between these two components can be any format; however, for the purposes of this book it will be an XML message.

The transportation layer is an optional component to an architecture. It may be omitted because the presentation layer may communicate directly with the business layer, or there may be another technology that will interface directly with the business layer, such as Web services.

Although the transportation layer is an optional component to an architecture, it does provide an extra layer or complexity and security to a system. Instead of the presentation layer having direct communication with the business logic and thus the back-end systems, it has a middleware that acts as a transport. The various available transportation mechanisms can be configured to accept traffic only from specific addresses and ports.
This extra layer will protect the business commands from unauthorized access.

When deciding on whether or not to use a transportation mechanism, consider the following:

- Ease of use
- Ease of integration
- Compatibility with other components
- Performance
- Implementation costs

This section will look at two types of transportation vehicles: WebSphere MQ and Web services.

WebSphere MQ

WebSphere MQ is a messaging agent that can communicate with almost any OS and platform. WebSphere MQ is unique in that it guarantees the delivery of a message once it has been received. This capability is extremely important in a mission-critical application.

WebSphere MQ works very simply, which is one of its keys to success. It has queues, which are used to store a collection of incoming messages. Queues will be discussed in greater detail later in this section. Applications connect to the queue and place messages within it; this action is known as *put*. Other applications connect to the same queue and retrieve messages; this action is known as *get*. These actions are shown in Figure 11.3.

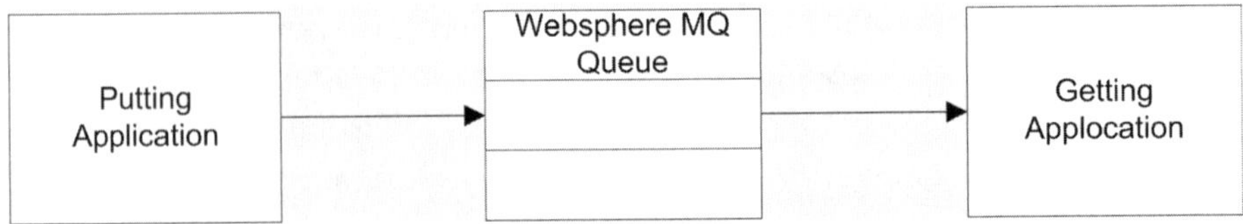

Figure 11.3: Putting messages in a queue and getting them out.

WebSphere MQ can also be set up to work in a request/response mode. In this case the application places a message in one queue and waits for a response message in another queue. On the other side, the waiting application processes the incoming message found in the first queue and puts its response to the other queue for the first application to get (Figure 11.4).

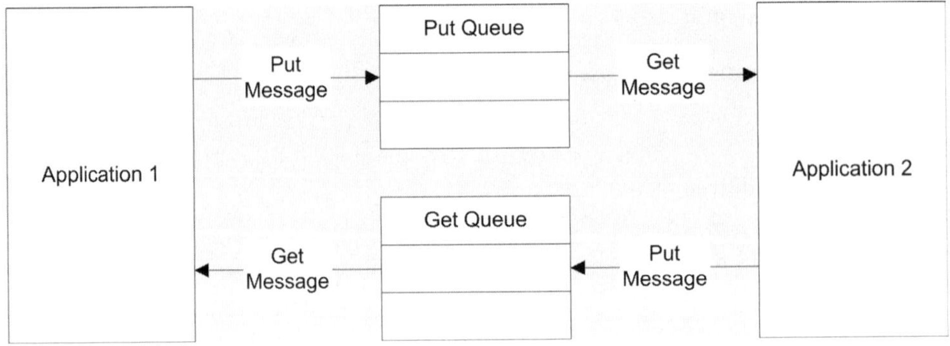

Figure 11.4: Request and response using WebSphere MQ.

Messages can be placed into a queue with specific priorities. This is extremely useful in a batch environment similar to Figure 11.3. When the next message is retrieved, the message with the next applicable priority will be retrieved.

To ensure the integrity of the data being sent, WebSphere MQ ensures that the message is free from errors. This in turn ensures that the application receiving the message has the correct data when it processes the request. Another guarantee is the correct delivery to the proper queue. In an environment that has applications monitoring specific queues, invalid messages are not welcome.

Using WebSphere MQ does not require any special network configuration. It can be configured to use TCP/IP or SNA for the iSeries. With TCP/IP, WebSphere MQ can be configured to use any port to accommodate any infrastructure. Version 5 Release 3 of WebSphere MQ currently supports 35 different platforms and has support for the following operating systems:

- AIX
- HP-UX
- iSeries
- Linux on Intel
- Linux on zSeries
- Sun Solaris
- Windows

This support allows applications to span farther than just the iSeries. In almost all network environments, there are more than just iSeries servers. Deploying WebSphere MQ within a network allows for the possibility to include other systems within applications.

To ensure high availability, WebSphere MQ has the ability to cluster queues. This enables applications to send and receive messages from what appears to be a single queue that is shared across multiple servers. The cluster acts the same as a normal queue, but the data spans multiple servers. This allows systems to go offline without any downtime and, more important, without any lost data.

WebSphere MQ can also be used with Secure Sockets Layer (SSL). With SSL, messages will be encrypted prior to transmission and decrypted once they have been retrieved. This feature ensures that unwanted eyes cannot see the contents of a message.

One of the advantages to using WebSphere MQ on the iSeries is the support for integrated languages and compilers. WebSphere MQ has support for C, C++, COBOL, RPG, and Visual Age C++ for the iSeries as well as Java. The Java integration also contains support for Java Message Service (JMS).

The following paragraphs discuss a few basic concepts necessary for understanding WebSphere MQ:

Messages

A message is simply a string of bytes. The message can be any format, although this book focuses on using XML. The message is a transmission of information from one application to another. The message is meaningful only to the applications that can understand it.

A message contains two parts: the application data and a message descriptor. The application data contains the content of the message. The message descriptor contains metadata regarding the message. The metadata can contain information about the message type and the priority of the message.

Queues

Queues are used to store a set of messages. Applications access queues by putting and getting messages. Messages are retrieved based upon two components: first in, first out (FIFO) and priority. These two factors are used in an algorithm to determine which message can be gotten next. Individual messages may also be retrieved from a queue. To get an individual message, the message ID must be known.

Queue Managers

Queues are managed by Queue Managers. The queue manager maintains the queues that it owns. It is also responsible for placing messages in the appropriate queue when the put action is performed. Messages are put into a queue, not into a queue manager. The queue manager just ensures that the message has been placed into the queue.

The queue manager will also ensure, when requested, that attributes have changed to items it owns, for example, when the priority of a message has changed. The queue manager also ensures the execution of *triggers*. A trigger can be fired when the appropriate criteria have been met. It is the responsibility of the queue manager to ensure that the trigger has been executed.

When queues are clustered, the queue managers on the various systems will communicate. Each system will have a local queue; however, the queue managers will ensure that the information is properly distributed.

Channels

Channels provide communication from one queue manager to another. Channels hide the underlying network communication from the application. Channels can be used to move messages from one queue to another.

Using WebSphere MQ with Java

Using MQ with Java requires the following steps for either put or get operations:

1. Establish the MQ environment.
2. Create a connection to the queue manager.
3. Open the queue with either *Input* or *Output* option set.
4. Set the put or get options for the message.
5. Get or put the message.

```
01 MQEnvironment.hostname = "myservername";
02 MQEnvironment.channel = "mymqchannel";
03 MQEnvironment.port = 1414;
04 MQEnvironment.properties.put(MQC.TRANSPORT_PROPERTY,
     MQC.TRANSPORT_MQSERIES_CLIENT);

05 MQPutMessageOptions putMessageOptions = new MQPutMessageOptions();
06 putMessageOptions.options = MQC.MQPMO_FAIL_IF_QUIESCING;

07 MQQueueManager queueManager = new MQQueueManager("myqueuemanager");
08 MQQueue putQueue = queueManager.accessQueue("myputqueue",
     MQC.MQOO_OUTPUT);

09 MQMessage putMessage = new MQMessage();
10 MQMessage putMessage = new MQMessage();
11 putMessage.expiry = MQC.MQEI_UNLIMITED;
12 putMessage.writeUTF(outMessage);
13 putQueue.put(putMessage, putMessageOptions);
14 putQueue.close();
```

Figure 11.5: Java code for putting a message in WebSphere MQ.

Figure 11.5 shows an example of how a message can be put into a queue. The environment must be configured before any communication with WebSphere MQ. Lines 1 through 4 set the server, the channel, the port, and any other properties. The next two lines, 5 and 6, set the put message options for the current execution. These options indicate how to place the message into the queue. Lines 7 and 8 open the queue manager and the queue. On line 8, the queue is opened with the output option, allowing messages to be added to the queue. Lines 9 to 12 ready the message for delivery. The next line puts the message in the queue using the put message options established on lines 5 and 6. Finally, the queue is closed on line 14.

```
MQEnvironment.hostname = "myservername";
MQEnvironment.channel = "mymqchannel";
MQEnvironment.port = 1414;
MQEnvironment.properties.put(MQC.TRANSPORT_PROPERTY,
  MQC.TRANSPORT_MQSERIES_CLIENT);
```

Figure 11.6: Java code for getting a message from WebSphere MQ (part 1 of 2).

```
05 MQGetMessageOptions getMessageOptions = new
     MQGetMessageOptions();
06 getMessageOptions.options = MQC.MQGMO_WAIT;
07 getMessageOptions.waitInterval = 30000;

08 MQQueueManager queueManager = new MQQueueManager("myqueuemanager");
09 MQQueue getQueue = queueManager.accessQueue("mygetqueue",
     MQC.MQOO_INPUT_AS_Q_DEF);
10 MQMessage getMessage = new MQMessage();

11 getQueue.get(getMessage, getMessageOptions);
12 String szReturnMessage = getMessage.readUTF();
13 getQueue.close();
```

Figure 11.6: Java code for getting a message from WebSphere MQ (part 2 of 2).

Figure 11.6 shows an example of how a message is retrieved from a queue. Lines 1 to 4 show the environment variables being initialized. In this section the server name, the channel, the port, and any other properties are established. The next section establishes the options for getting a message. In lines 5 to 7, the options that have been set mean that the application will wait for 30 seconds before exiting. Lines 8 and 9 create the queue manager and the queue. On line 9, when the queue is created, the queue is opened as an input queue. This option allows for messages to be read from the queue. Lines 10 through 12 get the message out of the queue and into a String variable. The final step, on line 13, closes the queue.

The current version of WebSphere MQ, available at the time of this book, is Version 5.3. To use this version of Websphere MQ with the iSeries requires V5R1 and either TCP or SNA as the network protocol. WebSphere MQ requires approximately 70 MB of disk space for the server portion of the software; the client, if necessary, requires approximately 10 MB. Other disk considerations must be made for the queues. The disk usage depends on the number of queues, the size of the queues, and the size of the messages.

If SSL is used to secure the message transmission, the following additional components are required:

- Digital Certificate Manager (DCM) - OS/400 option 34
- Cryptographic Access Provider AC2 or AC3
- IBM HTTP server

For more information about WebSphere MQ, visit *www-306.ibm.com/software-/integration/wmq/*.

Web Services

Web services were discussed in detail in the previous chapter; however, the focus in that chapter was on how they work on the Internet. The chapter showed how to expose core business commands to other organizations over using the Internet and other networks. This is not the only use for Web services, however.

Web services can be used as a transportation layer just as Websphere MQ can. The Web services would act as the middleware to the business commands so that the presentation layer does not have direct access to the core system. This is accomplished by using other Web service technologies such as WSDL and stub code.

To use Web services as a transport layer requires a separate Web service for each business logic command. The Web service acts as an interface to the business command. The Web Service Description Language (WSDL) from each of the Web services would be used to generate stub code. As described in Chapter 10, the stub code is responsible for the communication, parsing, and generation of the SOAP message. The stub code is compiled and included in the presentation layer. In Figure 11.1, the architecture shows a presentation layer as the only interface that would require communication to the back-end systems.

Once a particular piece of logic is required, the request values are sent; the stub code generates the SOAP message and sends the request to the Web service. The Web service accepts and parses the request, executes the business command, and awaits the results. The SOAP response is then assembled based on the results and sent back to the stub code, which exposes the results to the presentation layer. Figure 11.7 shows how Web services act within a transportation layer.

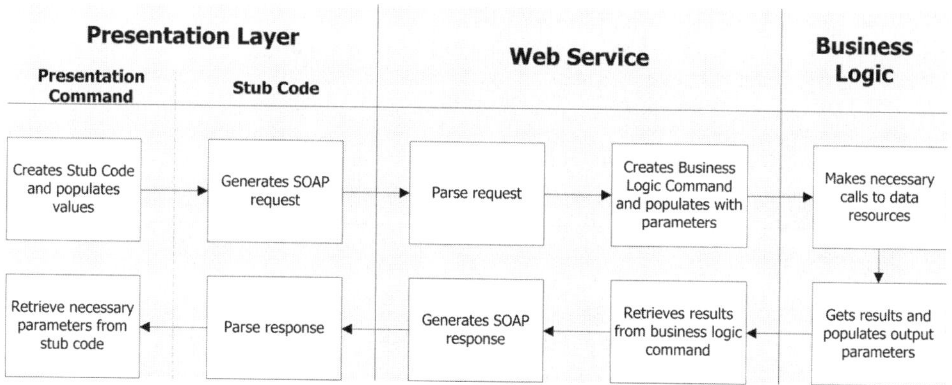

Figure 11.7: Web services as a transportation layer.

Web services work with other technologies to expose business commands. Web services work with various HTTP servers (such as Tomcat, IBM HTTP Server, and WebSphere Application Server) to expose the Web service to the necessary networks.

To use Web services, a Web service capable of executing Java code is required. IBM HTTP Server cannot execute the Web services; it requires a Java application server, for which it can act as a proxy. IBM HTTP Server would be used when the Web service must be exposed to the Internet. It provides a much more secure interface to the Internet. It also acts as another layer for the application; acting as an interface to the back-end processing.

Various measures can be used with an HTTP server to help ensure the security of communication with a Web service. The HTTP server can be configured to work with SSL to ensure that the data is protected while in transit. This prevents access to the data while it is in transit. Another security measure that can be taken is to restrict access by IP address. A configuration value can be set to the address of the systems that will need to communicate with the Web services.

To ensure that the Web services are highly available, load-balancing hardware may be put into place. If an architecture similar to Figure 11.1 were to be placed into a production environment, any downtime could be disastrous. Using a load-balancing hardware component would ensure that when a system is down for whatever reason, no further traffic is sent to that system.

Business Logic and Integration

Business Logic

The first thing that must be accomplished once a request has entered the back end is to ensure that the data is valid. This is the responsibility of the business logic layer, which contains the logic behind the business rules. It is very important that these rules be clear and contain all of the necessary validation. If the business layer attempts to pass inadequately validated information to the integration layer, it may result in loss of integrity of the data in question.

Does this mean that there should be no validation in the back-end stored procedures or iSeries programs? No. In fact, the more the merrier . . . as long as the rules are consistent. There are some rules that cannot be implemented inside the business layer but are crucial to the system. Those rules should remain intact in the database or the various programs.

Care should be taken when implementing rules in both the back end and the business logic layer. There may be situations when the rules can be in conflict. These situations can be avoided by implementing standards for where rules can and cannot be implemented. A diligent analysis of the project would determine the best location for the rules.

The business logic layer will get the request from the presentation layer. Once the request has passed all necessary validation, the application will make use of the integration layer to communicate with the core systems. Once processing is completed, the business logic layer will return the results to the presentation layer. Figure 11.8 shows, in an oversimplified way, how the business logic layer processes an incoming request.

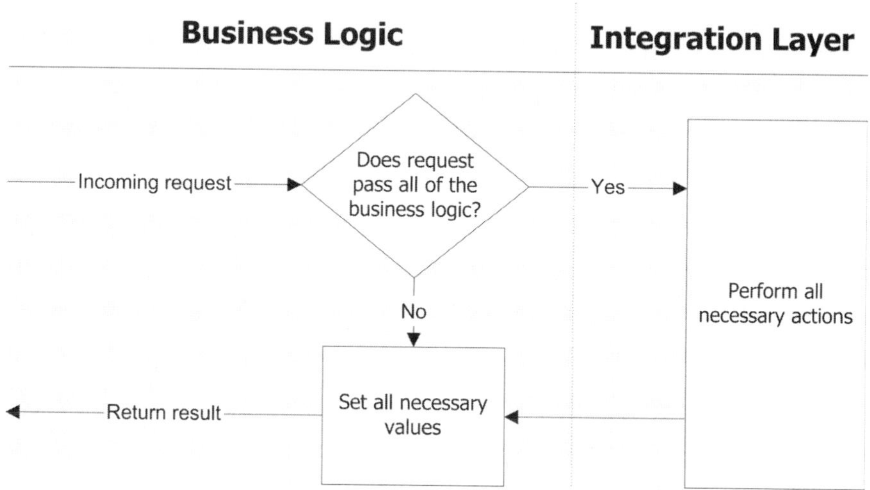

Figure 11.8: Oversimplified view of business logic.

Integration

The second step on the back end is integration to the core systems. Once the business logic has completed its validation of the data, it attempts to access the core systems by using the integration layer. Using a combination of iSeries programs, SQL statements, and stored procedures, the integration layer performs all of the necessary actions. These actions include read, update, insert, and delete actions.

One problem within organizations has been data synchronization. In many cases there is no single system that contains all of an organization's information. It is possible to have a customer relationship management (CRM) system, a transactional system, and a data warehouse, just to name a few, each containing the same information for customers or products. With the data in various places, it has become a challenge for organizations to ensure that this information is the same everywhere. To ensure that the data is processed on all the various systems, the integration layer executes an action on each system. The integration layer has a fine layer of granularity for all the operations, and it contains all the various unique commands necessary to execute the action on each system.

With all of the various systems the integration layer must update, another task it must perform is to ensure transaction integrity. It is its responsibility to ensure that all of the systems have the proper information, prior to committing the changes or updates. This will also ensure that each system will have information in the event that there is some problem during the operation.

As an example, suppose the integration layer shown in Figure 11.9 receives a request to update the information for a customer. The customer information must be updated in both system A and system B. The integration layer must begin the transaction and perform the updates on both systems. If there is an error, the transactions must be rolled back and an error must be reported. If there are no problems during the update, the transaction must be committed.

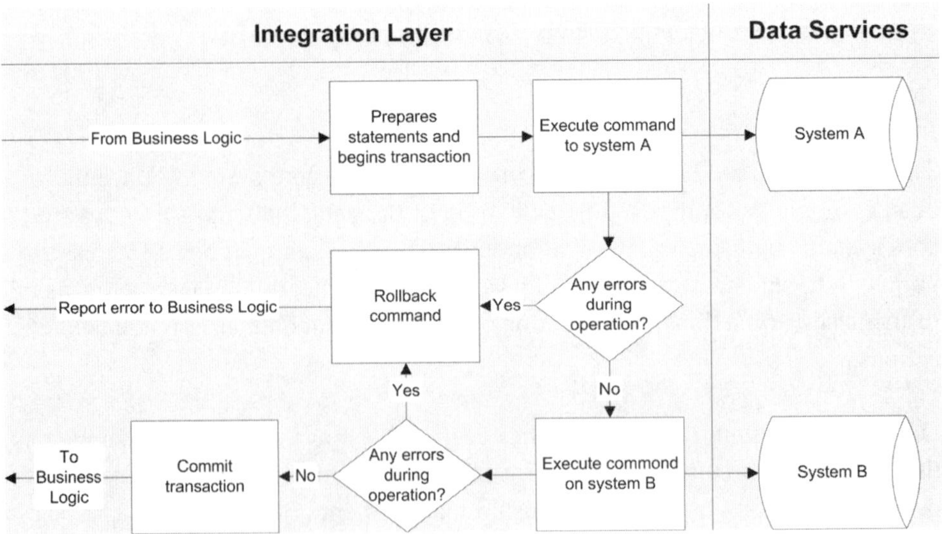

Figure 11.9: Integration to the core systems.

An option for solving such problems would be to develop a custom solution for the integration. This approach would provide the greatest amount of flexibility for accessing each unique system. Individual commands can be created for each system, each with its own unique attributes. They would be combined within a command that would call each individual command as required.

However, why would you want to build this integration when there are products already available that can do all these things? The time and effort required to build such a solution would require a great deal of planning, not to mention the resources required for development and unit testing. There are many products that can handle multisystem transactions. Each product is based on XML technologies that provide integration into iSeries systems.

WebSphere Business Integration Server

WebSphere Business Integration Server provides a suite of tools that ease the development for integration and business layers. It provides an environment that can integrate into the most complex systems. Transactions that span a single system or multiple systems can be executed with ease. It comes with a rich set of tools that allow the integration components to be tested, managed, and deployed.

WebSphere Business Integration Server takes advantage of other technologies to provide integration functionality. It can use WebSphere MQ to retrieve requests that have been submitted for processing and place a response message in another queue to complete the process if required. Use of WebSphere MQ for this solution is not required, although it does provide a great deal of flexibility and reliability.

The suite comes with the products listed in the following paragraphs, each with its own distinct qualities. All of these products operate very similarly though they provide solutions for different problems. Purchasing the entire suite is not required if only an individual product is needed.

WebSphere Business Integration Message Broker

Quite simply, this product is for processing a single unit of work. It accepts the incoming request from WebSphere MQ or another messaging agent. It parses the input from the queue and formulates the message into a new request for processing; hence the name "message broker." It acts as an intermediary between the calling application and the back-end applications.

The message formats supported are unlimited, providing that there is a mechanism to parse the values. The ideal format is—no surprise—an XML document.

WebSphere Business Integration Message Broker can be used to integrate existing applications with Web services. Messages can be submitted by existing iSeries applications to a queue. The broker accepts the request, formulates a SOAP message, and submits it for processing. The result can be placed in another queue to complete the request; it can also be used for routing SOAP messages to various Web services.

The current version of WebSphere Business Integration Message Broker is v5.0. It was previously known as WebSphere MQ Integrator Broker. It has undergone some updates to work with the Eclipse framework, which is used by the other members of the WebSphere family of products.

WebSphere InterChange Server

Websphere InterChange Server works very similarly to WebSphere Business Integration Message Broker. It accepts messages from WebSphere MQ, processes the messages, and, if necessary, generates the response and places it into another queue.

The difference is in the types of actions the products can perform. WebSphere Business Integration Message Broker simply parses the input and formulates a new request to be sent to another resource for processing. WebSphere InterChange Server, on the other hand, will do much more than just broker the incoming message. It can manage a transaction that spans across many applications and platforms, and it can also be used to integrate people into the business process. The transaction state information can be maintained with the InterChange Server.

The current version of WebSphere InterChange Server is V4.2.2. It was formerly known as IBM CrossWorlds.

WebSphere MQ Workflow

Like the previous two products, WebSphere MQ Workflow will retrieve message from WebSphere MQ queues. It can perform a set of predefined actions for a message found in a specific queue. At this point, it goes a little farther than WebSphere InterChange Server: It always places the message into another queue so that another step can take the message and perform another set of actions. It will continue processing and placing into queues until it has reached the end of a defined process, thus creating a process workflow that can span multiple months rather than a few seconds.

WebSphere Business Integration Adapters

Websphere Business Integration adapters provide connections to leading-edge technologies. They provide various methods for connecting to other technologies. The adapters would be used within a step on any of the Integration products to connect to backend resources.

Some of the available integration adapters include

- XML
- WebSphere MQ
- WebSphere MQ Workflow
- WebSphere MQ Integrator Broker
- JMS
- Web Services
- CORBA
- Data Handler for EDI
- iSeries

If none of these provides the required functionality, the Adapter Framework can be used to create your own adapters. This places a great deal of functionality in the hands of an organization. The ability to create custom adapters for systems that do not have existing adapters extends the range that the system can reach. The framework supports the creation of adapters using either Java or C++.

The iSeries adapter provides the ability to access iSeries resources. It also provides a mechanism for executing RPG programs. The iSeries system requires the IBM Toolbox for Java to access the programs.

Of the Integration products, each provides a means to process a message in a unique way. Table 11.1 shows the various scenarios in which each product should be used.

Table 11.1: When to Use the Various WebSphere Business Integration Products

Message Broker	Interchange Server	MQ Workflow
Handles a single piece of work sent to one destination	Is complex and has multiple activities	Contains multiple units over work spanning multiple systems/applications over a long duration
Can be simply transformed into a new format for execution on another resource	Will communicate with many systems	Requires following a predefined set of activities
Needs to be completed immediately	Needs to be completed immediately	May span a long duration

The various WebSphere products would fit into an architecture by having the products listen to the various queues for incoming messages. Once a new message arrives, the product would determine the next course of action and execute either directly to the back-end systems or through another technology such as Web services. It would then generate the response based upon the result of the execution and place it into the put queue. Figure 11.10 shows how this process would work for all of the products. Keep in mind that this process is generic and does not contain any of the advanced features that the InterChange Server or the MQ Workflow can provide. Essentially this will be the behavior that each product will have.

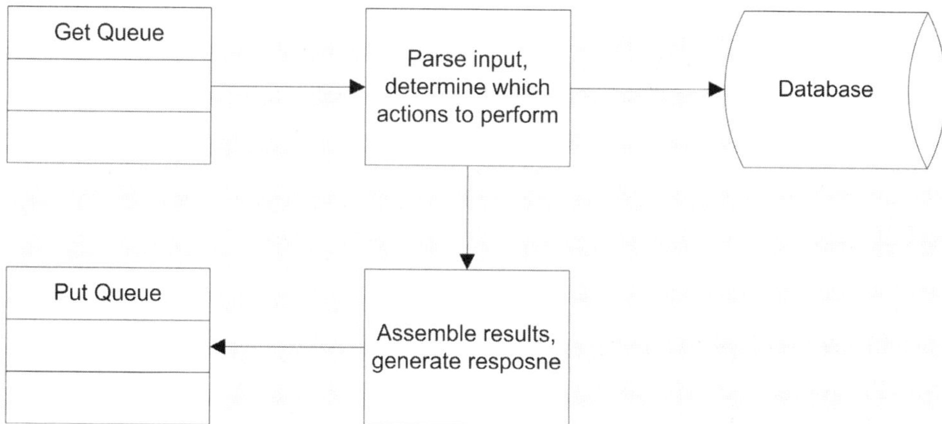

Figure 11.10: Using WebSphere Business Integration server components.

The WebSphere Business Integration Server is available for the following operating systems:

- AIX
- HP-UX
- Solaris
- Windows 2000, XP

For more information about WebSphere Business Integration Server and compatibility with specific operating systems and platforms, visit *www-306.ibm.com/-software/integration/wbiserver/*. Information about each of the subcomponents is available from this site.

PCML

Program Call Markup Language (PCML) is a markup language that provides a simple approach to calling iSeries programs. Based on XML syntax, PCML describes an iSeries program in a PCML source file. The PCML source file is used with the PCML Java package to create an instance of the program for use in Java.

PCML was designed to reduce the amount of development to connect to an iSeries program. By defining the program and all of its parameters, the PCML Java package automatically marshals the data from the program to the appropriate native Java class type. This eliminates the need for unnecessary development in the retrieving and casting of data that can result in unnecessary errors.

PCML describes how to communicate with an iSeries program. A document in PCML, known as a PCML source file, contains all of the information about the input and output parameters. PCML source files are typically stored in a location that can be accessed by the necessary Java applications. They can be packaged with the applications or in a central repository so that many applications can reference the same definition.

Once the source file has been created, it can be used to create instances of the program as required. When the iSeries program is created using the *ProgramCallDocument* class, the PCML source file is referenced. Figure 11.11 shows how the source file is referenced.

```
AS400 myas400 = new AS400();
ProgramCallDocument myPCD = new ProgramCallDocument(myas400, "myPCML");
```

Figure 11.11: Creating an iSeries program using PCML.

In the next step the Java application sets the necessary parameters for the program, using the *setValue* method of the *program* object. Figure 11.12 shows an example of how an integer value would be set for a program.

```
pcml.setValue(paramtername, new Integer(parametervalue));
```

Figure 11.12: Setting parameters for a PCML program.

Once the program has all necessary parameters set, the program is ready to be executed. To execute the program, the *callProgram* method is executed. The return value of this method is a Boolean value indicating whether a message was returned by the iSeries. The messages may be used to determine the success or failure of the execution as shown in Figure 11.13.

```
boolean bResult = pcml.callProgram(programname);
if (bResult) {
    // code to handle a successful execution
} else {
    // code indicating a message was returned by the iSeries
}
```

Figure 11.13: Program execution with PCML.

After execution, the values for the output parameters can be obtained. As the input parameter values are set with *setValue*, the PCML package uses the *getValue* method to retrieve the values. Figure 11.14 shows an example of how a return parameter can be retrieved. The overall relationships among the requesting program, the PCML Java package, the PCML source file, and the back-end legacy program are shown in Figure 11.15.

```
Object returnValue = pcml.getValue(parametername);
```

Figure 11.14: Retrieving a return parameter.

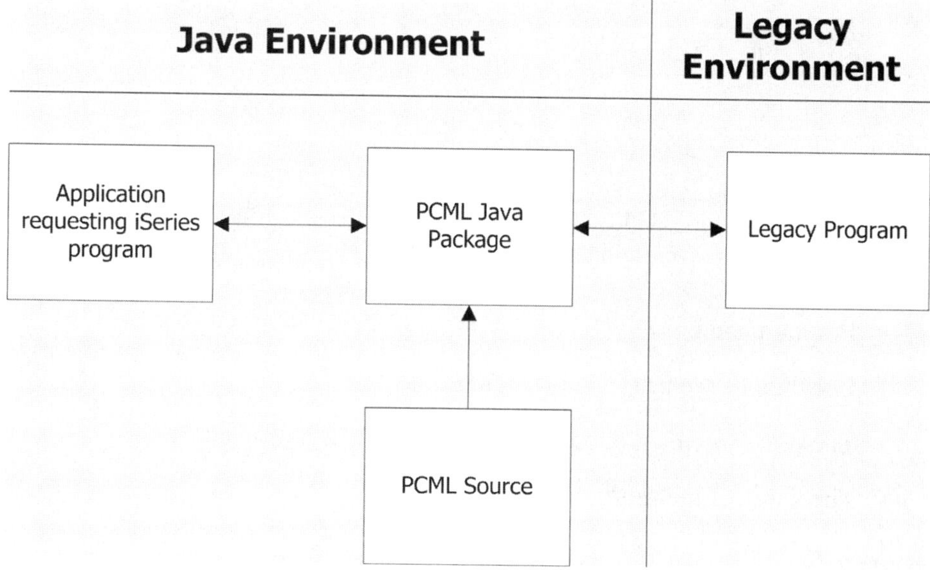

Figure 11.15: PCML basic operation.

It is obvious how the Java coding has been simplified using the PCML source file and the PCML Java package. It takes away the complexities of directly accessing iSeries programs as well as the retrieval and casting of the data. The PCML source file contains the all of the information on how to communicate with the iSeries program. The PCML source file, an example of which is shown in Figure 11.16, contains the following three tags:

- *program*
- *struct*
- *data*

```
<pcml version="1.0">
    <program>
        <struct>
            <data></data>
        </struct>
        <data></data>
    </program>
</pcml>
```

Figure 11.16: PCML source file syntax.

Program

The *program* tag contains the information about a single iSeries program. The *program* tag has the following attributes:

- Program name
- Location of the program on the iSeries
- The order in which the output parameters will be parsed
- The value of the return value if any.

The *program* tag can have both the *struct* and *data* tags as child elements.

Struct

The *struct* tag defines a named structure that will be used as an argument. The *struct* tag is a child element of the *program* tag. The structure can contain *data* elements or other *struct* tags. The *struct* tag has the following attributes:

- Structure name
- The number of elements in the structure
- The minimum and maximum OS version under which the element may exist (useful when the structure does not exist on specific OS versions)
- The offset for the structure
- Size of the output expected from the program
- The usage of the structure (input, output, both, or inherited from the parent element)

Data

The *data* tag is the finest level of all the PCML elements. It describes an individual field for a program or structure. The following are the attributes for the data tag:

- Data name
- Type of data for the field
- Length and precision of the data field
- Coded Character Set ID (CCSID)
- The initial value of the field.
- The minimum and maximum OS version under which the element may exist (useful when the field does not exist on specific OS versions)

- The offset for the field
- Size of the field expected from the program
- Indicator determining how the field is passed (either by reference or by value)
- The structure that contains the field
- The usage of the field (input, output, both, or inherited from the parent element are available values)

For more information about PCML, visit the IBM Information center for the iSeries at *publib.boulder.ibm.com/pubs/html/as400/infocenter.htm*. After selecting the geographical region, language, and OS version, view the section in **Programming → Java → IBM Toolbox for Java → Program Call Markup Language (PCML).**

Data Services

The last component of an architecture would be data services. These are responsible for communicating directly to the back-end resources such as files, tables, or even other XML technologies. These components perform typical operations on the data: read, update, insert, and delete, using familiar technologies such as RPG and SQL and new technologies such as DB2 Extender and even Web services to access data.

There are many technology options for this layer, all of which depend greatly on what is being accessed. The obvious choice for the iSeries is a native program such as RPG or COBOL. SQL objects may also be used on the iSeries if desired. Stored procedures provide a means of preparing a statement so that SQL statements do not have be generated on the fly. SQL statements that are generated on the fly are not as efficient as prepared statements and are not recommended.

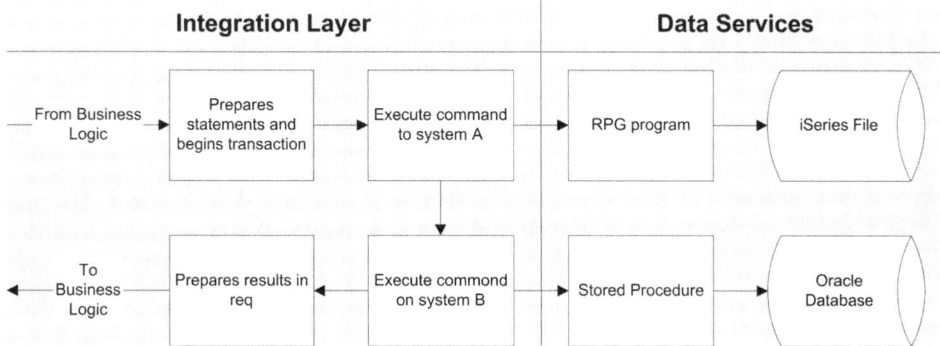

Figure 11.17: Data services execution.

Figure 11.17 shows how a single integration command would make two calls to the various data services: one to an iSeries RPG program and the other to an Oracle stored procedure. Although not shown, other means of communication may be used in this layer. Web services used with stub code can be used as a resource. Technologies such SAML, which was discussed in Chapter 9, can be referenced as a resource. Other databases, such as Oracle and Microsoft SQL Server, provide a Web service interface to the data.

DB2 Extender provides an additional means of accessing data inside a database. With this product, XML documents can be used instead of stored procedures or SQL to update data in the database. DB2 Extender could return the results as an XML document.

Conclusion

Where does the iSeries fit in this architecture scheme? Everywhere. The iSeries has all of the characteristics and the program support to fit into every layer of the architecture. With the supporting technologies and XML as the core message format, the iSeries can be used for every layer of the architecture. Whether it should is another discussion.

By dividing the communication into layers, each layer can use specific XML technologies to provide a reliable system capable of scaling to any size necessary. With XML as the message format, every layer can take advantage of the document format without having to manipulate and change it for each process. The presentation layer can simply apply a stylesheet to the XML and have rich HTML documents. The transport layer does not really have a preference what the message format is, but when a product such as IBM's WebSphere MQ product line is used, the XML document can be easily used to feed a workflow, communicate with back-end systems, or be transformed into other formats ready for processing.

Web services are an ideal fit for architectures. They provide a means of communication that can easily separate presentation from business layers, and they can integrate well with both ends. Stub code can be integrated into the presentation layer once it has been generated using the WSDL file from the Web service. The Web service can create business commands that will, in turn, create the integration commands that will ensure that all of the back-end systems get updated.

The layers defined have been carefully thought out and planned. With IBM's continually evolving WebSphere MQ product line, the architecture is able to provide a scalable and reliable system ready for any integration challenges.

References
jakarta.apache.org/struts/index.html
www.w3.org/Voice/
www-306.ibm.com/software/integration/wmq/
www.w3.org/2002/ws/
www-306.ibm.com/software/integration/wbiserver/
publib.boulder.ibm.com/

12

XML References

In this chapter you will learn:

- ✓ What organizations were used as references for this book
- ✓ Where to get more information about the iSeries and XML
- ✓ How to find information in the future

Now that you have a good basis of understanding of how the iSeries and XML work together, it is time to prepare for the future. One of the most difficult questions in moving forward after a long book is where to go next to get more information. This chapter is aimed toward showing readers where to go when there are questions or where to find out about new XML technologies.

IBM

IBM is continually supporting the available XML technologies within its applications, operating systems, and platforms. Look to the iSeries Information Center for a complete set of reference materials regarding iSeries specific documentation as well as XML references. Visit *publib.boulder.ibm.com/*; select **iSeries and AS/400 Information Center**, then select the continent, language, and version (currently V5R2).

The WebSphere Integration site, *www-306.ibm.com/software/integration/*, will always be updated with the most recent information. The section will contain iSeries-specific integration information specifically around WebSphere MQ and WebSphere Business Integration Server products.

W3C

Probably the best reference for XML technologies is the World Wide Web Consortium (W3C) at *www.w3.org/*. The W3C was founded in 1994. Its goals were and are to develop standards and protocols that promote interoperability. The W3C has over 400 members worldwide. This group has provided most of the XML-based recommendations used in this book, not to mention the original recommendation. The W3C has supplied the recommendations for XML including the original XML specification, DOM, XForms, XSL, XPath, XML Schemas, XLink, Web Services, P3P, SOAP, VoiceXML, XML Encryption, XML Key Management, XML Signature, and XPointer. These recommendations are just those used in this book.

The W3C is very active in most of the World Wide Web recommendation activity. It has also produced recommendations on topics that include HTML, internationalization, Portable Network Graphics (PNG), and CSS, just to name a few.

Note that the W3C group does not supply tutorials, products, courses, or any other information for their recommendations. They supply only the various recommendations, which tend to be very technical, although some of the recommendations contain primers.

OASIS

The Organization for the Advancement of Structured Information Standards (OASIS) Group, like the W3C, promotes the use of open standards. OASIS has produced many standards on a wide variety of topics that include security, XML, Web services, transactions, electronic publishing, and interoperability with marketplaces. In this book the UDDI, SAML, and XACML standards were examined; however, OASIS has produced many other standards, including many business-based XML specifications, the ebXML standard in particular. Developed with the United Nations, ebXML is designed to be a global framework for business interchange.

The OASIS group was founded in 1993, originally operating under the name of SGML Open, as it developed open standards specifically toward interoperability. Its members were vendors and users. In 1998 it officially changed its name to OASIS to reflect the wide variety of work it had come to encompass. It has over 600 members worldwide and spans over 100 countries.

For more information about the OASIS group and its standards, please visit *www.oasis-open.org/home/index.php*.

SAX

As described in Chapter 5, the SAX parser is an open-source standard. It has no licenses, because it has been placed in the public domain. However, David Megginson maintains the specification for the SAX parser. Any updates to the specification will be found on the SAX Web site.

For more information about the SAX specification, visit *www.saxproject.org*.

The Apache Software Foundation

The Apache Software Foundation has been responsible for many implantations of the W3C, OASIS, and SAX specifications. It has implemented both parsers, DOM and SAX, and has put together projects that will aid any solution.

The Cocoon project is geared toward component-based Web development. Its aim is to develop a product that is capable of delivering a multichannel Web site that separates data from the presentation. Java 2 Enterprise Edition (J2EE) solutions and portals can be easily integrated into the project. For more information on the Cocoon project, visit *cocoon.apache.org/.*

The Jakarta project is a Java-platform set of open-source products. They are available to the public at no charge and are distributed through various subprojects. Some of the available products include the Java-based processor Tomcat and the Struts framework. A complete list of all the available products is on the Jakarta Web site, *jakarta.apache.org/.*

Apache was formed in 1995, when it began producing the Apache HTTP Server. Since then, it has expanded its projects, and in 1999 it became a nonprofit corporation. To find out more information about the Apache group and its implementation, visit *www.apache.org*.

Microsoft

Although it has been mentioned very little in this book, Microsoft does have a very strong influence in the XML community. It has been involved with many of the specifications used today, including the XML, XSL, XSLT, Web Services, and XML Schemas recommendations, just to name a few.

Microsoft has also implemented both the DOM and SAX parsers for the Windows platforms. Web services can be written in any of the .NET technologies. Microsoft SQL Server has the capability of extending its database using Web services. SOAP messages can be sent to a Web server, which can be used to update, insert, delete, and retrieve information. For more information on Microsoft support for Web services, see *msdn.microsoft.com/webservices/.*

To find out more information about XML from Microsoft, visit *www.microsoft.com/xml/.*

Conclusion

These organizations are among a few that were used as references. There are many more that can be found just by simply searching on the Internet. The listed organizations, however, are the ideal place for the latest information on what is available. They are the trailblazers for XML standards. IBM, specifically, will be supplying the most relevant information for the iSeries and its support for XML.

Index

A

Note: Boldface numbers indicate illustrations or tables

E

I

J

K

L

S

T

U

V

W

X